THE PASSION AND THE FASHION

Popular Cultural Studies

Series editors: Justin O'Connor, Steve Redhead and Derek Wynne.

The Manchester Institute for Popular Culture was set up in order to promote theoretical and empirical research in the area of contemporary popular culture, both within the University and in conjunction with local, national and international agencies. The Institute is currently engaged in two major comparative research projects around aspects of consumption and popular culture in the City. The Institute also runs a number of postgraduate research programmes, with a particular emphasis on ethnographic work. The series intends to reflect all aspects of the Institute's activities. Current theoretical debates within the field of popular culture will be explored within an empirical context. Much of the research is undertaken by young researchers actively involved in their chosen fields of study, allowing an awareness of the issues and an attentiveness to actual developments often lacking in standard academic writings on the subject. The series will also reflect the working methods of the Institute, emphasising a collective research effort and the regular presentation of work-in-progress to the Institute's research seminars. The series hopes, therefore, both to push forward the debates around popular culture, urban regeneration and postmodern social theory whilst introducing an ethnographic and contextual basis for such debates.

Titles already published

Rave Off: Politics and Deviance in Contemporary Youth Culture.
The Passion and the Fashion: Football Fandom in the New Europe

(Cover photograph: Richard Davis)

The Passion and the Fashion

Footballl fandom in the New Europe

edited by
Steve Redhead

Avebury
Aldershot · Brookfield USA · Hong Kong · Singapore · Sydney

Published by
Avebury
Ashgate Publishing Limited
Gower House
Croft Road
Aldershot
Hants GU11 3HR
England

Ashgate Publishing Company
Old Post Road
Brookfield
Vermont 05036
USA

British Library Cataloguing in Publication Data

Passion and the Fashion: Football Fandom
in the New Europe - (Popular Cultural Studies)
   I. Redhead, Steve   II. Series
   306.4

ISBN 1 85628 462 X (Hardback)
ISBN 1 85628 464 6 (Paperback)

Printed and Bound in Great Britain by
Athenaeum Press Ltd., Newcastle upon Tyne.

Contents

Preface

This series of papers was produced by a 'football research' seminar in the Unit for Law and Popular Culture at Manchester Metropolitan University, held jointly with the Department of Sociology at the University of Salford. In addition to regular participants in the seminar, visiting speakers were also invited. The following speakers gave a public seminar as guest lecturers. Our thanks to all those who took part, especially:

Professor Ian Taylor, Head of the Department of Sociology at the University of Salford, who was joint organiser.

Also:

Pavel Slepicka, Charles University, Prague, Czechoslovakia, for his talk "Football Supporters in Czechoslovakia".

Andrew Ward, freelance writer on sports history for his talk "Oral History and Football Research".

Alan Clarke, Centre for Leisure and Tourism Studies, University of North London , for his talk "Putting the Boot in: A Critique of the 'Leicester' School".

John Bale, Department of Education, University of Keele, for his talk "Space and Containment in the Football Industry".

Alessandro Portelli, University of Rome, Italy, for his talk "The Culture of the Italian Soccer Terrace".

The photographs featured in this book are the work of photographer Richard Davis, to whom we would like to express our thanks.

The essays collected here focus on different aspects of spectatorship at football matches in Europe over the last few years. Famous clubs such as Leeds United, Manchester United, Napoli, Marseille and Juventus provide the territory for these original contemporary studies in sports fan behaviour. In 1985 the Heysel disaster led to a UEFA ban on English clubs which was lifted (excluding Liverpool) in the 1990-91 season. "Always Look on the Bright Side of Life" and "Ratfink Reds" provide accounts of a unique research project conducted by the Unit for Law and Popular Culture at Manchester Metropolitan University (formerly Manchester Polytechnic). It involved researchers following the fans of Manchester United and Aston Villa (the two English clubs allowed to play in 1990-91) as they travelled to the away games on their return to European competition. In the event Manchester United went on to win the European Cup Winners Cup and Aston Villa went down to defeat in Milan after a much acclaimed home victory against Inter in the first leg. Hooliganism, which was the ever present spectre for media coverage, failed to materialise. Indeed, the 1990-91 season was heralded (eventually) as a 'new era' in domestic football fandom in England. Our exhibition which celebrated (albeit critically) this conclusion of the research project - entitled *Football With Attitude* - was widely covered by the national and international media; it was also featured in a special BBC 2 *Newsnight* report on changes in football fan culture in the 90s.

The essays here also feature important, but hitherto little-known, contributions on research into European football fandom from Richard Giulianotti, Christian Bromberger and Alessandro Portelli. The focus is soccer terrace culture in France, Italy and Scotland, as well as England.

The remaining essays are by Richard Haynes who has researched the emergence of football fanzines for a unique project which aims to collect at least one copy of every football fanzine ever produced.

About the authors

Steve Redhead, is author of *The End-of-the-Century Party: Youth and Pop Towards 2000* (Manchester University Press, 1990) and *Football With Attitude* (Wordsmith, 1991). His first book *Sing When You're Winning: The Last Football Book* (Pluto Press, London, 1987) is now out of print. He is currently preparing a book on the regulation of popular culture entitled *Unpopular Cultures,* for publication by Manchester University Press. He is Reader in Law and Popular Culture at Manchester Metropolitan University, and Director of the Unit for Law and Popular Culture and Joint Director of the Manchester Institute for Popular Culture.

Richard Haynes, is a Research Assistant in the Manchester Institute for Popular Culture. His first degree is from Leeds Metropolitan University, where he graduated in Leisure Studies in 1988. Over the past two years he has carried out a research project into football fanzines and the regulation of popular culture. This research includes the maintenance and update of a unique archive of popular culture ephemera from the 80s and 90s. He has co-organised two exhibitions which have drawn from the Institute's archive: *Football with Attitude* and *Down At The Club.* When not being kicked across public parks while playing for Leeds Accies in the West Yorkshire Old Boys League, he 'marches on' for Leeds United.

Antonio Melechi, has written a number of articles and essays on youth and club culture, some of which have been published in the *New Statesman and Society* and *Marxism Today*. He is currently co-authoring a book on Europe and the Gulf War, and researching a book on Italian culture and politics in post-war Britain. During 1990-92 he was a Research Assistant in the Unit for Law and Popular Culture, Manchester Metropolitan University, where he also gained his undergraduate degree in English Studies in 1989.

Adam Brown, is a Masters degree student in The Manchester Institute for Popular Culture. He was formerly drummer with Ratfink, a Manchester based noise-pop band, and is a lifelong Manchester United fan.

Justin O'Connor, is Senior Research Fellow at The Manchester Institute for Popular Culture.

Alessandro Portelli, is Professor of American Literature, University of Rome, Italy. He is author of *The Death of Luigi Trastulli, and other Stories* (State University of New York Press, Albany, 1991).

Richard Giulianotti, graduated in Sociology from the University of Aberdeen with First Class Honours in 1989. Since then he has been employed by the University of Aberdeen and currently by the ESRC on research projects studying Scottish soccer fan behaviour at club and international levels, and related youth subcultures. He is editor of the forthcoming book *Football, Violence and Social Identity* (Routledge, London, 1993), and is co-editing a collection on soccer, modernity and culture for publication by Leicester University Press.

Christian Bromberger, teaches at the Centre National de la Recherche Scientifique, Université de Provence, Aix-en-Provence, France. He is author of numerous articles on football fan culture in Europe. This is the first time his work has been translated into English.

1 Always look on the bright side of life

Steve Redhead

Should football policy makers follow Eric Idle and "always look on the bright side of life"?[1] The 1990s in England certainly began with something of a surprise; at least as far as many commentators in the media have been concerned. English football fans at club level have largely managed to change their reputation as the world's most feared 80s 'football hooligans' into a band of committed law-abiding citizens who approached away matches abroad as members of a new European football community. Despite the trouble caused by some ethnocentric supporters of the English *national* team at the championships in Malmo and other Swedish centres it seems that *domestic* matches in England and Wales are continuing to underline the fact that the phenomenon of football hooliganism becoming less fashionable than in the seasons since Italia '90. Things in the field of football culture are of course never quite so simple; as has already been cited, violence by a small number of English, as well as Swedish and German, hooligans in various sites at the Championships confirmed that support for national teams in Europe in the 90s is often still associated with nationalistic, chauvinistic aggression. It is easily forgotten, too, that there was considerable public disorder in towns in England during the Italia '90 competition; especially after England's defeat in the World Cup semi-finals after a penalty shoot-out against the 'old enemy' Germany, the eventual winners.

Nevertheless, a research project[2] at Manchester Polytechnic[3] in the 1990-91 season, which provides the narrative contained in Chapter 3 of this book, suggested a number of reasons why, in an era of disturbing rises in neo-Nazi skinhead football violence (in, for instance, Germany), the 'English disease' - as it used to be called -

has proved a successful case for treatment when it comes to changing the outlook of fans of clubs such as Leeds United, Manchester United and others, who had justifiably bad reputations in various periods over the past two decades. A different 'attitude'(4) - light years from the ugliness of the Heysel debacle in 1985 appears to have manifested itself in *some* parts of English soccer fan culture since the mid-80s. Since, especially, Italia '90, the situation has received ever-less cynical media attention; critics and commentators have gone so far as to describe these as 'New Times'(5) for football.

Numerous fans in other European countries, as well as some in England and, as Richard Giulianotti shows later in this book, in Scotland, have continued, nevertheless, to follow a tradition for disorder and violence which was in the 60s, 70s and 80s, variously ascribed to English, or at one time, Scottish football followers. For example, six years after the Heysel disaster which killed 39 Juventus fans, Fiorentina (Florence) fans were still taunting Juventus supporters at a match in Turin by chanting the numbers from 1 to 39 - this enraged the Juventus fans so much that running fights started between two mobs and riot police in which an officer was stabbed and several fans injured. In another well publicised instance, only weeks after Manchester United and Barcelona fans had graced Rotterdam's De Kuip stadium (the home of Feyenoord) the Dutch Cup Final between Feyenoord and BVV Den Bosch on June 2, 1991, was marred by pitch invasions which halted the game and - at least initially - caused a civil court ruling that the second half of the game should be replayed with a 1-0 scoreline from the first half of the original match remair. ng.(6)

Whilst the mass m .dia in general has fashioned a consensus(7) around the idea that the English football hooligan problem that they once feasted on so greedily has, for the moment, largely gone away, the preference for a cyclical view of social history is prevalent. After a much publicised incident of hooliganism by some Birmingham City fans (which included a pitch invasion, an attack on the referee and opposing fans) in a Division Three League match against Stoke City in 1991 the popular press predicted that it would 'all come round again'. One paper, under the headline "More Aggro on the Way Say Experts", reported John Williams, joint director of the University of Leicester Sir Norman Chester Centre for Football Research as saying that "hooliganism occurs in cycles and there is a danger that the Birmingham incident may be the start of another period of problems." The problem with this argument is the failure to recognise that what is cyclical is the media reporting of such phenomena as 'football hooliganism', a social problem moreover which has no precise legal definition and remains more or less historical (and often hysterical) mass media construction. Those who argue that football hooliganism is waiting around the corner to spring out on us once again, end up defining a complex series of socio-legal behaviours - such as murder at one extreme and aggressive chanting at the other - with one catch-all label which seems to have little or no relation to the mass media coverage or sociopolitical conditions pertaining at any one time. It becomes an 'objective' social phenomenon, about which there is general definitional agreement, that can be measured, quantified, assessed and, importantly in this context of apparent decline of the phenomenon, predicted. Nothing in the content of the studies in this book should be taken as claiming that something called - especially in England - 'football hooliganism' has simply disappeared. Nevertheless, if our contemporary ethnographical studies - such as Adam Brown's personal account of following Manchester United abroad in 1991-92 in Chapter 3 - help to create a more balanced view of recent English football fandom in Europe a useful task will have been accomplished. Moreover, Richard Haynes' revisit to 'Leeds, the lads and the meeja' in Chapter 2 does not deny the involvement of some Leeds United fans in hardcore racist and fascist hooliganism over the past twenty years, but it *does* seek to question the orthodox view in deviancy theory that, in what Leslie Wilkins called the "amplification spiral", primary deviance is *necessarily* fanned by social (including media) reaction to *inevitably* create secondary deviance,(8) in this case a commitment to football hooligan behaviours. Indeed Richard's essay on his beloved Leeds United can be read as an instance of the opposite phenomenon occurring - the more the media and police and civil authorities stereotyped the fans as hooligans the more there was a determination, since 1985, to combat the 'image' of hooliganism which was being created, or, more correctly, continued. Football fanzines are placed at the sharp edge of this resistance, or defence, movement in Richard's essay on Leeds United, and his other essays in this book reflect the more general trend in the 80s and 90s in Britain for the mass of football fans themselves to reject the media stereotype of inarticulate, macho, hooligan imagery surrounding football fandom. This can be dated

3

historically; before the watershed year of 1985 (Bradford, Brussels and Birmingham all occurred in May of that year) there were only a handful of football fanzines. Then came *Off the Ball* (now defunct) and *When Saturday Comes*, which Richard subjects to a critical but empathetic analysis in Chapter 4. Chapter 5 is again a constructively critical study of football fanzines; in this case Richard draws on the unique collection which he and other colleagues in the Manchester Institute for Popular Culture have built. This public archive of football fanzines (mainly from Britain and Ireland) currently numbers over 900 examples of every football fanzine ever produced, in many cases comprising whole or part of fanzines. We gratefully acknowledge editors' (and indeed other collectors') generosity in their donations to the archive.

The fanzine collection which researchers have developed as part of a more general popular culture archive (containing a multitude of music and pop culture fanzines) stimulated an academic conference at Manchester Polytechnic in February 1991. Sponsored by the British Sociological Association's Leisure and Recreation Study Group, it attracted over forty academics, students and fanzine editors. Similar, but larger gatherings of those interested in football and society at the European University Institute, Florence, Italy in May 1990 and Aberdeen, Scotland, in April 1992, have shifted the focus of research into contemporary soccer culture away from *simply* the problem of violence to issues of the passion and the fashion surrounding soccer fandom throughout the world - its differences and similarities in each specific local or national social formation - and the variety of theoretical approaches which might help to grasp this pluralistic football culture. The writings and research projects of the likes of Alessandro Portelli and Christian Bromberger came to light for a number of scholars - such as our Greater Manchester colleagues Ian Taylor and Vic Duke - at several Florence meetings including the large convention on "Football and Europe", a conference convened shortly before Italia '90. The researchers in Manchester, in particular, have benefited greatly from the opportunity to welcome these two important writers - as well as others - to Britain, and to study their work. We are proud to present in this volume, in Chapters 6, 7 and 8, their original work on football and popular culture in the English language for, we think, the first time. Excellent translations are provided by researchers Justin O'Connor and Antonio Melechi. Similarly, we are delighted to include an equally stimulating essay by Richard Giulianotti from the Department of Sociology at the University of Aberdeen, in Chapter 9. Richard Giulianotti was responsible for organising the Aberdeen conference which introduced fresh thinking on football culture to another layer of academics and students from different countries including the USA where the World Cup will be held in 1994, and which provided an opportunity for a presentation of some of the Manchester Polytechnic research work on English clubs' return to European competition in the 1990-91 season. Richard Giulianotti has already written a number of papers which deserve a much wider audience. They are notable for both their theoretical and empirical focus. A writer on football culture who can innovatively combine the insightful, but disparate and confusing, theoretical approaches of such cultural icons as Pierre Bourdieu, Erving Goffman and Jean Baudrillard is rare indeed. To do so in order to illuminate the much misunderstood developments in the links between British 'casual' youth culture and soccer is a substantial achievement. In August 1985 *New Society* published 'Soccer Style Wars', a seminar essay by Steve Redhead and Eugene McLaughlin which attempted to explain the links in the chain up to that date. *Sing When You're Winning* by Steve Redhead - written at the same time but not published until several years later - parodied the media accounts of such 'casual' connections in a book which caught the plunge of football and much youth culture into the murky waters of the ugly Thatcherite surge in the mid-80s. However, it has taken several more years for academic sociology to come to terms with the implications of such studies. Giulianotti, drawing on his own ethnographic work with football casuals in Scotland, presents a wide-ranging and provocative view to counter the simplistic responses of those whose thinking - and research - on football and its culture remains wedged in the theoretical and political log-jam of the 70s.

In conclusion, it would seem that the two most important foci for serious study of football culture in the 90s and beyond are not football hooliganism and macho posturing as such, but the conflicting figures of 'participation' and 'passivity' which are picked up in a variety of ways in the chapters of this book. At the time of writing there is a welter of evidence to suggest a desire for a greater participation in fandom by the football fan him or, increasingly, herself. Whether this will lead to what Ian Taylor once called a "participatory democracy" around soccer becoming fully fledged is questionable; that it exists,

5

and is on the increase, is undeniable. Witness - in Britain - the growth of organisations like the FSA (Football Supporters Associations), the mushrooming of football fanzines, the popularity of women's soccer, the new tendency to conceive of football as a popular art form(9) instead of the lowest of low art, and so on. However, part of the reason for such changes in football culture is the counter tendency - sponsored by television moguls (such as Silvio Berlusconi and Rupert Murdoch) - to create an army of passive 'couch-potatoes' whose sole contact with 'real' football is through the mediation of television. Though it is mistaken to create a simple dichotomy - passive **versus** participatory - since many of those who have consumed BSkyB Premier League matches on satellite television in Britain have been committed, travelling fans wishing to imbibe even further their favourite mass 'opiate', there is undoubtedly a rationalising, modernising trajectory in motion which tends to create a more 'respectable', more affluent, audience for what is still (quaintly) referred to as the people's, or working man's, game, leaving outside its pearly gates a large section of the game's traditional following. The staging of the World Cup in the USA in 1994 is likely to further this transformation whatever resistance movements are thrown up in its wake.

6

Notes

1.   *Always look on the bright Side of Life?* the title of this Chapter, is taken from a song by Monty Pythons Flying Circus, originally released as part of the soundtrack for their film, *Life of Brian*, in the early 80s. In the 1990-91 soccer season in England it became a popular anthem amongst football supporters, especially Manchester United followers, and as a result the re-released single achieved considerable success in the pop charts. Inevitably anti-Manchester United chants bastardised the song, hence the version:

     "Always look on the runway for ice
     Munich, Munich, Munich."

2.   This is based on research by the Unit for Law and Popular Culture. The study actually focussed on the fans of English soccer clubs' returning to European competition for the first time since Heysel, for the 1990-91 season. Thanks are due to the Department of Law for sponsoring this unique research project. The interim report on this research was submitted, on request, to the Home Affairs Committee of the House of Commons (Chair: Sir John Wheeler) as they were preparing their influential report *Policing Football Hooliganism*, which was eventually published in 1991. The research method adopted by the research team was a combination of participant observation and interview. Researchers accompanied Manchester United and Aston Villa fans on the away legs of their respective European competitions in the 1990-91 season, travelling as ordinary fans. Contacts were made with many fans and interviews conducted with them on their return. In addition, club officials of Manchester United and Aston Villa consented to be interviewed about various matters, e.g. ticket allocation and travel arrangements. We are grateful to the officials who gave their time and assistance. The decision by UEFA (European Union of Football Associations) to allow English clubs back into European competition following the lifting of the ban imposed after the Heysel tragedy in 1985 was fully vindicated, as our research showed, by the exemplary behaviour of English clubs' fans. In 1991-92 other English

clubs, including Liverpool, were, rightly, allowed to compete again. The research also included interviews with those charged with policing football and drafting 'football legislation'. The former Minister of Sport, Colin Moynihan, was interviewed at length immediately prior to the introduction of the Football Spectators Bill in January 1989. The full text of the interview is available in a Working Paper (*The Last Football Bill?* Manchester Law Working Papers No. 1, by Steve Redhead) from the School of Law, Manchester Metropolitan University. Furthermore, the researchers interviewed Superintendent Adrian Appleby, the Head of the National Football Intelligence Unit (NFIU). In general, it had been felt by government ministers and senior police officers that the problem of English football hooliganism has declined since the time of the Heysel debacle *as a result* of the 'law and order' clampdown on football since 1985. Our contention would be different - that a new football and popular music fan culture emerged in the 80s (partly as a consequence of the clampdown on ordinary, law-abiding fans) which made 'football hooliganism' less fashionable. Nevertheless, during the first Premier League season it has been suggested that a number of factors (mass unemployment, rampant regionalism, long term Imperial decline, and so on) have continued to contribute to a persistent 'Little England' attitude amongst many football supporters at English clubs' home matches in European fixtures during the 1992-93 season.

4.   *Football With Attitude* (Wordsmith, Manchester, 1991) by Steve Redhead, examines the changing contemporary relationships between football, popular music and youth culture in the 80s and 90s - in short, soccer fandom as pop culture. The photographs from the book, by rising portrait photographer Richard Davis provide snapshots of the forever changing channels of football into pop, and pop into football. The book portrays a contemporary supporter culture where, increasingly, young football fans are music fans and vice versa; visually they are often indistinguishable. Many of those involved in the pop music industry (writers, producers, DJs, singers, players) are obsessive football fans themselves. Moreover, football-related popular music is no longer the

lowest of low art, but right at the cutting edge of dancefloor sounds, as proved by Adrian Sherwood's Barmy Army productions on the On-U Sound label. Gary Clail, Sherwood's vocalist and 'toaster' even made the charts, albeit with a non-football song.

5. *New Times for Football?* was a one day seminar held at The Centre for Extra-Mural Studies, Birbeck College, University of London, on Sunday, March 10, 1991. Thanks to Richard Haynes for his notes on this conference and his subsequent Working Paper, published by the Unit for Law and Popular Culture, which discussed the issues raised by participants in the seminar. One aspect of these so-called 'New Times' was Channel 4's decision to show live Italian football on Sunday afternoons in the 1992-93 season in its programme *Football Italia*. This bold decision not only confirmed that the new Premier League fare was relatively dull - if very fast moving - but exploded the myths that:

    (a) Italian League football was defensive or dour, and
    (b) English League soccer was the best in the world.

    It also provided us with an excellent new theme tune, Definitive Two's *I'm Stronger Now*, on the Deconstruction label.

6. Feyenoord won its appeal against the original court decision in Holland to replay the game. In the 1991-92 European Cup Winners Cup, which Feyenoord therefore entered, the Dutch team beat Tottenham Hotspur over two legs. Thanks to Gonnie Rietveld, Research Assistant at the Unit for Law and Popular Culture, Manchester Metropolitan University, and Michael Day, postgraduate student at the Manchester Institute for Popular Culture, for all their work on the details of the case.

7. Witness its wide but generally sceptical coverage of *Among the Thugs*, a book by the editor of arts magazine *granta*, Bill Buford, published in hardback in October 1991 (and in paperback in 1992), which painted an wholly out-of-date, and

by 1992, inaccurate picture of the extent and style of football related violence in England in the 90s. See Martin Amis: 'Adventures of Bovver Boy Bill' in *The Independent on Sunday,* October 27, 1991; Catherine Bennett: 'An Eye to the Main Chants' in *The Guardian,* October 28, 1991; Chris Maume: 'Where Are They Now?' in *The Independent on Sunday,* November 3, 1991. Other voices remain unconvinced about the extent of the change which my work has suggested: see Gavin Hills 'Whatever Happened to the Likely Lads?" in *The Face,* November 1991, and John Williams' confused contribution to *When Saturday Comes,* January 1992.

8.   See Stan Cohen, *Folk Devils and Moral Panics,* (Blackwell, Oxford, 1987); Stan Cohen (ed.), *Images of Deviance,* (Penguin, Harmondsworth, 1971) and Laurie Taylor and Ian Taylor (eds.), *Politics and Deviance,* (Penguin, Harmondsworth, 1973).

9.   For example, see 'The Passion of Football' a television programme by producer Mick Gold made for Granada TV's arts section 'Celebration' in 1992 which was based on the contentions of *Football With Attitude* and focussed on the football fandom of classical music luminaries Michael Nyman and Nigel Kennedy as well as the football-related music of New Order and On-U Sound records. Nyman is currently scoring a musical for television based on Stan Bowles, a former player with Queen's Park Rangers, Nyman's favourite team. Nigel Kennedy explains his devotion to Aston Villa in *Nigel Kennedy: Always Playing,* (Mondovia, London, 1992) especially Chapter 7.

The following photographs, by Richard Davis, are from the original research into Manchester United fans travelling abroad for the Rotterdam Final, May 1991.

2 Marching on together

Richard Haynes

> Leeds got to the top the hard way...and people have never forgiven them for it. They developed a new professionalism; holding onto the ball; tackling hard, using the rules, gamesmanship if you like.
> (Eric Carlisle, Secretary of Leeds United Supporters Club).(1)

The 'woollybacks'(2) of Leeds have had to endure two decades of derision and scorn from within the football world, among supporters, and in the media, ever since Don Revie assembled one of the greatest teams in English football, bringing the name of Leeds United into the broader public domain. 'Hardness' has long been associated with not only the style of play, but also with the temperament of Leeds fans in general. The emergence of the Leeds Service Crew in the early 80s, often seen by the media to epitomise Leeds fans, whether real or mythological, compounded the public fear and hatred of any young males following the club. A catalogue of incidents involving Leeds fans, the 'Bournemouth Riot' being the most recent appendage to the list, is frequently trotted out by tabloid and quality press journalists alike, to justify further abomination of the club and its support.

The quote by Eric Carlisle which begins this Chapter, was taken from an article by Martyn Harris entitled "Leeds, the lads, and the meeja" which appeared in *New Society* in 1982. The article attempted to describe the rise of the Leeds Service Crew, their affinity for media attention, and the contrast between United fans with Leeds Rugby League fans. It is an archetypal piece of journalism on Leeds fans; many more were to follow throughout the 80s and early 90s. This Chapter is about Leeds fans' relationship with the media and the club they love. Moreover, it is a study of the broader relationship of fans with other fans, the media, the law, and the changing perceptions of football in wider society. The Chapter also attempts to develop from previous studies of media treatment of the fans, specifically 'football hooliganism'.(3) This means not only analysing the simple dialectical relation between fan behaviour and media images (using the concepts of 'amplification spirals' and 'moral panics'), but turning to 'postmodernist' theories of 'hyperreality' where (especially in the case of 'football hooliganism') as Jean Baudrillard has argued "there is an increasingly definitive lack of differentiation between image and reality which no longer leaves room for representation as such."(4)

From the glory years to the gory years

The style of Leeds United, both on and off the field of play, is of central importance in understanding the ideas and mythology that surrounds the club. Revie's decision to copy the all white strip of Real Madrid (to create an aura of intimidation) and his penchant for professionalism, aroused a form of aversion to Leeds United amongst many football followers. In an article entitled "Is Modern Football Too Rough?" Revie himself captured the spirit of the 'modern' Leeds team:

> I wince when I watch the Leeds United players in training - they put as much into it as Olympic athletes. Afterwards, they will sit in the dressing room picking each other to pieces, and its like music to my ears! You see, they constantly analyse each other's weaknesses, discussing ways to overcome them. And this shows they are striving for perfection all the time. Their lives revolve around Leeds United because they realise that the sky's the limit if the club is successful. They are prepared to devote themselves fully, sinking their individual ability into the general team pattern, even though it may mean that they might not stand out as past stars like Stan Matthews and Tom Finney did.(5)

Further innovations to the United strip: the sock number tags, and the plundering of the 'smiley badge' as the team emblem, added greater annoyance among anti-Leeds fans.

However, by the late 70s, Revie had left to manage the England national squad, and after losing the European Cup Final of 1975 in Paris, the team's influence at the top of the First Division faded. Yet the fans still persisted with the chant "Champions of Europe". This chauvinistic expression, and last ditch attempt to retain some of the 'glory years', emerged as Leeds fans became synonymous with the rising political influence of the National Front and other neo-fascist groups within football. Leeds frequently appeared top of the league table of racist hooligans appearing in *Bulldog* a magazine produced by the Young National Front. As the 80s came along and Leeds departed the First for the Second Division, racist and fascist material was increasingly available outside Elland Road. Among the publications was a 'skinzine' called *Wonderful World* which revelled in the covert activities of Leeds fans, and carried articles such as "A day out with the Leeds service crew". The skinhead style appeared to have a residual effect on football in Leeds while other working class fans, particularly in the North West of England, had moved onto the 'casual' style of support. This so-called 'backwardness' amongst Leeds fans in the soccer 'style-wars' is best documented in the adroit pages of the early 80s' fanzine *The End*. Coming out of Merseyside, *The End* captured the early 80s terrace culture, and its format can be seen as the forerunner to the plethora of football fanzines that emerged in the late 80s. The self-styled label wearers from Liverpool, known amongst themselves as 'scallies', took to labelling all Leeds fans as 'woollybacks' because of the Yorkshiremen's supposed affinity for sheep! Leeds fans came in for a particular slating on the letters page; the following from 'worried of Seaforth' is a classic example:

> I wonder if you can help me. I'm desperate you see although I pretend to be a real scally I have a secret overwhelming desire to be a 'woolly'. It started last year when I went to the Liverpool v Leeds match with my scally friends. I found myself identifying with the Leeds fans and started to wonder how I would look in their clothes. I couldn't wait to get home and try on some of my brother's

old clothes, as he was older than me and I was sure he must have some left over from that time. Bricking the Leeds coaches which had been such fun in the past now seemed like an unnecessary delay.

As soon as I got home I raided my brother's wardrobe and to my delight I found a 3 star jumper, a pair of birno's and a pair of beige and brown platforms. I hurriedly tried them on and looked in the mirror, but somehow I didn't quite look right, so I parted my hair, my image was complete; I realised that I had become a 'closet wool'.(6)

Not surprisingly Leeds fans rose to the bait, sending letters of resentment for being ridiculed, the replies often boasting about the exploits of the Service Crew, much to the amusement of *The End*'s editor and leader of The Farm pop band, Peter Hooton. Indeed, it approached the stage where Hooton comically commented that they sold "more mags in Leeds than Birkenhead." The playful dialogue between Leeds fans and the supporters of the North West, was not as vindictive as the rivalry between Leeds and Chelsea fans. Stemming from Chelsea's F.A. Cup victory over Leeds in 1970, a hatred had developed to mythological proportions between the two clubs. As one recent Chelsea supporter put it in the fanzine *The Blues Brothers*:

I always thought every club had its best behaved supporters reserved for places like the main stand, but it seemed at Leeds that the whole place was totally hostile and antagonistic to everything to do with Chelsea.(7)

While not denying the reality of such feelings and events as experienced by Leeds fans and their rivals, it is clear that the mythologies that surround this terrace culture have been increasingly used and amplified by the media. By doing so the media create their own narratives, focusing on the particular fan rivalries, the 'hooligan menace', the 'scum' of Elland Road. By anticipating, like the fan, where to expect trouble, the media set out to report it. As Baudrillard asks in a different context: "what else does the media dream of if not raising up events by its very presence."(8)

The events in Bournemouth at the end of the 1989/90 season where Leeds secured promotion back into the First Division, offer a prime example where the media's scenario of events preceded, and ultimately coincided, with what happened on a hot summer Bank Holiday. So how and why did the media stage the 'Bournemouth Riot' in May 1990?

Staging the 'Bournemouth Riot'

In November 1990 South Leeds Youth Theatre staged a play called 'Leeds United' developing the experiences of Beeston teenagers, using the weeks before the match with Bournemouth and the break-up of a love affair as its backdrop. As one reviewer put it:

> Into the framework of place names and local detail, the Youth Theatre throw acid trips, raves and riots. A band plays anti-poll tax benefits, a young woman is pressured into sex, fascists organise football supporters and parents lecture on condoms.(9)

Essentially fictional, borrowing stereotypical images of youth culture and male football fans, the play at least offered a broader narrative of young people's lives in Leeds, portraying the way in which their leisure practices intersect with or contradict others. More importantly the play illustrated that going to the match is only part of a young person's experience of following football. In many ways the Youth Theatre production could have been written before the event; to a certain degree it was.

For the media, police and other legal authorities, the only story that could unfold centred around stopping Leeds fans causing trouble, and like a self-fulfilling prophecy, that eventually became the outcome. Eleven months before the Bank Holiday game the Dorset police had approached the Football League asking for the date of the game to be changed. One week before the game, Assistant Chief Constable Allan Rose proposed the game be moved to the Thursday. Following the events of the weekend *The Daily Star* proudly announced that it had warned of trouble 72 hours before "Leeds fans mounted their shameful south coast invasion" with the headline

"WE TOLD YOU SO."(10) Because of several incidents on the Friday evening before Saturday's game, hundreds of police from Dorset, backed by forces from Hampshire and Wiltshire, provided a strong police presence at the ground and in the town. In the words of Chief Superintendent Richard Danbrey, they were "prepared for the worst scenario." As fans congregated on the seafront, any thoughts of celebrating the prospect of their club's return to Division One were quickly dashed as the police moved the fans off the beach towards Deans Court. The 'running battles' that resulted were almost assured, but not as predictable as the headlines of the following couple of days:

> **UNITED THUGS RUN RIOT; WELCOME BACK LEEDS**
> (*Sunday Mirror*, 6/5/90.)
> **SOCCER IN THE GUTTER:** We'll rip your car to pieces if you don't give us some tickets. (*The Sun*, 7/5/90).
> **BATTLE OF BOURNEMOUTH:** Leeds hooligans kick team's reputation into touch. (*Yorkshire Post*, 7/5/90).

Under the heading "Leeds have a smashing time by the seaside" football reporter Joe Lovejoy was horrified enough to write:

> Leeds promotion back to the mainstream after an eight year absence was achieved against an appalling backdrop, the riff-raff of the Ridings having turned Bournemouth into Beirut for 24 hours with an orgy of mind numbing violence... The First Division is about to gain a hooligan army and a moderate team whose most effective weapon this season has been a tedious offside trap. Some bargain....At the final whistle the Leeds hordes, gathered under the racist banners proclaiming their white origins, some in full ku-klux klan garb, poured on the pitch with the nihilistic chant: 'Let's go fucking mental'. Unfortunately, for the rest of us, they are.(11)

Vociferous support by the anti-Leeds fan club continued at the highest level. David Evans, M.P., a prominent deprecator of 'football hooliganism' proclaimed:

The blame attaches to incompetent football administrators and the failure to treat people from Trafalgar Square to Strangeways and Bournemouth in a strictly disciplinary way. I'd take the lot of them to the Leeds ground for a good public flogging.(12)

As if the Football League had control over Poll Tax riots and aggrieved prisoners! Less bombastic commentators tried to find a more subversive reason for the violence. The then Shadow Minister for Sport, Dennis Howell, M.P. argued:

Somebody, somewhere organised this which is proved by the fact that some of them were wearing T-shirts emblazoned with the words 'Bournemouth Invasion - 1990'....We now have this National Intelligence Unit supposed to be operating. We would like to know how it has proved to be so ineffective.(13)

To suggest that the T-shirts constituted some sort of preorganised crime is clearly nonsensical, as they were freely available outside Elland Road at previous home games. However, such conspiracy theories about the subversive nature of 'hooligan gangs' and 'generals' have been a favourite theme when talking about football related violence, not only by M.P.s, but the media, the police and sociologists alike. Moreover, the constant labelling of troublesome fans associated with particular clubs gave credence to the establishment of a National Football Intelligence Unit in the summer of 1989, to co-ordinate a strategy of covert operations against the 'hooligan generals'. The NFIU and Dorset police did have prior intelligence reports from the West Yorkshire police, which were put forward as a major reason why 700 police, the majority in riot gear, along with horses, dogs and helicopter surveillance, were deployed to police approximately 5,000 football supporters. The NFIU is the latest in a series of legal interventions into the social and public domain of football, which have significantly altered the game's contours since the early 70s. The events in Bournemouth became a catalyst for further interventions. Dorset Chief Constable, Brian Weight, called for power to veto potentially 'troublesome' football fixtures. The Association of Chief Police Officers followed up his argument and Alan Eastwood, chairman of the Police Federation, lobbied the Home Secretary, then David Waddington, to set up a top-level Government inquiry into the rioting. The Football League subsequently bowed to government pressure, pledged to give the police (in practice) veto over fixtures, shelving any plans by the Government to introduce legislation to make veto a statutory right for the police. This left the Football Association to carry out its own internal inquiry into why the Football League had ignored police advice and, further, to arrange some form of punishment for Leeds United. The eventual outcome of the inquiry reserved its strongest criticism for the Football League, suggesting the programme for the last Saturday of the season be reviewed at least six weeks in advance. Leeds, for their part, did not have to pay any compensation to Bournemouth, but received a suspended sentence which requiredthem to play four home matches behind closed doors should there be further misdemeanour. Any further trouble would have cost the club its affiliation to the F.A. and therefore membership of the League. Prior to this, Leeds United were given a civic reception with 5,000 fans gathered in front of the Civic Hall, which was draped in a banner proclaiming 'BOURNEMOUTH WE'RE SORRY'. In the *Yorkshire Post*, May 14, 1990, Leeds City Council Leader, Councillor John Tricket, said:

> We don't accept responsibility for what happened in Bournemouth but it was done in the name of Leeds. Today we have proved we are not a hooligan city.

However, Bournemouth's chairman, Jim Nolan, was not so impressed with the outcome of the inquiry.

> Leeds have got off lightly, with a slap on the wrist, and they know it. They spent £4m on players this summer. I would have liked them to have put 10% of that into a Bournemouth council fund so it could have been distributed among those people who had property damaged by their fans, or who lost business as a result of damage.(14)

The above legal and political meanderings regarding the Leeds versus Bournemouth game are indicative of the narrative structures within which the football authorities, the police, and the Government are played out in the realm of the media. Superseding the apportioning of blame worthiness in the pages of the press (usually on the back page) is a meta-narrative which makes English football fans (particularly from clubs such as Leeds) seem synonymous with violence and criminal behaviour. It is here that an alternative view of events needs to be put; a counter-story challenging the hegemony of received wisdom about Leeds fans in Bournemouth, and football supporters in general since the mid-80s.

We love you Leeds, Leeds, Leeds!

> Without warning the riot police charged into every Leeds fan they could see, banging their riot shields and batoning everyone. I've waited 8 years for this promotion but what happened broke my heart. I was virtually crying on Saturday night.
> (David Brown, accused in the 1988 'Wild Boar' trial.) (15)

Until the mid-80s the voice of the football supporter was virtually unheard. With the tragedies at Bradford, Heysel and Hillsborough, fans have nudged their way into the mainstream media partly through the vociferousness of the Football Supporters Association and myriad soccer fanzines. This unprecedented explosion of literature, written by supporters themselves and containing a variety of stories and humorous anecdotes, has expressed a very widespread disillusion with the manner in which professional football is being organised. Fanzines provide an insight into the football milieu, offering an alternative network of ideas and lifestyles compared with the usual portrayal of fans in the tabloid, and even serious, press.

It was difficult, in the aftermath of the events at Bournemouth, to find any interviews with, or representation of the opinions of, the fans in the press coverage. The only space given over to fans either listed the names and addresses of those arrested or quoted a fan who simply reiterated the demand for punitive action proposed by the television, media and press themselves. For instance, an article in *The Daily Star*, May 9, 1990, under the heading "FAN BACKS

LEEDS BAN", reported that lifelong Leeds supporter Ray Hallett agreed with *The Star's* lead article which argued that Leeds should remain in the Second Division; he declared, "I feel disgusted and have made one decision: I won't be going to Elland Road next season."

There appeared to be only one alternative description of the events in the press, that of the regional *Leeds Other Paper*. In an enlightened attempt at a balanced report, *LOP* highlighted the availability of a large number of forged tickets, explained the large scale condemnation of violence by fans who tried to calm down the situation and stressed the point that the violence on the Saturday was provoked by over-zealous policing. Moreover, Nick Stringer from the Leeds fanzine *The Hanging Sheep* was used as a key eye-witness in the report, an idea that has since been adopted by many of the national newspapers as fanzines have gained more recognition. Stringer was quoted as saying:

> We are obviously very annoyed they wouldn't let us in. There were more people with proper tickets outside the ground than inside. Then the police over-reacted.(16)

In the subsequent months, several articles and letters appeared in fanzines, all criticising either the police, the media or the football authorities. One of the most articulate arguments appeared in the Leeds fanzine *The Square Ball*:

> In the case of Bournemouth, the attitude of Leeds fans was to have day out by the sea even if ground admittance was out of the question....Every club has a contingent of 'nutters' and the hype generated before the game must have attracted other clubs' undesirables. All they had to do was don a Leeds shirt. Of the hundred or so arrests only a small percentage were United away club members. The police tactics were also up to their usual brilliance. Riot gear and cavalry charges seem to be the accepted norm for the 80s/90s, countering everything from striking miners to acid house parties. More often than not this leads to an escalation of violence and will always injure the innocent as well as the guilty.(17)

When Saturday Comes, one of the most widely read fanzines, carried an article by Nick Varley entitled 'Not Quite Riot'. He argued that anyone returning to this country after a spell abroad, would still have guessed which team's supporters were responsible for the events in Bournemouth. The media came in for some severe criticism, especially Joe Lovejoy of *The Independent,* who he claimed had:

> Deduced that the various banners supporting the whites were racist (Don Revie's real motives for changing the kit colour now became clear - he was a covert NF agent!)[18]

Even more annoying for Varley was the myopia of the media to the positive steps taken by Leeds and their fans to prevent trouble: the away club members scheme 'The Red Card'; live screening of the match at four venues in Leeds; and the work of Leeds Fans United Against Racism and Fascism. Finally, Varley best sums up the way in which the press exacerbated the problem, suggesting:

> Journalists have to be prepared to go beyond the cliches which pervade football reporting. Headlines such as 'Soccer At War' don't help anyone. The aim of everyone involved in football must be to marginalise the hooligans as a step towards a peaceful nature. The media, so swift to identify others culpability have to realise they also have a role to play in overcoming hooliganism. Don't believe (all) the hype.[19]

From being kicked to where it's 'kickin'

> I do believe there is a connection between what happened in Bournemouth and the fact that Leeds is the least hip city in Britain.[20]

Going to football for young Leeds fans is a similar experience to that of their contemporaries in the North West: having a laugh with your mates; wearing 'cool' clothes; and supporting your club, not through fighting, but through colour and singing 'your heart out for the lads!'. Bournemouth was the end-of-season party, where beer, music and football met sun, sea and sand to produce what many Leeds fans wanted to be part of a spectacle, a carnival to remember. The all-white dress - baggy Leeds shirt, and sun hat - helped to produce a summer spirit, a youthful hedonism, and, significantly, an identity that said, 'We are Leeds'.

Despite the label of 'woollies' and being criticised for being 'five years behind fashion and five years ahead of music',(21) Leeds took up the scally look with enthusiasm. Football and music in Leeds in the late 80s and early 90s was embodied in the fanaticism for Leeds-based 'Indie' pop bands, The Wedding Present, CUD and The Bridewell Taxis, along with James, Happy Mondays, The Farm and The Stone Roses. Fashion and clubbing was greatly influenced by what *The Face* termed 'The Manchester Effect';(22) heavy policing of clubs and illegal parties in and around Manchester causing a spreading of all-night raves over the Pennines into West Yorkshire. Young people in Leeds once again became victims of legal intervention, the most widely reported incident occurring in Gildersome near Leeds, where there were 836 arrests. In many ways, as far as their relationship with the police was concerned, 1990 was no 'Summer of Love' for young people from Leeds, especially football fans.

However, by way of a postscript to the events of 1990, the summer of '92 tasted quite sweet in Leeds. Both the football and dance club scene had blossomed in a city which is entering the New Europe not only economically but culturally. Forgetting the recession and a further term of Tory administration, young people in Leeds party on the back of Leeds United's League Championship success and the city's booming night-life. Arguably the best terrace chant of the season came from Elland Road, the disco rhythm of "ooh aah Cantona" in celebration of the enigmatic and inspirational French footballer Eric Cantona, subsequently recorded by Oo-La-La on North Speed Records. The free-spirited Frenchman, who has a love of poetry, showed verve and passion which, in the words of David Hopps of *The Guardian*, "created a celebratory mood which contrasted with the debilitating nervousness at Old Trafford",(23) something which ultimately influenced the 1991/92 title race. Celebrations in the city on the Sunday as Leeds clinched the title were described by police as being "livelier than New Year's Eve."(24)

Throughout the year a new unbridled hedonism had taken a hold among young people in Leeds, which manifested itself in the carnivalesque atmosphere of the terraces and plethora of 'top' nights in the city's club. Britain's leading dance and clubbing magazine *Mixmag* welcomed its readers to "planet Leeds" and stated in March 1992:

> It's another world up there. And there's certainly no recession as the club scene goes barmy. Clubs like Kaos, Back to Basics and Ark are booming away, with Leeds striding through the winter blues, packing the best club scene in the land.(25)

The Corn Exchange, a shopping arcade by day, transformed itself into a ravers paradise by night, a huge open plan venue with people crammed on balconies and benches. DJ Terry Farley went as far as to liken his experience there to the early days of the rave scene on the island of Ibiza.(26)

The revitalised night-time economy in Leeds and the success of Leeds United are now important for shaping the city's public image. What is usually considered to be 'low' culture is, in fact, creating an enhanced cultural ambience in the city, constructing alternative images and possibilities, moving towards a cosmopolitan regional capital. Leeds is an example, along with other industrial cities across Europe, of youth celebrating life in the city, creating a positive mood, which in turn markets the city for future investment and tourism both locally and nationally.

The importance of the image of the fans in relation to the image of the city cannot be understated. The media coverage of Leeds in winning the 1991/2 Championship tended to spotlight favourably on the fans.(27) But comparisons with the Revie era and the cliched scenarios of the teams 'resilience' and the 'fighting spirit' still pervaded the match reports. Throughout both seasons back in the top flight, match reports emphasised the tenacity and fast moving football Leeds played. David Batty was singled out as epitomising the club, showing "the sort of pride that underlies the passion of the support."(28) Gordon Strachan, the Football Writers Player of the Year for 1991, summed up the problem the club had with its media image in an interview he gave after a game with Crystal Palace:

We've tried to change. We knew there was a style to get out of the Second, but you can see we are trying to be a better team. You can't simply say we're aggressive - it's like saying you don't like Des O'Connor records - it's just a music hall joke.

Leeds are the 'music hall joke' of football, due to the media focus on particular tactics of the team and past antics of their massed support, re-representing and short-circuiting reality, causing what Baudrillard would call the "implosion of image and reality."(29) This is not to argue that Leeds fans have not in the past, and are never likely to in the future, cause trouble, but merely to recognise that things have changed and the prevailing mood is now far more carnivalesque than in the 80s. What has happened in the postmodern, media-saturated scene we have described here is an increasing lack of differentiation between the image of the club and its fans, and any separate, autonomous, prevailing reality, giving no time or space for a 'true' or 'false' representation.

Football fans, and especially 'hooligan' fans, are part of, and to some extent structured by, numerous discourses. Football for so long came to signify not a game of beauty and skill but a troublesome blackspot of 'society' that the majority of 'decent' people had to reluctantly put up with. The work of fanzines, the FSA and other independent fan organisations act to build up oppositional discourses in the football world and the processes of mass media re-representation. Unlike the scenarios posited by early theories on football fandom, where young people were seen to take on the deviant media role prescribed for them, fanzines invariably defend the integrity and good nature of fans against the deviant discourses posited by the media, the police, the government and frequently the football clubs themselves. Fanzines represent an inversion of received scenarios of discourse on fans; of the crowd perceived as 'threatening youth'. The Leeds fanzine *Marching Altogether* produced by Leeds Fans United Against Racism and Fascism represents a form of cultural contestation within football, and moreover sport in general. Striving towards a form of democratisation within the game, fanzines - whether they are humorous, anecdotal or political - and the emerging good nature among masses of football supporters in general in the 90s - provide the way forward to combat the popular image of football fans as 'hooligans'.(30)

References

1. *New Society,* November 25, 1982.

2. A term of derision often used by people from the North West to describe people from out of town or Yorkshire. Epitomised in the early 80s fanzine *The End.*

3. See, for example, Stuart Hall 'The Treatment of Football Hooliganism in the Press' in R. Ingham, *Football Hooliganism: The Wider Context,* Inter-Action, 1978; Gary Whannel 'Football Crowd Behaviour and the Press' in *Media, Culture and Society,* 1979, Vol. 4; and P. Murphy, E. Dunning, J. Williams, *Football on Trial,* R.K.P., 1990.

4. Jean Baudrillard, *The Evil Demon of Images,* Power Publications, 1987.

5. Don Revie, 'Is Modern Football Too Rough?' in *The Park Drive Book of Football 1967/68.*

6. *The End,* Vol. 9.

7. *The Blues Brothers,* No. 4.

8. Baudrillard, op cit.

9. *Leeds Other Paper,* November 9, 1990.

10. *The Daily Star,* May 7, 1990.

11 *The Independent,* May 7, 1990.

12. *The Independent,* May 1990.

13. *The Yorkshire Post,* May 7, 1990.

14. *The Independent,* August 1990.

15. *Leeds Other Paper*, May 11, 1990.

16. *Leeds Other Paper*, May 11, 1990.

17. *The Square Ball*, No.5.

18. *When Saturday Comes*, No. 41, July 1990.

19. *When Saturday Comes*, ibid.

20. Quoted on the 'Propaganda' page of *The Square Ball*, No.5.

21. Pete Naylor 'In Search of the Scally', *Unpublished Paper*.

22. *The Face*, October 1990.

23. David Hopps, *The Guardian*, August 25, 1990.

24. *The Guardian*, May 2, 1992.

25. *Yorkshire Evening Post*, April 27, 1992.

26. *Mixmag*, March 1992.

27. On Sunday, May 3, 1992, more than 100,000 people came out onto the streets of Leeds to celebrate the clubs success. The Lord Mayor of Leeds, councillor Ronnie Feldman, told the crowd at the civic reception, "The players and supporters have been a credit to this city and their club."

28. *The Guardian*, August 25, 1990.

29. Baudrillard, op cit.

30. In March 1992, a pitch invasion at St Andrews occurred at the end of a game between Birmingham City and Stoke City due to the high stakes of a promotion place between the Midland clubs. St. Andrews had been the scene of a fan's death at a game involving Leeds United in May 1985 immediately prior to

the Heysel disaster. The media took the opportunity to remind its readers of such spectres from football's 'hooligan' past and The *Sunday Express* chose to focus on the words of John Williams from the Sir Norman Chester Centre for Football Research at the University of Leicester, who was quoted as saying, "our experience is that hooliganism occurs in cycles and there is a danger the Birmingham incident may be the start of another period of problems." See Chapter 2 for a discussion of the cyclical nature of mass media presentation of the problem of football hooliganism.

3 'Ratfink Reds': Montpellier and Rotterdam 1991

Adam Brown

On the one hand, the images from Manchester United's European Cup Winners' Cup games in Montpellier and Rotterdam are similar - the ranks of the United faithful celebrating famous victories. On the other, they illustrate different approaches to the regulation of fans and different aspects of fandom - the front of a nightclub in Montpellier smashed and fans being chased up the street by riot police, as opposed to supporters dancing with policemen and women draped in red and white, on rainy Rotterdam streets.

My experiences were unusual in that they combined two obsessions, music and football. As drummer in a Manchester band, Ratfink, I travelled to both games to not only watch the football, but also to play gigs specifically designed for the supporters. In a sense, however, it was less unusual than might first appear. Magazines like *The Face* and the *New Musical Express* began talking of a football/music crossover in 1990 - after all Manchester's New Order had just recorded the England World Cup song, *World in Motion*, and a plethora of bands emerged making reference to their other interests in their names and songs, from Pele, Eusebio, Mexico '70, to On-U Sound. As has been written elsewhere,

> ...the new culture of post-punk influences on football fandom continue to make their presence felt. Various 'street' styles have been disseminated across the nation's young football fans...in a never ending procession of phases...

and in this sense, our experience was an example of a trend that the "football/pop crossover reached an inevitable peak in the 1990/91

33

season following Italia '90."

The gig on the night before the game in Montpellier was arranged by us completely independently, once the draw was known. We never played due to the club being closed by the CRS riot police after some heavy handed security and police sparked off trouble with some of United's followers. We were, in contrast, invited by Dutch police, through Rotterdam Arts Council, to play a special outdoor concert for United fans on the afternoon before the final, illuminating a different approach and different understanding of fan culture in the 90s.

Allez Les Rouges! - Montpellier, March '91

Gordon Taylor of the PFA talks of football's "dream factor", and of the "footballing democracy" inherent in the game, the element of chance. For me it was the coincidence that United drew Montpellier in the quarter finals of the Cup Winners' Cup, and that the away leg was at the same time as Ratfink were scheduled to be on tour in France.

Immediately the draw was known a gig was arranged, to coincide with the tie, at The Rockstore club the night before United's game. Using all the enabling technology of desk top publishing and cheap duplication, along with a fair dash of entrepreneurial self-publicity - "do it yourself pop" 90s style, in Iain Chambers words - we made sure everyone would know about the gig. Using the informal networks around the anzines *United We Stand* and *Red Issue* we distributed publicity. This involved leaflets, a phone-in competition for tickets, and word of mouth, the fact that I was deeply involved in both aspects of the event, as a football supporter as well as drummer for Ratfink, certainly helped.

The local press also came to our aid: *City Life* ran information on the gig and the competition, and *The Manchester Evening News* ran the story "Ratfink Will Paint Montpellier Red", claiming that, "Even if Manchester United don't batter Montpellier into submission tomorrow, I'm sure Ratfink will tonight." The language, as it turned out, was all too appropriate.

It is worth detailing the events about the Montpellier trip, as a useful illustration of what can go wrong with football fandom from a seemingly near perfect situation.

Arriving in the centre square of Montpellier at lunch time on Monday, March 18, was a marvellous experience - hundreds of United fans singing, dancing, drinking, playing football and swapping scarves with the 'opposition' in the French sunshine. It was a 'carnivalesque' fans celebration of 'just being there', and being there unofficially, not on one of the Manchester United's organised tours, and despite the obstructiveness of the club and the British government.

The pleasure of being there was only heightened when we realised that everyone knew about the gig, recognised our T-shirts and that the club was less than a football pitch's length from where the burgeoning groups of fans were gathering.

The only blot on the blue horizon was the problem of tickets. As a good example of an attempt to sanitise popular culture, to regulate and control events as tightly as possible (motivated by a deep fear of what fans might do), United had only got 500 tickets from Montpellier, all available as part of an official package trip; most fans were seemingly excluded from the chance to follow their team.

It is sad that, given the tremendous support from fans, who were prepared to dig deep into their pockets in the heart of a recession, United seemed so obstructive about having their supporters with them. It was, after all, the first away leg abroad, of the competition that most fans could get to - the previous rounds had been in Hungary and Wales - and fans wanted to mark the return of English clubs to European competition. To be asked to pay £50 on the black market - transferred from Wythenshawe to Montpellier for the week - seemed to increase a sense of alienation, and the promise of some fans that, "we'll storm the ground if we don't get in", illustrated the unnecessary potential flashpoint.

The first hint of any trouble as far as we were concerned, was that one person said to us that he and a friend had been refused entry into The Rockstore the night before because they were United fans. Knowing what problems it would cause, given the interest in the gig, I tried to make sure that it didn't happen on the night. Both myself and one of the tour's organisers spoke to the manager of the club, and got firm assurances that no such policy would be pursued on the night. This seemed to be clearly understood by all parties, and indeed, the management of the club seemed pleased that so many fans were likely to turn up.

However, at about 8 p.m., whilst we were still soundchecking,

35

everyone suddenly left the auditorium and rushed to the bar at the front of the club - which was open all the time - because of a disturbance. We followed them out and the staff and security were in a state of some panic, with two of the windows at the front of the club broken. There were bottles broken on the steps in front of the club, and CRS riot police were charging after United fans in the streets.

Staff told us that very drunk and aggressive fans had been refused entry into the bar and reacted by throwing bottles and other missiles. An early attempt to talk to the police was met with a sharp poke in the ribs from a truncheon. However, a rather different version of events emerged from the fans we spoke to outside. It appears that although there were a very few who were very drunk and who wanted to take bottles into the club, most had be queuing in an orderly manner. There were not large numbers outside the club at this time (perhaps as few as 25) so there should not have been any problems in controlling the crowd. Indeed, it appeared that some of the fans with cans and bottles had bought them precisely because they had not been allowed into the club.

What is more, the club's 'bouncer' seemed to have been determined to cause trouble, and although there had been some argument because no fans were being allowed in, there was not a violent reaction by those outside. Not, that is, until the bouncer sprayed some gas (probably Mace gas) into the faces of those outside in an attempt to get them to disperse. I met a number of people with very sore skin and swollen eyes from the gas, who, it should be pointed out, were in no way violent or drunk.

Predictably, this provoked a reaction from the fans, a small number of whom (perhaps just two or three) threw bottles at the club, breaking two panes of glass. The CRS then arrived in force, using truncheons and dogs - where they thought they were chasing the supporters was not clear. It was also reported by a number of people that the club security had fired some form of plastic bullets at the crowd. This was not only ridiculously heavy handed and entirely indiscriminate, but was also highly counter productive. It very nearly resulted in disturbances on a much greater scale.

Later, after repeated assurances from the management that there was no discriminatory policy toward English fans, provided they were not drunk, the security were still not letting any fans in. Eventually, at about 10 p.m., the CRS entered the club and closed it down. The night which promised so much was over without a note being played.

This incident raises important questions about the policing of football supporters. Most notably because the French police and the club's security seemed to base their actions more on the, at the time, hysterical media image of English supporters, all of whom, they presumed, were infected with the 'English disease'. The attitude was to treat supporters as thugs when all the evidence pointed the other way - the pervading atmosphere was one of celebration, as this was after all a holiday for many, a break from the drudgery of working of - in many cases - unemployed lives. It was not necessary for the CRS to be in attendance all day in full riot gear, or for the club's security to be armed with tear gas , a knuckle duster and plastic bullets. It seemed that the authorities had already decided what was going to happen and their actions merely ensured it.

This suspicion and fear of English fans was not, it seemed, localised; supporters I spoke to later the same evening had been thrown out of bars in which they had been drinking happily all day. Also, at the match itself the following day the policing amounted to downright provocation, as supporters were hit, searched and had possessions stolen. The suggestion over those two days was that the only thugs in evidence were dressed in blue and not in red.

It is fair to say that other factors played a part - for instance, with hindsight it would have been a good idea to have an English representative on the door of the club. But, at most, our gig provided the situation, and the responsibility for the flashpoint lay with the club's security.

The complexion of the supporters was an influence also, in that it seemed to be made up of young males in their late twenties rather than late teens, and as such included those who had been on the European campaigns in the late 70s and early 80s. In an important sense, it represented an older 'style' of football supporter - one showed me his commemorative tattoo from St. Etienne, next to his Inter City Firm tattoo - to whom the changes since Heysel, and the changes in youth culture, for instance, meant little.

These are only minor qualifications, however. The determination of the media to focus upon violence was illustrated on the day of the match when I was interviewed on French radio. Although I said that I only wanted to talk about Ratfink, the interviewer persistently asked about the trouble the night before. What is more, the only section of the interview broadcast was my comments about the violence, and they were broadcast on a news programme and not a music show!

The determination of the fans was no less remarkable, however. Considering the provocation and discrimination faced, it was a credit to their ability to celebrate a special occasion that there were no more serious disturbances. Their reward was fittingly given in the form of a famous victory for United and the fact that everyone found their way into the match one way or another. The sheer pleasure that football can bring, the 'jouissance' in Barthes' word, could not have been clearer than on that evening. It is perhaps fitting that it was at this game that the fans first started singing *Always Look on the Bright Side of Life*. The 'New Times' in football were not only marked by the fact that two of my friends were supplied with tickets by a Manchester City fan, in Montpellier for the fun of it, but also that the whole tenor of the crowd was celebratory. Given the experience of the previous 24 hours, this was very refreshing.

We're the famous Man United and we're going to Rotterdam!

I had already resigned myself to the fact that I would have to go on one of the official trips organised by the club to the final in Rotterdam on May 15. However, the joke of "Ratfink off to Poland/Holland then?" became a reality at the last minute.

Through contacts with the FSA (Football Supporters Association) made in Montpellier, I heard that the Dutch police were wanting bands from Manchester to play a special outdoor festival for the fans. After a hectic day's telephone calls it was confirmed. Thel Brekelmans, Deputy Chief Constable of the Rotterdam police, had showed an imagination and fresh way of thinking that had been sadly lacking in France.

What is more, it is no coincidence that he looked to music as the way to entertain the fans - the global media phenomenon of 'Madchester' had been in full swing for the previous year and more, and the status of Manchester as a music, as well as a footballing city, was well established. 808 State from Manchester played a gig in Holland while the fans were there for the final.

It is interesting, also, that the main obstacle to us going was the obstructiveness of the North Sea Ferries, who had banned any football supporters from using their ships. Fortunately we were able to use our identities as musicians, plus a fax from the Rotterdam Arts Council, to get around them. One friend who had been with us in Montpellier evoked religious imagery to sum up our situation; "Going to the final and playing a gig there! It's like going straight to Heaven and cutting out the middle man!"

Obstructiveness greeted us once more when we arrived in Belgium two hours late, as Belgian police wouldn't let us stop to make a telephone call. Having reached Rotterdam we were bombarded with a series of amazing images. First was an impromptu interview with *The Manchester Evening News* in the mini-bus en route to the venue. Then there was the sight of thousands of United fans all dressed up; red, white and black was everywhere. The feeling of being a participant in such a spectacle was tremendously uplifting. Backstage were the somewhat contradictory images of a police officer armed, yet draped in red and white, enforcing an alcohol ban on site, yet overlooking the widespread use of soft drugs by the fans - Europe, '91 style!

It was perhaps not surprising that the gig itself was flawed: we had to use the venue's equipment, had numerous technical hitches and the rain poured down. Nonetheless it was a memorable gig - starting 'Charge' with a blistering Hendrix-style rendition of *We're on the march we're Fergie's army*, Chris booting footballs back into the crowd, and seeing the flags come out for an anarchic rendition of *The Boys are Back in Town* were the highlights.

We were provided with tickets for the game and, once all the Ratfink business was dealt with, there was the agony and ecstasy of waiting for the evening to come - a feeling every football fan the world over is familiar with. The impact of how many United fans were there wasn't really made until we were in the stadium itself. Looking up at the tens of thousands who had made the journey from one post-industrial rainy city to another was a sight not to be forgotten. It was football as a spectacle at its best - with a sea of red and white banners at one end, and the purple and blue flares of Barcelona at the other.

The events of that evening are well documented elsewhere; suffice it to say that United had to take us all through every possible emotion, from joy to despair, before lifting the trophy, and marking a remarkable return to Europe for English clubs. Yet it was striking that the occasion was made as much by the fans as by the players on the pitch, and in this sense it is correct to see popular culture's participants as John Fiske does as "cultural producers and not merely cultural dupes."

The whole occasion in Rotterdam had a completely different feel to it than Montpellier, and it wasn't just that we got soaked instead of sunburnt! The supporters were different in a number of ways. There were, of course, much greater numbers in Rotterdam - United made it practically a home game. Easier access also gave the crowd a different complexion, with a greater variety in ages and more fans in their teens and early twenties. It would be wrong to labour this point, however.

Montpellier had been the first 'big' European game for United for a number of years and in some respects people did not know what to expect. By the time of the final, however, the scaremongering newspaper stories - from German skinhead gangs, to prison in Poland - were no longer really credible, despite the attempt being made at that time in the British media to rename 'Madchester' as 'Badchester' in the nation's press.

The attitude of the police forces marked a huge difference. The French police watched the supporters from a distance, suspicious and waiting for trouble. The heavy handed and militarised policing looked like it would cause more problems than it would solve - fencing fans in, and pointing automatic rifles is not really going to establish a good rapport with the fans. It felt in Montpellier that things could have gone quite differently and the fact that it didn't had more to do with changes in fan behaviour and fan culture than with policing methods.

This was a point that one felt the Dutch police appreciated to a greater degree. As our experience goes, we went from having our gig cancelled by the French police to actually being invited to play by the Dutch police. Although it seems that the concert in the park was something of a last minute decision, and the venue was under threat for a time, it was an altogether more thoughtful and, ultimately, more successful approach. The pictures of police men and women dancing with United fans and wearing scarves and shirts were a vivid visual display of a more refreshing "football with attitude."

Of course, these are just two examples of contemporary fan and police behaviour, and so contain many generalities. Also, they are an account from someone who was very much a participant of events as

40

well as an observer. However, I think that there are important lessons to be learned and differences to be seen. At its most basic level there is the lesson that, if you treat people like animals there is a greater chance that some of them will behave like animals. Fortunately, on *both* these occasions that did not happen, largely as a result of changes in football fandom since the mid-80s.

As an illustration of where fan culture is these experiences offer a number of pointers. The football/music crossover hype naturally disappeared as quickly as it came. But the fact of ever more diverse and interlinked fan cultures and fan identities is still a feature of the 90s. The rave/dance culture and its associated drug use is still in evidence on the terraces and despite a persistent ethnocentrism in English football culture has many implications. As Anthony H. Wilson has said:

> No one's getting pissed anymore. They're doing soft drugs and dancing, and still going to football or whatever, but it's taken the edge off culture in many British cities.

What is also remarkable is the continuing ability of fans to defy dominant images in the media and in wider society. The ability to get hedonistic pleasure from a game with the authorities trying to prevent, or at least severely restrict and regulate, their presence is surely what Fiske means by the pleasure and politics of these instances of popular culture being the important ones, "for they are the articulation of the interests of the people."

But in the year since these events, fans have found it necessary to organise themselves into protest groups to protect 'their' game from clubs whose financial motivations are putting it beyond their reach; this has happened at United as well as elsewhere. The continuing exclusion of fans from decision making is a typically perverse way of rewarding them for 'upholding the good name of English football' as the TV pundits and football administrators insist on putting it.

It was perhaps fitting that it was Manchester United who provided this example. It is a club who pioneered the English game in Europe, and whose capacity for drama and sense of occasion is perhaps unequalled in any football club. It is also a club whose supporters have formed an integral part of its identity, a support which exhibits "sustained levels of fanaticism" and so it was fitting that they provided the spectacle in Europe in 1991.

References

1.   Redhead, S., (1991), *Football With Attitude*, Wordsmith, p.103.

2.   Taylor, Gordon, Chief Executive, Professional Footballers' Association in interview with author, June 10, 1992.

3.   Chambers, Iain, (1986), *Popular Culture and the Metropolitan Experience*, Methuen, p.172.

4.   *Manchester Evening News,* March 18, 1991.

5.   Turner, Graeme, (1990), *British Cultural Studies*, Unwin Hyman, p.218.

6.   Ibid, p.218.

7.   Fiske, J., (1989), *Understanding Popular Culture*, Unwin Hyman, p.181.

8.   Redhead, S., op cit, p.106.

9.   Ibid, p.168.

10.   *Manchester Evening News*, February 19, 1992.

11.   Crick, M. and Smith, D., (1990), *Manchester United: The Betrayal of a Legend*, Pan, p.165.

12.   The original photographs in the Chapter are by Richard Davis who was commissioned by the Department of Law to cover Manchester United's fans behaviour at the final in Rotterdam.

43

information

RATFINK

WEDNESDAY 4 APRIL 1991

Ratfink play THE WITCHWOOD, Old St., Ashton Under Lyne
on their return from their 'eventful' visit to France
and Montpellier. The gig is on Tursday 11 April and
entry is free.

Along with hold-ups at customs and nearly losing their
van in the Atlantic, Ratfink never got to play their
Montpellier date planned to coincide with United's game.
The CRS Riot Police — not known for their diplomacy or
timidity towards English soccer fans — closed the Rock
Store club after an incident when the band were sound
checking. A door policy of not letting English people
into the club, and prventing entry with use of some
kind of tear gas and it appears plastic bullets didn't
help matters. The band had previosly spoken with the
management to make sure United fans would be allowed
entry, as they knew that numbers of United fans attending
the gig would be in the hundreds. These words were
obviously ignored.

The band would like to say to anyone who came to the gig
that they are very sorry it did not take place and that
those who were in France will be able to come to one of
Ratfink's dates in the near future. A gig in Warsaw
anyone??

44

4 Vanguard or vagabond?
A history of 'When Saturday Comes'

Richard Haynes

The 5th birthday and 50th edition of *When Saturday Comes* (not a fanzine, but 'The Half Decent Football Magazine' as it prefers to call itself) provided an opportunity for reflection, both serious (by the 'quality' press) and tongue-in-cheek (by itself). The current editor, Andy Lyons, instead of 'a self-indulgent trawl' through back issues gave a satirical account of 'The True(?) Story of *W.S.C.*' entitled 'When Saturday Came'. He confessed:

> *WSC* began as a twelve-page supplement to *Cardigan*, a short-lived magazine aimed at the thousands of middle-aged men who rediscover childhood hobbies once their marriages have ground to a standstill. (*When Saturday Comes*, No. 50, April 1991).

In the 'quality' press Dave Hill in *The Independent on Sunday,* April 7, 1991, described the magazine as "The half-decent defender of those long-suffering supporters" and "the exemplar of a phenomenon." Simon Barnes in *The Times,* April 10, 1991, suggested that "*WSC* has not gone legit: not in any establishment-loving sense. This is a fanzine that has grown up and lost its pimples and started to shave." To celebrate the magazine's transition from stapled photocopied sheets to finely produced and well distributed football monthly, a party was held at The Rocket, London, with guest Adrian Sherwood (producer of the classic football record, Barmy Army's *The English Disease,* and owner of On-U Sound records, where Gary Clail achieved chart success in 1991). What is important about these anniversary celebrations is that they stem from a football fan organising around an enthusiasm, without any prior knowledge of

45

writing about football and with no conception of making a living out of doing so. In what he termed as 'Surely Emotional Farewell of the Season?' Mike Ticher (founder of *WSC* and beleaguered Chelsea fan who loved to hate Ken Bates) gave a brief and nostalgic look back to the beginning of his fanzine:

> When *WSC* first started, equipped only with a wobbly typewriter and a lovingly-nurtured sense of outrage, it was inconceivable to us that so many other people would share our frustration at the way football was run, and written about. It's inevitably been a slow process establishing contact with those people, but the realisation from the start that we weren't just isolated eccentrics is the one reason why the magazine is still here after two years, against the odds. (*When Saturday Comes*, No. 18, August 1988).

From its 'bedsit origins' in March 1986, the first issue of 200 copies had twelve pages and cost 15p, the magazine (as its editors have always preferred to call it) has a readership approaching 40,000. When the magazine began Ticher and Lyons were working in a record shop, and at the time of Ticher's emigration to Australia in the summer of 1988 they each received an allowance of approximately £40 per week. By this time they had recruited student Bill Brewster (avid Grimsby Town fan) after advertising for someone to help out during the day. By the 89/90 season, after the publication of their first book, the 96 page *Offside*, they tried to get the magazine on a more permanent footing, paying each other £300 a month. This gradually increased until quite recently, when they joined PAYE as fully fledged employees of *WSC*. There are now eight employees, either full or part-time. Apart from the magazine and the books (of which there are now three) *WSC* indulged in commercial spinoffs such as T-shirts. But the editors were conscious of not making a lot of money out of the name of the magazine, keeping *WSC* merchandise within reasonable limits, not wanting to appear too commercial, and of promoting something that would not detract from people's interest in the game itself. Lyons gives his reasons for such fears:

> The only problem with making a bit more money out of the people magazine, in theory, is the more stuff we do the more people we need to work a bit more and there is a chance that

we might get a bit more remote from our readers.

Such an attitude, of maintaining a small-scale staff and managing the conflict between progress and principle, reflects the wider principles of the intelligent football lobby with which the magazine openly identifies. But the tension between the modernisation of the game and football nostalgia is also mirrored in *WSC's* resistance to change, which to Dave Hill:

> Sometimes seems inspired by a kind of aesthetic conservatism as well as a dislike of being steamrollered by power brokers. This can lead the magazine, fleetingly, into the same camp as those they most dislike: that Bates fellow for instance. (*Independent on Sunday*, April 7, 1991).

The economic potential of the magazine has been recognised by none other than the editors of *Viz* who launched a takeover bid, with the promise of a circulation of up to 150,000 a month. But *Viz* to Lyons and his co-editors is the very antithesis of what *WSC* is all about. By July 1989 the first musings of taking on advertisements was mentioned. But it was not until April 1990 (*WSC* 38) that adverts were introduced. Lyons explains the difficulties over this issue;

> With advertising we'd been holding off for a couple of years. It basically paid, and brought in enough money to pay somebody's wages. It was quite a big thing to do. We'd been mentioning it for a while about advertising and I think we thought it was the way we should go and nobody really complained about it. We were concerned about the idea, but decided we needed to do it as long as the adverts were tied in with the outlook of the magazine. We weren't going to take adverts for South African airlines for instance.

The rise of *WSC* from its makeshift beginnings to the shelves of major newsagents can be likened to other magazine subcultures which organised around the enthusiasms and leisure practices, for instance, *Hot Rod Magazine* in America, and the numerous scooter magazines in Britain.(1) Similarly, these magazines played a pivotal role in their subcultures. Bert Moorhouse has suggested that such specialist magazines have a two-fold significance: firstly, that they organise demand by telling people what they wanted to know, arranging matters so that the pastime was available to them;(2) secondly, they present the sport/pastime to a greater constituency of readers who were not active in the subculture, but feel some affinity to the pursuit. Hence, the effect of *Hot Rod Magazine* was to change 'hot rodding' from a casual pastime into a participant and spectator sport, 'drag racing'. *WSC* to a certain degree follows this theory in the way that it has captured a new audience that was hitherto unrecognised amongst the football milieu that were fed up with what Ticher called "cliched, hackneyed, lazy journalism" (*WSC*, No.1) and later helped the cause of the Football Supporters Association as it campaigned against the ills of the game. However, it was with its fanzine counterparts *Off the Ball* and *The Absolute game*, that *WSC* made its greatest impact on British football culture. By listing the names, addresses and price (and an occasional review) of many of the club based fanzines, *WSC* kick started the blossoming of a whole new phenomenon. They also began to list sales outlets which were invariably record shops or specialist sports book shops. As Steve Redhead(3) commented on the habit of listing:

> ...has proved to be a successful format for building an alternative local cultural network in an age dominated by hi-tech global media.

As new fanzines continually emerge they are subsequently listed amongst an update which also includes fanzines which are defunct, or changing name and address. John Robinson, editor of *The Best of the Football Fanzines*, also praised the three aforementioned fanzines:

> It was these three which were to prove the most influential in inspiring the wide range of contemporaries now available in a way that *Foul* for all it's relative success, strangely, never did.

And in the *New Musical Express* (May 27, 1989) an article on football fanzines argued:

> In the same way that the best pop fanzines make you want to go to the gigs, *WSC* will have you returning to the terraces.

It is the magazine's attempt to maintain a balance between humour and serious articles about contemporary happenings that has ensured its survival. After the inaugural issues, where the magazine in Lyons' words "got a lot off its chest", the magazine settled down into a familiar format with the emblem of a crusading footballer of 'The People' as its masthead. Although the magazine relied (and still does) on outside contributors, the 'in-house' writers showed considerable journalistic flair. John Duncan, who joined the magazine as a co-editor just before Ticher departed, took care of the business side of things, and later moved on to be a full-time freelance football journalist with *The Observer* and *The Guardian*. However, although Lyons has written a column for an American magazine on the topic of European football, he has never been interested in using his experience at *WSC* as a springboard into football journalism. He was happy to co-exist alongside the mainstream media, not particularly interested in writing match reports.

In February 1990 (*WSC* 36) the magazine carried out a survey of its readers, to try and establish who their readers were, and what they liked or disliked about the magazine. Questions attempting to ascertain where, when and how often readers bought the magazine were accompanied by questions designed to find out what other literature (magazines/newspapers) fans bought, and how they would like to see the magazine improved. The survey found that from a sample of 949 (they eventually received over 2,000 replies) nineteen per cent claimed to go to 50 games or more a year, with forty per cent going to between 20-49 games. Eighty per cent watched from the terraces. The majority of the sample suggested they were happy with the magazine, but wanted it "to edge away slightly from soft focus nostalgia towards a more hard hitting, investigative stance" (*WSC* 39). Andy Lyons sets out who he believes the magazine is aimed at:

> ...the average reader is probably someone in their 20s, may be ex-student, or quite likely to be a student, and the *Guardian/Independent* reader....Someone that grew up watching football in the late sixties, early seventies. Predominantly male. We have got some women readers, but not that many really. But in a way there's not a great deal you can do about that. Probably not that many readers over fifty. Probably not that many under sixteen. An adult readership....We only ever really thought about stuff that we

find interesting ourselves; if other people are interested then fair enough.

The majority of nostalgic articles now tend to appear in the *WSC* books which act as a repository of unpublished material. The magazine still relies on its readers to send in articles and as the readership has grown, so the magazine has developed a wide network of contacts that it can draw upon. For instance, many English fans now living in other countries regularly keep the magazine apace with goings on around Europe and the world game in general. So in many respects the magazine, although employing full time staff, acts as a forum for other people's views; pretty much how the magazine was envisaged as being from the beginning. The magazine only publishes ten per cent of the articles sent in, but boasts four pages of letters. Articles that are offensive, either racist, sexist, or of a sectarian type, are immediately dismissed. Slanderous local rivalry is considered by the magazine to be contrary to the original idea of the football fanzine, which was that partisanship was acceptable as long as an article that expressed such views was constructive or had something positive to say about the game in general. Lyons argues that many of the newer breed of fanzines are produced merely to impress their friends. He considers standards to be dropping, mainly due to the number of teenagers producing fanzines who don't know enough about the history of their own clubs.

This selective, almost moralistic viewpoint as to the standards of certain fanzines came to a head in the magazine's 50th edition. Following a debate on the letters page about fanzines, the magazine carried an article under the heading 'Out of Print' which aimed to highlight what it called a "disturbing trend". The article drew upon a letter from the father of a Liverpool fan who had read copies of the Manchester United fanzine *Red Issue* and was "extremely depressed and angered" at the contents of the fanzine. Citing other fanzines, such as *The Square Ball*, (Leeds United) and *Mi Whippet's Dead* (Rotherham United), as other examples of poor taste, the article (which remained anonymous) argued that:

> Two years ago, most fanzines appeared to be fighting the same battles, and railing against the same people. Clearly that is no longer the case. There was always a danger that the broadly

accepted principles underpinning fanzines could be abused by people publishing magazines that openly peddle prejudice. The hope is that such fifth columnists will be exposed for what they are. (*When Saturday Comes*, Issue 50).

The article suggested that *WSC* was not in favour of censorship, but could not condone blatantly offensive material. *Red Issue* was removed from the *WSC* listings, forthwith. Lyons gives his reasons as follows:

> *Red Issue* is just like *The Sun* I suppose....But there was stuff in there we just thought was crap. It just wasn't enough to ignore it. If people wanted to buy it OK, but we don't want to be associated with it. From his point of view he is a football fan, and he's got a right to express his views. But it seems to me that he's actually maintaining stereotypes. Like going on about Liverpool being thieves all the time, which people believe that is the kind of stuff that goes on. The longer you say those things, the more it becomes like an accepted thing. I just thought they've really not got anything to say.

Both the article "Out of Print" and the dropping of *Red Issue* from the listings prompted several complaints and an apology. The apology came from *The Square Ball* for making homophobic comments and suggested they were looking to "improve and develop" their content at all times. However, T. O. Walker, a Manchester United fan, argued that there are two sides to the rivalry between United and Liverpool. Referring to chants about 'Munich '58' and 'Hillsborough '89' he commented:

> Perhaps your correspondent would be well advised to look up the word 'provocation' in his dictionary. I for one am certainly fed up with the pusillanimous attitude shown by many of the people who discovered that in April 1989 cheap football disaster jokes had become a double-edged sword. (*WSC*, 50).

The most vociferous retort came from *Red Issue* themselves, who carried a cartoon of *WSC* (in the words of *Red Issue* "Whinge, Slag and Criticise: The Half Interesting Football Mag") which was billed as being:

As hard-hitting as Gary 'Fair Play' Lineker
As controversial as the United Review
As Dull as Don Howe's Arsenal
For everything you need to know about football in Swaziland.

Suggesting that *WSC* was the "Mary Whitehouse of the fanzine world" and that it was "hypocritical", "sanctimonious" and "self-righteous" the fanzine argued that:

> By not advertising our address they are denying their readership a chance to buy *Red Issue* and form their own opinions. Instead, they're more than happy to let people read their views with the attitude, "What we say must be right, you don't need to read *Red Issue* to see if what we say is correct."

This iconoclastic view of *WSC's* idiosyncrasies reflects a growing feeling among certain fanzine writers that the 'half decent football magazine' is becoming too respectable. However, *WSC's* movement into the mainstream of football publications reflects a broader shift in the respectability of football fanzines in general. Fanzines have established themselves as a vital source of information not only to fans but to the media. Herein lies the major success of *WSC* in helping to persuade the football press, and to a certain extent society as a whole, that all fans are not hooligans. Several mainstream football writers have been keen on promoting fanzines: Patrick Barclay of *The Observer* and Phil Shaw of *The Independent* for instance. However, there is a certain antagonism to fanzines, partly due to a generation gap between those who write fanzines and those at the top of the football journalist profession. People like Brian Glanville of *The Times*, and *The People*, for instance, have been dismissive of fanzines, defending the 'professional' credentials needed to be a football journalist. Yet, this does not seem to bother Lyons who argues that *WSC* is quite happy to co-exist alongside figures such as Glanville, believing the magazine's approach to be valid in its own right.

Finally, the magazine has made excursions into television, sometimes used as alternative spokespeople on the game, or in the case of BBC 2's *Standing Room Only* taking a consultant's role in advising the programme's producers of ideas of who to contact. But Lyons is sceptical of the BBC's attempt to simulate the fanzine on television, believing that the humour does not quite come across, and seems a bit smug. It is clear that Lyons does not want the magazine to broaden its horizons too far, allowing himself and his co-editors to keep in control of their livelihood. Moreover, this is made even more evident from his final quote:

We're not desperate to get into TV. We might get some money but we quite like doing what we do, we don't like say "this is a means of stepping into the media" particularly. A bloke from the Labour Party affiliated newspaper *The Socialist* did an interview a couple of weeks ago and he asked us a lot of stuff about what's behind our magazine, what's our agenda and all this kind of stuff. And we really haven't got one. We're just thinking towards the next issue all the time. I think once you start to step back from the magazine and analyse what you're trying to do with it, who is reading it, all that kind of stuff, you just go round in circles, you know. You just end up doing nothing. We never really think in any concise way about what we do. It's like we drifted into it as a full time job. It's a ridiculous, absurd job really; it's quite a silly sort of thing for an adult to do. But at the same time we might as well do it, for the simple reason that I enjoy football.[4]

Sources

1. See collection in our archive in Manchester.

2. H. F. Moorhouse *Organising Enthusiasm: Specialist Magazines and Subcultures*, in L.S.A. Conference Papers No. 26, 1984.

3. Steve Redhead, *Football With Attitude*, (1991), Wordsmith, Manchester.

4. This essay is based on a textual analysis of the magazine *When Saturday Comes* and other fanzines held in the archive of the Manchester Institute for Popular Culture. It is also based on an interview with the magazine's editor, Andy Lyons, which took place at their offices on November 6, 1991.

5 Every man (?) a football artist: Football writing and masculinity

Richard Haynes

> Mrs. Elizabeth Charlton is a grey-haired, handsome
> woman now. It is said in Ashington that when she was a girl
> she could dribble with a football as well as most of the boys.
> She was born into football and she knew the game and its
> ways as theatre mums make-up and stage-doors.
> (A. Hopcraft, (1968), p.87).

The Mrs. Charlton referred to in this passage is, of course, the
mother of England's (in)famous footballing brothers Jackie and
Bobby Charlton. Given the above, and the fact that the Charlton's
came from a 'footballing family' (Elizabeth's cousin was Jackie
Milburn of Newcastle United), it is hardly surprising that the
Charlton's took to football like ducks to water - the rest is history. Or
more correctly, part of a mythology built on boyhood dreams, from
kicking a football in a back-alley to playing on Wembley's sacred turf.
For the boys who didn't 'make the grade', the contemporary football
experience invariably means sitting in an armchair watching the
spectacle of football on television, with a commentator confirming
the faith in a 'man's game'. Whatever the scenario, the obsession and
passion football arouses amongst a large section of the male
population in Britain is difficult to ignore. So why didn't Elizabeth
Charlton get to play at Wembley? And if she'd have had two
daughters, would they have played football? The answers to the
above are not so important, and would not be that surprising. What
is surprising is that the above passage appeared in Arthur Hopcraft's
eloquent book *The Football Man* (the title itself a giveaway as to
whose game it is!) Hopcraft's little anecdote about Mrs. Charlton
clearly has novelty value, as is usually the case when men talk or

write about women in football. The most important question to pose then, is why men have claimed football as their own, and why does it arouse such passion and energy? This is not to ignore the fact that many women play and watch football, a point I shall return to later, but to recognise the raison d'etre of my analysis: that football shapes male identity.

Football's popularity amongst men has been inextricably bound up with its reportage in the media. As the social historian James Walvin pointed out in *Football and the Decline of Britain:*

> Newspapers, magazines and boys comics were active at an early stage in promoting and exploiting the manifest interest among males in football.

Coverage was compounded by the screening of football on television from the early 60s, setting the scene for the creation of a generation of armchair fans. By a banal twist of fate, fans have had to suffer the well-rehearsed jibes of television's most unlikely double act, star players from that era, 'Saint and Greavsie'. Yet it is this 'sports chatter', referred to by Umberto Eco (1986), which marks out the terrain of my analysis. As Rowe (1991) has argued:

> It is this assumed affinity between the world of sports journalism and that of its target audience which requires analysis (p.84).

More specifically, for the purpose of this Chapter, it is the major site for analysing the reproduction of masculinity in football and through the sphere of football into the wider society.

Theories of football and masculinity

After twenty years of serious sociological research on football, it is as if the contemporary history (and in some instances the complete history) of British football since the 70s consists of narratives of the 'football hooligan'. Academic myopia, possibly symptomatic of the broader 'crisis' in society concerning 'law and order', has provided a skewed contemporary history of football in this country. Hence the need for a novel and broader approach to football culture and its place in society. This does not mean abandoning previous studies on 'football hooliganism', but it does require incorporating these ideas in an interdisciplinary approach to football culture.

Not surprisingly, studies of 'football hooliganism' have attempted to analyse football and masculinity, albeit in the context of violence. The Sir Norman Chester Centre for Football Research is the pre-eminent centre for research on 'hooliganism' in Britain. They have developed theories of male aggressiveness in the working class by looking at the social roots of 'aggressive masculinity'. Their own interpretation is based on a synthesis of Suttle's theories of 'ordered segmentation' and 'the defended neighbourhood', and is a contribution to Norbert Elias' theory of 'civilising processes'. In their own words they attempted,

> ...via the construction of a general model to shed some light on the structural features of lower-working-class communities which lead to the recurrent generation within them of male adolescent gangs, an aggressive masculine style and relatively narrow bonds of identification. It does not attempt to take account of social change or nuances of 'lived experience'. (Dunning et al, (1988), p.212).

Dunning et al, recognise that such 'extreme forms of masculinity' pervade many aspects of popular culture, including popular newspapers, and argue that the press "played a part of some importance in directing hooligan behaviour into the football context" (Murphy et al). More recently the 'Leicester Group' have turned their attention to the role of women in football. On Granada TV's *World in Action* programme 'Send For the Sisters', Patrick Murphy (accompanied by his son in the programme!) was critical of discrimination in football:

> Football in this country is predominantly a male preserve - possibly one of the most attractive features of the game to football hooligans. I think an influx of females would undermine this masculine imagery and change the atmosphere at matches. (*The Guardian*, January 17, 1990).

However good Murphy's intentions, such an analysis is couched in the context of hooliganism and influenced by the theory of the 'civilising process'. Julie Welch of *The Times* had got her retaliation in first regarding the presence of more women to end the battles on the football terraces. She argued:

> Women a civilising influence at football matches? What women? Even if we wanted to form the 'manners police', I doubt there would be enough of us for a quorum.

It is clear that women should be treated as spectators in their own right, than dishonestly used as a social control mechanism. The perspective of Murphy et al, ignores broader aspects in the construction and reproduction of masculine identity in football, specifically because the focus is on aggressiveness and overt machismo, rather than the subtle nuances of the majority of young men's lived experiences and their passion for football.

More recently, research carried out by Jackie Woodhouse at the Sir Norman Chester Centre for Football Research has distanced itself from previous accounts regarding female football fans. In her survey conducted amongst female members of the F.S.A., while accepting that the sample is skewed towards the more 'activist' female football audience, Woodhouse argues:

> ...the theory of 'feminisation' is based upon stereotypes of female characteristics, of passivity, non-aggression, etc. (1991, p.23).

and continues

> ...it is assumed that the 'use' of women to pacify male football crowds is justified for society's benefit without consideration of the effect it may have on women. (1991, p.23).

The broader synthesis adopted by the Sir Norman Chester Centre of late (Rogan Taylor's history of football supporters organisations, published as *Football and Its Fans*, by Leicester University Press, in 1992: the surveys carried out by Information Technology Trainees into F.S.A. members and fanzine readers; and John Williams' turn to a broader cultural analysis of the 'hooligan' phenomenon, acknowledging previous critiques, for instance Clarke, 1991) is part of an even wider and ever expanding field of academic interest in football. It is to this body of football writing I would now like to turn.

The increased forms of research into football has occurred in conjunction with the explosion of football fanzines and assorted literature relating to football. While not to ignore the continuation of violence in and around football stadiums up and down the British Isles, fanzines have helped to create a new 'structure of feeling' among fans, moving towards a positive image away from that of fans as 'hooligans', and countering the misrepresentation and lack of authenticity that has been prevalent between the popular press and its audience. However, what has not been asked, of the emergent fanzine phenomenon or academic writing on football, is whether or not there has been a significant shift in masculine identity, or if the new football writers merely operate in a male cul-de-sac. After all, fanzines are, in many respects, another form of 'sports chatter', their content reflecting many conversations amongst men to be heard in the pubs across the nation. It would be naive to suggest that the form and content of this type of conversation (football discourse) has not changed over time, or its meaning among its participants. Masculinity in the post-punk era has taken on a new meaning around football, its articulation a major influence in the transition of recent sexual politics: fashion consciousness. As Steve Redhead argued in the 80s:

> Soccer in Britain, for a century the opiate of the working *man*, is a surprising location for designer menswear and its specific connotation of a crisis in masculinity. (*New Socialist*, No.47, 1987).

Frank Mort has also documented the changing surfaces of male youth as they make their way to the turnstiles:

> Individuality is on offer, incited through commodities and consumer display. From jeans: red tabs, designer labels, distressed denim. To hair: wedges, spiked with gel, or pretty hard boys who wear it long, set off with a large earring. And the snatches of boys talk I pick up are about 'looking wicked' as well as the game. Which is not to say the violence is designer label. (1988, p.193).

Redhead also picks up on this last point arguing that the "skin-deep

59

body politics of football chic" in the 80s and early 90s have still seen the affirmation and reassertion of traditional masculine styles in the reign of the Conservative government. As Janice Winship neatly puts it, "under many a new man fashion look lurks a diehard wolf" (1987, p.153). So to what extent do these 'atavistic desires persist' within the 'New Football Man', the F.S.A. member, the fanzine editor and the regular 'man on the terraces' in a post-modern world of hi-tech and avid consumption?

Feminist cultural theory and football

Gazza's tears may have launched a thousand cliches about why 'boys don't cry' and 'New Men' do, but they didn't drown the myths that underlay masculinity and football. The World Cup, Italia '90 mix, was a watershed with regards to women's interest in football, yet the interest for many women may have stopped at mum singing along to Pavarotti and big sis' dancing to *World in Motion* by New Order, bringing a whole new meaning to 'playing for England, Eng-a-land!' Fashion in football was turned on its head to football in fashion as John Golan, one of Italy's top designers, sent out the world's top models wearing customised Umbro football shirts with a Man City badge, paired with striped trousers. In an article by *The Independent's* fashion writer, Roger Tredre, entitled 'Designer stripes on the ball - The World Cup has kick started soccer style for women', designer Helen Storey was said to have taken up the football theme for her Autumn '90 collection. In true fashion writer style, Tredre commented on Storey:

> Not content with customising soccer shirts, she has developed a complete 'football for women' look. She has designed high-cut soccer shorts with beads around the thighs and turned footballs into hip-bags. For evening, she has come up with striped satin hooded bomber jackets and evening dresses with players numbers on the back. (June, 1990).

Finally, as if to make Storey's intervention into football seem less threatening and even more farcical, she was quoted as saying:

Football is a very male-dominated game. I liked the idea of the swapping of roles, making football clothing sexy. (*The Independent*, June 1990).

Whether or not such an idea undermines male sexuality within football is open to interpretation. Such an exercise merely reinforces stereotypical images of whose game it is, by implying that women have no part to play in the game itself, as it is played, watched and managed. 1990 did represent a year in which there were some positive images of women in football; Channel 4's screening of the Women's F.A. Cup and the series *The Manageress*. However, statements abounded about the unlikely event of a woman managing a football team. Few men in the game took the idea seriously, which was epitomised by Gary Lineker, England's foremost striker and the nation's favourite son who, when asked if he could envisage working with a female manager, replied: "I could if she looked like that", referring to the actress Cheri Lunghi. Given such provocation and ammunition it is not surprising that feminist discourse has turned its attention to football and sport in general.

The majority of studies on football which have tried to theorise about the game, have often over-simplified the many variants that have made it such a popular sport amongst men. Much has been written about football and its relation to class, but there has often been a neglect of the 'unseen' or 'unheard' discourse of gender and sexuality (along with ethnicity). The earliest forms of sports feminism grew out of the desire for equality of opportunity with men, and its liberal attributes were essentially pragmatic. The Women's Football Association has campaigned along the lines of equal opportunities, with the incentive for women to get into a traditional male sport. While not to ignore such a positive strategy as increasingly influential and a success in encouraging more women to play football, recent socialist feminist perspectives on sport would argue that it fails to offer any radical alternatives. Women's football does have some element of 'separatism', an ideology that intends to "give women access to the most masculinised sports, create wider definitions of femininity and provide women with experiences to administer and control their own activities" (Hargreaves, 1990, p.292). Yet such an ideology threatens to exclude not only men but women too. Again, as Hargreaves (1990), argues such 'unnecessary divisions' neglect;

...to look at ways in which women and men are exploited *together* in sport and how gender relations articulate with capitalist relations. (1990, p.295).

Following on from this argument Hargreaves suggests three strategies for change in female sport:

(1) Co-option into a male sphere of activity.
(2) A separatist all-female strategy.
(3) A co-operative venture with men for qualitative new models in which differences in the sexes are unimportant.

These strategies, especially the third, are of vital importance to understanding the way in which male identity is constituted in football. It highlights the fact that identities of football fans, players, managers, etc., are not reducible solely to the single logic of class. It is important to recognise that "class is gendered and our gender is classed" (Rutherford, 1990, p.19). Heterosexual masculinity evades becoming the object of discourse, especially in the football world where it has asserted itself as the mainstream in male cultural life. As is often promulgated, football is the 'last bastion' of male identity. The problem for men and women who attempt to change the dominant meanings of masculinity and the mythologies of patriarchy, is that such threats to myths and illusions of superiority produce stronger male bonding. Cynthia Cockburn highlights such ironies when she says:

Since male power is not merely ideological but also based in wealth, social organisation and physical might, femininity has had little power of its own to force adaptations in its complementary oppressor. The initiative normally lies with masculinity. That is what is so startling about feminism, and why our project so often seems unlikely to succeed. (1988, p.321).

To return to the idea of 'feminising' football, in the survey by Woodhouse (1991) it is apparent that many women who go to matches at the moment are indifferent to the prospect of more women attending games. This highlights a further irony, where the 'masculine atmosphere of the game' is all important to the football

62

experience. Has there got to be some fundamental shift in the game, the way it is played, watched, organised, etc., for there to be any balanced, non-sexist game? There is a fundamental problem in trying to (re)introduce women into sports, predominantly male, and constructed as a male domain. Is it possible to deconstruct football? Or must women challenge men at their own game? Woodhouse comes to the conclusion that the survey suggests:

> ...male attitudes towards the whole relationship between women and football need to be challenged and altered before any real progress could be made. (1991).

An analysis of fanzines and the plethora of football literature which has emerged in the past few years, might give an indication as to 'any real progress' in the gender relations within football.

Football, consumption and masculinity

Joyce Layland has pointed to the "latent effect of seeing feminist research as exclusively about women's lives"; the very fact that men's lives often go unquestioned; and that what is left is, inevitably, 'male-as-norm'. What Layland calls for is a demystification of power and its components, the major culprit in feminist discourse being the production of 'masculinity' and 'masculine behaviour'. She contends that:

> ...the production of 'masculinity' or 'femininity' is in part, the result of individuals being presented with different sets of possibilities of how to make sense of a given social situation. (1990, p.129).

Magazines play a major role in the production of such 'possibilities' of making such a sense, specifically in young people's lives through the realms of sport, music and fashion. Richard Hoggart in his *The Uses of Literacy* demonstrated the interconnection between public culture, including magazines, and the structure of an individual's private everyday life, gender relations, and a community's 'common sense'. Under the sub-heading 'The Newer Mass Art', Hoggart examined the 'Juke-box boys' who he characterised as:

...those who spend their evening listening in harshly lighted milk-bars to the 'nickelodeons'...boys aged between fifteen and twenty, with drape-suits, picture ties and an American slouch. (1957, p.250).

Hoggart asks of the 'hedonistic but passive barbarians', the portent of the 50's:

What are such men likely to read, apart from picture-dailies, the more sensational Sunday papers and newspapers /magazines? (1957, p.250).

This early analysis of youth and what they read, moving from literary to cultural theory, whilst it is one-dimensional and nostalgic for a lost working-class culture, did help to frame the work of cultural theorists and feminists in the study of girls and women's magazines. For some reason magazines specifically produced for, and consumed by, men have rarely been the subject of analysis, but the feminist studies of magazines enlighten and inform any attempt at forming a critique of men's magazines and how men relate to such texts. A dominant theme running through many feminist studies of popular magazines has been the 'open' or 'closed' nature of the text. Closure within the text suggests the successful establishment of hegemonic relations of class, gender and race, where a popular cultural form is the vehicle for the maintenance of dominant social meanings. For instance, Pleasance's (1991) study of women's magazines highlights how feminine identity is fixed in magazines through particular representations of consumption. Gendered narratives of consumption, appearing to offer choice and freedom, in fact hid the lack of material choice for women. The flip-side of this gendered narrative of consumption is epitomised in the new men's magazines *GQ, Esquire, For Him* and *Cosmo for Men*. Collier (1991) and Winship (1987) both argue that such magazines have not met with unqualified success. In an attempt to develop non-sexist ideology, the magazines still push products for men with an emphasis on power, money, business and sporting success, and invariably dodging the issue of male sexuality. As Winship concludes of the difference between men's and women's magazines:

Our lives as women and men continue to be culturally defined in materially different ways, and both what we read and how it is presented to us reflects, and is part of, that difference. (1987, p.6).

Nowhere is the distinction between the sexes more starkly illustrated than in the consumption habits of boys in relation to football. It is not to suggest that many girls and later women are not involved in the consumption of football related goods and memorabilia (indeed, as argued earlier, replica football shirts are often a required fashion accessory for some women), but to recognise that women are usually on the periphery of such consumption patterns. Consumption around football has its historical antecedents: the early sporting press (Mason, 1980), match programmes, and the cigarette cards of football players. However, the plethora of football publications did not start in earnest until the 60s with *Roy of the Rovers, Goal* and *Shoot* - to name but a few - targeted at young boys. Football bubblegum cards and later the Panini football sticker album series, created a whole schoolboy subculture, as young boys gathered to barter and swap to capture the elusive card or sticker to complete their collection. Moreover, fans could delight in the relentless publication of football annuals, inane biographies, and books to improve soccer skills. The link between football and tobacco companies continued with *The Park Drive Book of Football* series emerging in the mid-60s to the early 70s. These books consisting of articles written by players ('Football is a Man's Game' by Derek Dougan), managers ('What I Expect from My Players' by Don Revie) and celebrities ('We're all Footy Mad in Liverpool', by Ken Dodd) helped to fuel young male appetites for the game and reproduce the image of the 'man's game'. For instance, Derek Dougan's account of the 'modern' game in the 1970 edition epitomised the kind of philosophy which has kept football a male preserve.

Emancipation is one thing: a man's sport another - and professional football is a man's game. If by the term we mean physically exacting and tough on the muscles. I don't know what the game was like when the Football League was founded. Life in these days was tough to the point of being grim. People were used to hardship, but I doubt if footballers had the sinews and the capacity for endurance that are needed and demanded today. (1970, p.109).

He continues:

> To say that football is 'a man's game' does not imply that it is ruthless, brutal, and insensitive. It means that skill has to be forged on an anvil of physical endurance. And they say a woman's work is never done! (1970, p.109).

Contemporary female football players would, I am sure, have something to say about their skill and physical endurance. But the point to be made is that such language has been consistently used within football literature and reportage. In today's era of varied leisure practices and entertainments, it would be naive to suggest that all boys are seduced by the need to consume their football fantasy. Yet the continued success of a game like Subbuteo attests the fanatical desire among new generations of boys for anything and everything related to football. The recent phrase 'armchair supporter' has taken on a whole new meaning with the explosion of football videos, so that fans can recount their favourite memories, both old and new, providing the ideal Christmas or birthday present for male members of the family. Football video and arcade games provide the ultimate simulated experience, without even pulling on a pair of boots or standing on the terraces. Fanaticism for anything football-related often develops into the collection of memorabilia, especially programm s and more recently, fanzines. Women are virtually excluded from such a 'football world' as the many comics, magazines, games and stickers are targeted at a male consumer. As far as club merchandise is concerned it is not surprising that the larger clubs cash in on young fans allegiance, in particular. It is not uncommon to see a Liverpool shirt being worn outside of Merseyside, for instance, due to the displacement of club allegiance in relation to locality, mainly because of intense television coverage of top clubs (see Bale, 1991).

Football fanzines have provided a further twist to football consumption. Not only do fanzines disseminate news, views and anecdotes, they subvert the dominant, commercial football media because they are produced by fans for fans, servicing what Rowe (1991) calls "a need for intense localised communication founded on orality rather than literacy". Fanzines have been cited as one area of political contestation in sport, something that many sociologists of sport have thought improbable. However, in terms of gender politics, as Woodhouse (1991) argues, fanzines are invariably edited, written and read by men. A case in point is the much lauded fanzine (or more correctly 'the half decent football magazine', as it prefers to call itself) *When Saturday Comes*, which we examined in Chapter 4. Their target audience is predominantly male, and grew up watching football in the late 60s and early 70s, the era characterised as the birth of the 'modern' professional game and, as we have seen, which saw the mushrooming in the consumption of football-related commodities. With the professed target audience in mind, many of the articles contained in the fanzine have cultural references with which men in their twenties and thirties can identify. For instance, humour is often derived from television, fashion or music of the 60s and 70s, references that conjure up nostalgia for past stars and teams and boyhood football dreams. While not openly sexist, *WSC* and football fanzines in general offer a subtle brand of male bonding; one glimpse at the letters page gives the male game away. Ironically, fanzines offer another all male line-up in keeping, rather than in contrast, to the predominantly male television football panels and press reporters. Furthermore, according to the survey by Woodhouse (1991) the media image of football as masculine and 'warlike' was given as the area most in need of change. In arguing that women fans and players have a genuine interest and knowledge of football Woodhouse states:

> Female writers are able to offer an alternative perspective on the game and provide an important vehicle for the articulation of the views of female fans. Equally as important, by gaining respect and recognition through writing about the game in a knowledgeable and entertaining fashion, such women can play a key role in challenging the macho attitudes and image of British football. (1991, p.48).

The reading of football literature and consumption given so far has been strictly limited and offered no conception of the complex meanings and pleasure young men obviously derive from the game. I have raised only one side of men's relation to football magazine texts. It is one thing to describe the construction of masculinity in such texts, another to argue that readers readily identify with each, or behave in the manner advocated. Theories focusing on readers' active appropriations of media texts are instructive when attempting to move away from a concept of ideology that infers that subjects are its passive dupes. Pleasance (1991) has highlighted the need for a 'postmodern' reading of popular texts, which are open, incomplete and constantly moving. Neville Wakefield (1990) has likened "The smile that crosses the faces of those who read the *Sunday Sport* as a form of 'postmodern sensibility'. By 'hyperbolising tabloid conventions' the *Sunday Sport* creates a new 'media space'. Instead of taking the traditional left's view of an irresponsible gutter press, a 'postmodern' sense of 'knowingness' is needed, where the readership refused to be the 'duped mass' of social theory. For Wakefield the *Sunday Sport* belongs to:

> an intertextual space which, in shedding its mortgage to the real, appeals to the sort of ironic sense of play...and also, perhaps more straightforwardly, a newly invigorated sense of the comic....Humour emerges in a form that is neither elitist (dependent on exclusion and the community of laughter that such exclusion entail), nor is it 'lumpen' in the sense of being without sophistication or subtlety. (1990, p.15).

This intertextuality, where cultural practices are produced through the interconnection of a range of texts, and 'newly invigorated sense of the comic' is central to the success of football fanzines. The actual production of fanzines relies on the humour and sense of fun they provide, thriving on the misuse of language, revitalising conventional football media speak, using puns and cliches to convey a multiplicity of meanings. Football fans are both discriminatory (through support of a particular team) and productive. As fanzine readers they are cultural producers not only cultural consumers. The fanzine is polysemic, offering a variety of potential meanings, depending on how the text connects with a fans social experience. Football's popularity can be identified with pleasures that resist and stand outside the forces of ideology. To this end, can it be argued that football offers some pleasure from a physical source, located within the body, as opposed to the way we give meaning to the world by social activity? Many football commentators, including fanzine writers, have attempted to write about the essence of football, the illicit pleasure obtained from the game. An example of this attempt to capture the 'jouissance' of football is captured in Rogan Taylor's recent lament to the Hungarian player Ferenc Puskas, illustrating just how positive the draw of the game can be:

> By some freakish accident, no one in my family was particularly interested in football. Located on the south side of the town, we were far away from Anfield and Goodison, and never witnessed the huge crowds of up to 80,000 of the faithful gathering for their Saturday afternoon rite. The great names and players of Everton and Liverpool were never mentioned at our fireside, and there was no television in the corner to incite an interest. Consequently, as a kid I lost my heart to the game itself, without confusing that affection with a local football club. I fell in love innocently, with only a tennis ball at my feet and no red or blue shirt in my imagination. (1990, p.33).

Taylor's love of the game, whether it is played in the street or at Anfield, hints at the possibility of positive, productive pleasures to be found within the game, as opposed to hegemonic pleasures derived from masculine posturing on the pitch or on the terraces. Women derive a great deal of energy from playing and watching football. Women's devotion to the game, and the intensity of the pleasure it offers is typified by an interview in *The Guardian* (November 21, 1991) with a life-long supporter of Bolton Wanderers, Jean Thomasson, who 'had the game in her blood', and stated:

> Football occupies quite a lot of my life. When you get to the end of the season, you get withdrawal symptoms just like from a drug.

Football offers an everyday pleasure (plaisir) and special moments of carnival (jouissance). Football's evasive pleasure empower the production of meanings of self and social identity. The increasing legal regulation of the game and its appropriation by global media/corporate wealth, has led to a defence by fans of the pleasure and meanings produced by football. Moreover, the unequal power relations of gender within the structure of the game, have also been resisted. As Fiske (1989) points out the "politics of popular culture is that of everyday life", at a micropolitical level, "concerned with the day-to-day negotiations of unequal power relations" (p.56). A women's football fanzine *Born Kicking* represents one attempt to challenge male hegemony in football by drawing on women's involvement in the game as both fans and players. As a passionate believer in the women's game Jane Purdon, the editor, launched the fanzine at a crucial time in the game's development, towards the end of 1990.

The main objectives of the fanzine were fourfold: to publicise women's teams and leagues, helping women who want to play find teams and coaching; to give support to and report on the national teams; to provide a forum for women whose main interest is not as players but as spectators, giving a valuable contribution to current debates on football in Britain; and finally to campaign on rights wherever possible, from pushing for a national women's league to the provision of tampon machines at grounds. Unfortunately, there have been only a few issues to date, the content not always fulfilling expectations. But the fanzine does provide a positive instance of cultural contestation to dominant ideologies of masculinity in football. An even more inventive idea to highlight the role women play in football was an event called *Blowing the Whistle* an electronic animation which paid tribute to female fans worldwide. Commissioned and presented by Moviola, a Liverpool media arts group, and Oldham Art Gallery, the animation inspired by a Victorian photograph of a woman pegging out 12 football shirts on a washing line, was shown simultaneously at Goodison Park, Everton, and Boundary Park, Oldham. Recognising the supportive roles women play in football the press release read as follows:

> *Blowing the Whistle* shows that football really is a funny old game, and most definitely a game of two halves - men and women. The 15 second animation see gyrating washing machines, steaming irons and jostling team shirts triumphantly parading across the screen. Interspersed with statistics on women and football, it aims to symbolise what every wife, mother or girlfriend knows; that without them the game would never have gotten off the ground.

Both of the innovative ideas mentioned above are visible attempts to challenge male identity as it is constructed in football. Indeed such ventures highlight the fact that sexual identity is not fixed. There is no specific 'position' for men and women to achieve.

This argument leads to the final issue regarding the discursive construction of sexuality in football: homosexuality and homophobia. Organised football as we know it today, grew out of the rational recreation movement and the public schools of the nineteenth century (Bailey, 1978). Embodied in the construction of organised sports was the conception of manliness associated with muscular Christianity. As John Hargreaves has pointed out, this cult of athleticism had the desired effect of "disciplining or 'normalising' the male youth of the dominant classes" (p.4), the strenuous sport making it less likely that boys would indulge in indecent behaviour. Muscular Christianity was influenced by Evolutionary theory, the triumph of mind over body, but where "the first requisite of life is to be a good animal" (Hargreaves, 1986, p.41). As the game was appropriated by the working class in the late nineteenth century, it is not surprising many of the newly organised League clubs had their roots in the church. The purpose of highlighting the roots of the modern game is to show how the rational attempts to discipline the body and populations were, as Foucault has argued, responses to the urban crisis of this period, and that such disciplines have their parallells in contemporary society, specifically in football. Football, as we have seen, still holds strong the virtues of manliness, acting as a regulator of homosexuality, marginalising it as 'perverse' or 'queer'. Eco (1986) in his polemical essay on football likens his early encounters with the game to a 'terrified young homosexual' who forces himself to like girls. Eco describes why some boys don't get involved in football, invariably to receive the label of 'sissy' or 'puff'.

> I don't love soccer because soccer has never loved me, for from my earliest childhood I belonged to that category of infants or adolescents who, the moment they kick the ball - assuming that they manage to kick it - promptly send it into their own goal or, at best, pass it to the opponent, unless with stubborn tenacity they send it off the field, beyond hedges and fences, to become lost in a basement or a stream or to plunge among the flavours of the ice-cream cart. And so his playmates reject him and banish him from the happiest of competitive events. (p.167).

Conversely to Eco's aversion to the game, homosexual men, being brought up as heterosexual boys, accept that they are men like any other and often behave as such, which includes playing and watching football. As Metcalf argues:

> Gay men are caught in the double bind of being told that we are not men yet being expected to behave as men. (1985, p.74).

However, the 80s has seen the rise of many homosexual men and women 'coming out' to affirm their gay or lesbian identity, a political act which is in direct opposition to the homophobia of the Thatcher years. The attempt to redefine notions of nationhood, of the active citizen and the nuclear family were government's response to the threats to the new British respectability. The spectre of AIDS creates the 'pathologization of homosexuality' (Stacey, 1991, p.286) attacking its associations with promiscuity, disease and a risk to public health and morality. 'Section 28' encapsulated the attempt to sustain the institution of the family. The introduction of this homophobic legislation rather than silencing lesbians and gays, put homosexuality high on the political agenda.

Football has been touched by the increased politicisation of sexuality in the wake of Section 28 of the Local Government Act, 1988. Justin Fashanu, one of Britain's earliest million pound signings, is the first footballer in this country to 'come out' and openly state his gay identity. This brave move, unfortunately exploited on the pages of *The Sun*, prompted an article by Andy Medhurst, a gay football fan, on the pages of *WSC*. Promoting the erotic attraction of football, Medhurst wrote:

> Sport provides one of the few spaces in our anxious, repressed culture where one man can openly admire the body of another, as you'll find out by visiting any gym or standing on any terrace. This appreciation is, of course, heavily disguised and coded, but that doesn't make it any less real. (*WSC*, No.47).

There now exists a Gay Football Supporters' Network, said to be the biggest special interest group by the Gay Times (Redhead, 1991). Moreover, the football fanzine *The Football Pink* produced in Manchester, is for gay and lesbian football supporters, the title playing on the many football newspapers produced across the country on pink paper. The assertion of gay politics in football is a clear retort to the muscular Christian ideals of the late nineteenth century, and offers further possibilities for the game's future.

Conclusion

Football fanzines may have emerged out of the events at Heysel and Bradford, attempting, to some extent, to change the way the game is controlled, but they also enable male producers and readers to redefine their ideas of masculinity when watching football. At a time of men's anxiety in relation to issues of sexuality, fanzines and the other means of contestation cited above, offer a way in which they can reveal or explain their social identities. This changing condition, which some describe as postmodern, destroys traditional and modern football myths. There are no permanent identities to unproblematically take on, cultural differences yielding further openings and possibilities. Although football is a dominant cultural form, obeying the non-discursive factors of class formulations and the strictures of late capitalism (from the fans on the terraces to the corporate members in the executive box), it does not necessarily sentence the fan to lifelong gendered social imprisonment.

Bibliography

Bailey, P. (1978), *Leisure and Class in Victorian England*, Hutchinson.

Bale, J. (1993), *Space, Sport and the City: Football and the Urban Environment*, Routledge.

Chambers, I. (1990), *Border Dialogues: Journeys in Postmodernity*, Routledge.

Clarke, A. (1991), 'Figuring a Brighter Future' in E. Dunning and C. Rojek (eds.), *Sport and Leisure in the Civilising Process*, Macmillan.

Cockburn, C. (1988), 'Masculinity, the Left and Feminism', in R. Chapman and J. Rutherford, (eds.), *Male Order: Unwrapping Masculinity*, Laurence and Wishart.

Collier, R. (1991) *Repositioning the New Man: Sex, Work and the New Men's Magazines*, occasional paper, Faculty of Law, University of Newcastle.

Dougan, D. (1970), 'Football is a Man's Game' in *The Park Drive Book of Football 1970 Edition*.

Dunning, E., Murphy, P., Williams, J., (1988), *The Roots of Football Hooliganism: An Historical and Sociological Study*, R.K.P.

Eco, U. (1986), *Travels in Hyperreality*, Picador.

Fiske, J. (1989), *Understanding Popular Culture*, Unwin Hynman.

Hargreaves, J. (1986), *Sport, Power and Culture*, Polity.

Hargreaves, J. (1990), 'Gender on the Sports Agenda', *International Review for Sociology of Sport*, No. 25.

Hoggart, R. (1957), *The Uses of Literacy*, reprinted by Pelican 1966.

Hopcraft, A. (1968), *The Football Man*, reprinted by Sportspages, 1988.

Layland, J. (1990), 'On the Conflicts of Doing Feminist Research into Masculinity', in L. Stanley, (ed.), *Feminist Praxis: Research, Theory and Epistemology in Feminist Sociology,* Routledge.

Mason, T. (1980), *Association Football and English Society 1863-1915,* Harvester.

Metcalf, A. 'Gay Machismo', in A. Metcalf and M. Humphries, *The Sexuality of Men,* Pluto.

Mort, F. (1988), 'Boys Own? Masculinity, styles and popular culture', in R. Chapman and J. Rutherford, (eds.), *Male Order: Unwrapping Masculinity,* Lawrence and Wishart.

Murphy, P., Williams, J., Dunning, E. (1990), *Football on Trial,* Routledge.

Pleasance, H. (1991), 'Open or closed: popular magazines and dominated culture', in S. Franklin, C. Lury, J. Stacey, (eds.), *Off Centre: Feminism and Cultural Studies,* Harper Collins.

Redhead, S. (1987), 'When Men Were Men', *New Socialist,* No. 47.

Redhead, S. (1991), *Football with Attitude,* Wordsmith.

Rowe, D. (1991), 'That Misery of Stringers' Cliches: Sports writing', *Cultural Studies,* Vol, 5. No. 1.

Rutherford, J. (1990), 'A place called home: identity and the cultural politics of difference', in J. Rutherford, (ed.), *Identity: Community, Culture, Difference,* Lawrence and Wishart.

Stacey, J. (1991), 'Promoting normality: Section 28 and the regulation of sexuality', in S. Franklin, C. Lury, J. Stacey, (eds.), *Off Centre: Feminism and Cultural Studies,* Harper Collins.

Taylor, R. (1990), 'Puskas and the real thing', in H. Lansdown and A. Spillius, (eds.), *Saturday's Boys,* Collins Willow.

Wakefield, N. (1990), *Postmodernism: The Twilight of the Real,* Pluto.

Walvin, J. (1986), *Football and the Decline of Britain*, Macmillan.

Williams, J. and Wagg, S., (eds.), (1991), *British Football and Social Change*, Leicester University Press.

Winship, J. (1987), *Inside Women's Magazines*, Pandora.

Winship, J. (1991), 'The Impossibility of Best: Enterprise meets domesticity in the practical women's magazines of the 1980s', *Cultural Studies*, Vol. 5, No. 1.

Woodhouse, J. (1991), *A National Survey of Female Football Fans*, Sir Norman Chester Centre for Football Research, Leicester.

6 The rich and the poor in the culture of football

Alessandro Portelli

Editor's preface

Alessandro Portelli is Professor of American Literature at the University of Rome. He is the author, amongst other works, of *The Death of Luigi Trastulli and other stories: form and meaning in oral history*, (State University of New York Press, Albany, 1991). He presented a paper on 'The Culture of the Italian Soccer Terrace' to the joint football research seminar run by the Unit for Law and Popular Culture at Manchester Metropolitan University, and the Department of Sociology at the University of Salford held on Monday, July 22, 1991, at the John Dalton Extension, Manchester Metropolitan University. This was a revised version of another paper 'The Rich and the Poor in the Culture of Football' given at the Football and Europe Conference in May 1990, at the European University Institute, Florence, Italy. He has retained the earlier title, but the essay printed here is substantially the paper delivered at Manchester Metropolitan University on July 22, 1991, and at the British Criminology Conference at the University of York a few days later.

Starting with the 80s, football in Italy has become both more respectable and more disreputable. The respectability derived, most of all, from Italy's victory in the World Cup in Spain in 1982. The presence and sheer enthusiasm of President Sandro Pertini at the Cup Final became an icon of national unity, and politicians who had never had anything but spite towards football and its fans jumped on the bandwagon, trying to cash in on a hypothetical revival of football-inspired patriotic nationalism. The language of politics and journalism became increasingly replete with soccer metaphors: to offer a 1991 example, the EC's warning that Italy's status in the community was threatened unless we do something about our economy was rendered as "we are in danger of being demoted from A-league to B-league".(1) Sponsoring football clubs (and sports in general) became a rewarding enterprise for industrialists and financiers, in terms of direct profits and, even more, of image, popularity, and political pull. Football became an expressive arena for the elites.

Meanwhile, football also continued as an expressive arena for the masses - but rather than reinforcing its new-found respectability, mass action in football was a threat and a danger. The question of football violence was, in fact, central to discussion of the game: if anything exists in contemporary society to remind us of the 'popular and dangerous classes' of the industrial revolution, these must be the football fans in the cheapest hustings, the 'popular classes and dangerous classes' of the information revolution.

In this Chapter I will attempt to sketch some of the relationships between these two apparently opposite developments. The theoretical tool I will use (partly in metaphor) is the concept of the 'culture of poverty' as developed by Oscar Lewis. Among the traits of the culture of poverty, Lewis includes the lack of actual participation and integration in the institutions of society at large, a sense of crowding and promiscuity, a strong internalised sense of being marginalised, powerless, dependent and inferior. All these attitudes are to be found in the relationship of fans (whether financially poor or not, but more frequently amongst the less privileged) to the institutions of football.

On the other hand, Lewis makes it clear that one precondition for the existence of a culture of poverty is that it develops only in societies where not everyone is poor. You cannot have a culture of poverty without the rich for the bearers of the culture of poverty to feel inferior to, and dependent on. Our discussion, therefore, must necessarily start with a look at the rich.

The economist and football scholar Paolo Caselli has sketched a dramatic change in the role and identity of the football rich in the last twenty years. In the 60s, it was customary to describe owners of football clubs as 'ricchi scemi' ('stupid rich'): second-rate billionaires who squandered their money on football, which they hardly understood to begin with. From the 80s onwards, they have been replaced by what Caselli styles as the 'ricchi furbi' ('smart rich'): modern competent entrepreneurs who *invest* their money in football and attempt to introduce in its administration some of the principles of modern business.

The dramatic progression from stupid to smart rich is likely, however, to make us forget the one element of continuity: that is, indeed, the *rich*. As Francis Scott Fitzgerald was fond of saying, the rich are different. They are different "from you and me", he went on, "because they have more money." I would argue that they are also different from capitalists, even though capitalists may have 'more money' than the old-fashioned rich, and even though the rich and the capitalist tend to be one and the same person. Berlusconi and Agnelli as *rich* owners of Milan and Juventus are different from Berlusconi and Agnelli as *capitalists*, because they entertain different relationships with their respective constituencies.

The basic difference is that, while capitalists and workers are bound by contracts, which regulate legal rights and legal duties between formal equals, there is no contract between the rich and the poor. The poor have no rights, but may receive gifts; the rich have no legal duties, but are bound by a 'noblesse oblige' moral obligation to their social inferiors.

This is precisely the type of relationship that exists between the owners of the football clubs and the supporters. Supporters have no voice in running the club and the team with which they identify, nor are the owners in any way responsible to them. On the other hand, if our owner is rich enough, he might buy us Paul Gascoigne (in the case of my team, Lazio in Rome).

Hence, the typical relationship, hinged on dependence, which structures the cultures of poverty around an ambivalence of i) *identification*, and, ii) *resentment*.

Let us begin with identification. Football becomes a vehicle of a cult of personality which cuts through all institutional mediations and legal structures, turning the rich into some kind of pop stars on the one hand, and modern day monarchs on the other.

One need only look at the humiliating slobbering of sportscasters running after Agnelli on TV every Sunday as he walks to his car after the game, begging for some gem of football wisdom from his august lips, to see manifestations of the personalised cult of the rich. That Agnelli's wisdom is no wiser than what you or I could say about the game, reinforces the myth by projecting a 'plain folks' image which, by its very 'humanising' effect, underscores the 'superhuman' stature of the charismatic hero. As John Kenneth Galbraith once said, "Even the commonplace observation of the head of a large corporation is still the statement of the head of a large corporation. What it lacks in content it gains in power from the assets behind it."(2)

Agnelli, in fact is central to this mythology because he combines the aura of the modern capitalist with the semi-feudal, paternalistic relationship to the club and its fans: as opposed to football's nouveau riche of the 80s and 90s, his family has controlled Juventus for generations. In an article which describes the mass fans of Juventus as "the Tuareg of black-and-white fandom", the most sober and highbrow of Italian newspapers, *La Repubblica*, combines in Agnelli's image the role of the competent entrepreneur, the passionate fan, the blue-blooded aristocrat:

> Yesterday, the Avvocato Giovanni Agnelli awoke with a great yen for Juventus. He looked out of his window and St. Moritz's glorious dawn encouraged him...(A few hours later) Agnelli's helicopter lowered on a field near (the team's) hotel, and offered to the people the awaited, expected and reassuring vision of the sovereign visiting his troops. Wearing jeans, Agnelli climbed into one of the (Fiat) Group's cars which immediately carried him to the training field, where Juventus stood waiting for him in tight orderly ranks.(3)

Agnelli's visit is a king's progress and a general's inspection, but also the trip of a plain, jeans-wearing fan checking on how 'his' team is coming on. Agnelli, however, able to express his passion through the (rumoured) promise of a Ferrari apiece if they win the pennant, as is fitting for the mythical rich: "the fanta Avvocato", as the article designates him. The writer goes on to report Agnelli's technical views on the state of football worldwide, and concludes with a memorable statement of his: "Nowadays some people just up and buy a club. I, myself, was acquired by Juventus fifty years ago...." Agnelli implies that, while the vulgar 'buy' mere monetary ownership, old money 'acquires' a relationship which includes responsibility and noblesse oblige duties. With this re-statement of the paternalistic role of the truly rich, "the Avvocato takes off. Like dreams do."

In the recent discussion on the state of the economy, Agnelli has also used the football 'demotion' metaphor: "I know one sure way to be demoted to B-league status", he said, "that is, playing like a B-league team, losing away games and tying home ones." (4) It is a hackneyed image, but Agnelli's use is more powerful than others, because he is supposed to 'know' both about the economy and about football. The myth comes full circle: because he is an economic power, our media have made him an authority on football; because he is an authority on football, he has a double authority on economic matters.

Agnelli's direct counterpart, and the man to whom he is probably referring in his statement about buying clubs, is of course Milan's Berlusconi, who bought Milan in the late 80s. Berlusconi pioneered in transferring to football the business principles which accompanied his meteoric rise to an empire, first in the construction industry and then in a monopoly of commercial television stations. Milan's spectacular victories and playing style were geared to refashioning football to suit TV programming, enlarging the audience, attracting advertising. In fact, Berlusconi's interference in technical matters stems not only from every Italian male's belief that he knows more than anybody else about the game, but by his insistence that Milan's game must be based on a spectacular attack rather than utilitarian defence, because the former shows better on television. It was after Berlusconi's arrival on the scene that football became the crucial arena of competition between private and public television, making football now so pervasive on the TV screen as to become actually boring. Berlusconi was so successful that even Juventus attempted (and failed) to imitate his business methods; others, more vulgar nouveau riche types, like Roma's Ciarrapico (a mineral water magnate with extreme-right leanings) or Fiorentina's Cechi Gori (a cinema producer) are attempting to imitate him in direct mass appeal.(5)

It was Berlusconi who raised the ante so high that money became more crucial to the game than it had ever been: there is now so much money in 'the world's greatest football tournament', that no regular club can afford it on gate receipts only. Having a rich owner becomes more important than having a good centre-forward, because only the owner can buy us the player. Thus, for football fans, having a rich owner becomes a matter of pride and security precisely like a rich master has been for servants and slaves: in fans' conversation, the financial assets of owners are discussed as passionately as the merits of players, and the enthusiasm of Roma's supporters when Ciarrapico bought their club surpassed that which accompanied the arrival of great players like Falcao or Rudi Voeller.

A variant of the 'my master is richer than thine' motif is 'my company is bigger than your company', in what passes in the West for the 'Japanese' model of industrial relations. This reminds us that the rich men as pop stars - Agnelli or Berlusconi, Lee Iacocca or Donald Trump - are capitalists after all. The personalised appeal of the owners becomes part of a broader re-feudalising of social relations, in which industrial/financial conglomerates draw an internalised allegiance not unlike nations, parties or churches. Football is but one of the most effective and visible vehicles of this process: one need only think of the sponsorship of private firms for cultural events (from art exhibitions to the restoration of monuments) to see another example geared to another sector of the public.

It is not merely coincidental that precisely when the 'Japanese' model - intended to win the workers' inner allegiance - is being launched at Fiat. Mr. Romiti, Fiat's chairman of the board, has intensified his appearance at football games and on sports pages of newspapers. In the Italian context, it appears that the intense mass appeal of football makes an ideal vehicle through which the rich masters of certain capitalistic conglomerates attempt to create among consumers the same type of allegiance that the 'Japanese' model is supposed to generate among workers. Before Napoli's last game a banner across a street in Sorrento read: "Boycott Channel Five" (the key network in Berlusconi's TV empire) - the apparent assumption being that there is a correlation between being Milan supporters and watching Berlusconi channels. The personal, semi-feudal, direct relationship with the masses that they seek, and the allegiance they receive, is ultimately part of a corporate strategy.

Subordination, as I have already pointed out, is mixed with resentment. One theme in the cultures of the poor is the sense of living in a cosmic order which is unjust but unchangeable. While you depend on, and identify with, Agnelli and Berlusconi, you also resent that they have all the power and the freedom - let alone all the money - and they get to make the decisions about the club, and you can do nothing about it. Rogan Taylor, of the Liverpool Football Supporters Association, has described the average football supporter as "the Cinderella of the game...alienated from the whole process of decision making" even though they are "the single and the most important asset that the game possesses". A character in Ricky Tognazzi's 1991 film on football fans, *Ultras*, voices the same feelings: "they treat us like the least wheel in the wagon, while we're the ones that keep it rolling."

Precisely like the poor, the resentment of football fans is heightened by the awareness that the rich and the owners could not ultimately survive without them. But the fact that they need you only gives you very indirect, roundabout means of pressuring them, emotionally expensive, often illegal, rarely effective. Fiorentina supporter may call a 'strike' against the Pontello family - but only a fraction of the arena will go along with them and, as soon as the team scores a goal, its all over. Like the poor, supporters are easily divided and bribed.

I would suggest that this attitude is reinforced by the nature of the game itself. Here is this event, in which you have a huge emotional stake, unfolding under your eyes - and you can **do** nothing about it. As the phrase goes, "you can look, but you'd better not touch"; you can exert moral pressure, you can create an atmosphere, make a noise, but anything beyond that is either fraud or violence.

One response consists in the fans' attempt to replace the pitch event with the hustings, to become the event themselves, rather than being spectators to the game. This is expressed in the visual and oral creativity of banners, fireworks, choreography, slogans, chants - as well as in the strategy of seizing the headlines and the eye of the camera by disrupting the order.

Another, more deep-seated attitude, is that of the typical powerless poor; a restless subordination, an unruly mob behaviour, occasional flares of destructive violence - riots, 'jacqueries' - which are shows of resentment but no challenge to power.

So, the world is stacked against you, it is unjust, it is inevitable. And yet....

Christian Bromberger has pointed out certain factors in the culture of football - most of all, the role of *chance* and *cheating* - which I also

83

have in mind, though with a slightly different focus. We can see how these concepts operate by a look at the random example: the Florence newspapers of May 1990, reporting on Fiorentina's defeat by Juventus in the European Union of Football Associations Cup Final. All the headlines are variants of one of three themes:

- Fiorentina lost *undeservedly*
- Fiorentina lost *unfortunately*
- Fiorentina was *cheated*

Although, as Bromberger shows, chance and cheating are no strangers to the culture of capitalism, they are absolutely central to the cultures of poverty. In Ralph Ellison's novel *Invisible Man*, during a ghetto revolt in Harlem, a woman sings the following blues verse: "If it hadn't been for the referee, Joe Louis woulda killed Jim Jefferie".(6) It is a cosmic sport's metaphor: life is a crooked game, in which the 'referee' is biased against us. Yet, we *could* win, *if....* A narrative theme which I have found and analysed both in oral histories and in science-fiction novels is that of *uchronia* - "what if...", "if only...." History is wrong, but it *could* have been different 'if only' one key event had chanced to (or been made to) go differently. Science-fiction writers contemplate what the world would be like if the Spanish Armada had not sunk or if Hitler had won the war; oral history narrators insist that 'if only' the leaders had not stopped 'us' in 1921 (or 1943, or 1948, or 1953, or 1968...) then history would be different and the workers would be in power.(7) And football fans revel in 'if only' uchronias: "if only Zenga hadn't left the goal during the game with Argentina, allowing Caniggia to score, we'd be world champions now." Or, in a beautiful example I heard in a pub in Manchester in the summer of 1991: "if Gordon Banks hadn't been sick when England played Germany in Mexico, England would have been world champions - and the Labour Party wouldn't have lost the election."

More than any other game, football is ruled by the imponderable. Seen from above, from the point of view of the wielders of power, this is one of the reasons why business methods which work very well in industry and finance do not transfer automatically to the administration of football: it is the degree of imponderability which differentiates a football club from a business concern.(8) Seen from below, from the point of view of the fans (especially of those who,

84

like me as a fan of Lazio - perhaps until now in 1992 - root for chronically losing teams), it means that - contrary to the puritan ethic of the spirit of capitalism - merit does not guarantee success, and success does not necessarily signify merit. Therefore, though we may be the defeated, yet it was not necessarily our fault. On the other hand, thanks to chance, every dog has its day. We may be weak and small, but we are not defeated in advance. My team, Lazio, can go to San Sire, play a very indifferent game, and beat Milan: and the pleasure is doubled precisely by the fact that we know they are a better team (of course, they have more money) and we did not 'deserve' it (they scored an own goal). Our subordination and inferiority has its occasional moments of consolation and even glory, but no cosmic structure is upset. The strong will ultimately prevail: all the 'small' clubs which have won the championship in the last twenty years (Lazio, Cagliari, Verona) paid for their *hubris* by dropping out of the A-league within five years.

The occasional victory of the weak over the strong has a powerful mythic appeal, going back to cosmogonic mythologies. After all, the most powerful uchronias concern the story of creation, and the shape of the world: if only Eve and the snake had not caused Adam to eat that cursed apple, there would not be so much evil in this world. Small, wily creatures of deceit known as tricksters interfere with the Almighty's plan, and introduce disorder in the world; and the trickster is a folk image of the poor and weak who deceive and cheat to beat the system (the player who 'steals' a penalty by deceiving the referee; the 'scally' who makes it a point of honour to get into the arena without paying) or simply to survive (as we hear from John Williams, the theme of 'coming through adversity' is very important for the Liverpool supporters - as well as for folk spirituals: "How I got over"). The hope and rationalisations of chance, the pleasures of cheating are the consolations of those who know that they stand no chance in ordinary rules of the game and the general setup of power.

To conclude, football is not a culture of poverty, but traits of cultures of poverty are found in football because they are generated by specific aspects of the organisational framework and of the structure of the game. On the other hand, these traits of the culture of poverty are not the whole thing, football does not cater to the poor alone, not everyone in it is powerless, and even the attitudes and behaviour of the most alienated supporters cannot be explained entirely and only in terms of the culture of poverty analogy. Finally, because there are many cultures and identities within the world of football, the same traits can be interpreted in culture of poverty terms by some supporters at certain times; and in other terms by other supporters, or by the same supporters at another time.

The *"mors-tua-vita-mea"* philosophy which Bromberger describes, can be, as he explained, a metaphor of competitive capitalism, but is also a powerful image of the world view of the poor. While capitalism kept telling us that development and energy had no limits and we need not worry about the distribution of wealth because progress would give enough to everyone, folk cultures remained painfully aware that we live in a world of limited goods. As the Italian anthropologist, Alberto M. Cirese, discovered in his study of a ritual in the Sardinian town of Ozieri, in folk games the winner did not take all but survived at the expense of others less lucky than him (sic).

By attempting to win everything, Berlusconi's Milan violated both this basic folk rule (you always leave something for the others) and "an old rule in Christian Democrat politics, which says you may win, but never attempt to wipe out the opposition." Identifying himself with the 'winner' - the folk hero of the 80s - Berlusconi convinced himself that he was 'virtually undefeatable', and wound up losing the pennant, the Cup, and his bid for the monopoly over the publishing industry.(9) But then, although it is men like him who cause it to exist, Berlusconi does not belong to the culture of poverty.

Sources

1.	This metaphor is endemic, *La Repubblica*, September 14 and 15, 1991, used it in several banner headlines.

2.	John Kenneth Galbraith, (1975), *The Great Crash*, Penguin, p.159.

3.	Murizio Crosetti, 'Piacere Juve, non deludermi', *La Repubblica*, August 7, 1991, p.37. All the newspapers that day carried spreads on Agnelli's visit to his team; the sports papers featured it in banner headlines on the front page. I am using *La Repubblica* precisely because of its reputation for soberness. The article consistently refers to Agnelli as 'the Lawyer' (l'Avvocato). Agnelli has never practised law, but one cannot name him without some deferential title. Most regular lawyers in Italy are addressed as 'dottore', which designates anyone with a college degree.

4.	Nino Sunseri, 'L'Italia é in A, ma gioica da serie B' é, *La Repubblica*, September 14, 1991.

5.	A two-page spread in *La Repubblica*'s business section: 'I padroni in fuorigioco', July 12, 1991, describes in detail the ties between business moguls and football clubs.

6.	Ralph Ellison, 1965, *Invisible Man*, Penguin, p.438.

7.	See Alessandro Portelli, 1991, 'Uchronic Dreams: Working Class Memory and Possible Worlds', in *The Death of Luigi Trastulli and other Stories. Form and Meaning in Oral History,* State of New York University Press, pp.99-116.

8.	See Mario Sconcerti, 'I padroni in fuorigioco' *La Repubblica*, op cit.

9.	A. Cal, 'Quell 'ebbrezza da record', *La Repubblica*, Business Section, July 12, 1991.

7 Fireworks and the ass

Christian Bromberger and others
Translated by Antonio Melechi

Editor's preface

Christian Bromberger's pioneering work on football, place and
identity is founded on empirical research into various clubs in Italy
and France, including Naples, Juventus and Marseille. This working
paper is translated by Antonio Melechi, formerly a Research
Assistant in the Unit for Law and Popular Culture. It is translated
from the Italian with the permission of the author on the grounds
that we believe Christian Bromberger's work deserves a wider
audience.

The following references to Bromberger's other essays may be of
interest to those reading this Chapter:

'L'Olympique de Marseille, la Juve et le Torino. Variations
ethnologiques su l'engouement populaire pour les clubs et les matchs
de football', *Esprit*, 4, 1987, pp.174-195.
'Sur les gradins, en rit...aussi parfors: faccetie et moquerie dans les
stades football', *Le Monde Alpin at Rhodanien*, 3/4, 1984, pp.137-156.
'Les Dieux et L'Ohéme', *Autrement*, February, 1989.pp.160-171.
'Le stade de football: une carte de la ville en réduction',
Mappemonde, 2, 1989, pp.37-40.
'Lo spettacolo delle partite di calcio. Alcune indicazioni di analisi
etnologica', in *Il calcio e il suo pubblico*, (1992), P. Lanfranchi, (ed.),
Naples, ESI, pp.183-219.
With A. Hayot and J-M. Mariottini, 'Allez l'O.M.! Forza Juve! La
passion pour le football a Marseille et a Turin', *Terrain*, 8, 1987, pp.8-
41 (translated by Justin O'Connor in this volume of essays).

Investigations into the dialogue between the Neapolitan football team and the city. The style of play and the style of support. The division of territory between groups of supporters. Discourses against the 'compensatory illusion' of football and its real effects on society.

The Neapolitan imaginary through its football

In an entertaining episode in *Roma* a student calls on Fellini and urges him to finally address the most serious problems of the capital: unemployment, the housing and university crisis, etc. The master slips away, leading us to a classic sequence lasting a quarter of an hour, to an antiquated theatre in which second rate comedians perform their fantasy in turn. To understand Naples through its football, the events which accompanied the recent championship victories in 1987 and 1990, the rituals of the fans reunited in the San Paolo stadium, may seem even more incongruous, in that neither is an *auteur* film nor a documentary, but an essay on various aspects of the local culture of a damaged city. A strong sociopolitical tradition in fact invites us to carefully assess the popular passion for sporting competition as a means to distract from, and forget, the real problems and values of society. Opiate of the masses, fleeting unanimity disguising tensions and oppositions, manipulation and entertainment distracting us from the essential.... These are the disparaging appraisals that commonly stigmatise the function of these spectacles.

This manipulatory conception has some justification. With reference to Naples, it will be remembered, for example, that Achille Lauro, 'O Commandante' (The Commander), used his managerial role in the squad to affirm proper political hegemony. One of his slogans during the campaign in the 1952 municipal elections was: "With Lauro for a great Naples [the town], for a great Naples [the club]." It could even be claimed - but the argument is deceptive - that the two championships provided a symbolic or even illusory compensation. The existence of similar processes cannot be denied, but the passion for football serves many other functions and has many other meanings. In general, if a match fascinates it is because it condenses, like a philosophical drama, the essential values that model our society: it speaks of merit, successful enterprise, solidarity (team spirit), the role of luck in individual and collective destinies, of promotion and recession; it reminds us of some essential truths and that basically the misfortune of some is the condition of happiness for others (your death, my life); ultimately it offers an expressive support for the affirmation of collective identity and local, regional and national antagonisms. It is with this last aspect that we will consider the passion for football in Naples, attempting to glimpse, over the shoulders of football players and fans, many of the salient features of local culture. What do they tell us of the real and imaginary identity of the city, the style of play that has been adopted and the forms of support in action?

The style of the game as a metaphor of a collective identity

Every great team, local or national, is known for its style of play, perceived by the fans as a representation of a specific collective existence. This style, which the fans take pleasure in identifying with, does not always correspond to - in fact is often far from - the practical reality of the footballers, which renews itself annually according to the many tactical decisions made by the managers, but rather corresponds to the stereotyped imaginary through which a community identifies itself and which it likes to give of itself. In this sense, the local style is part of a 'collective imaginary', or of a 'mentality' in the sense that M. Vovelle gives these terms (M. Vovelle, 1982): not only the way in which men (play and) live but the manner in which they like to narrate their team's game and their own lives. For the young fan, progressively discovering the nature of the local style is a kind of sentimental education in the values which model the city's and the region's imaginary. What can be said about the Neapolitan style? It appears - and the opposition is revealing - as the inverted image of that of Juventus of Turin, represented by the three S': 'Simplicity, Seriousness and Sobriety', the motto coined by E. Agnelli, President of Fiat and the Football Association in the 20s and 30s, which reflects the project of an industrial society built on rigour and efficiency. In Naples, contrastingly, they particularly value the imaginative game, full of thrills and skills, the eye-catching move, the spectacular feat. Against the sober and restricted game which the Juventus style imposes, Naples champions the imaginative, embodied in recent years by Giordano (or Carnevale), Maradona and Careca, the last of whom celebrates his exploits in the steps of a samba. For a

91

foreign observer, the revelation of the taste for a skillful game reveals itself in the jubilant expression of the spectators beholding the sheer skill of one of the players which may finally prove ineffective. Mauro, who has played for both Juventus and Naples, underlined in an interview the vivid contrast between these modes of understanding football and life. To many of the stylistic ingredients marking a sense of spectacle, and cultural scene, we can add craftiness, the jest in the game, or cunning, all traits which reinforce the parallel that can be made between the Neapolitan and Brazilian styles, undoubtedly illustrating the common ideal of a golden life (on the Brazilian style of play see R. da Matta, 1982).

The popularity of players, past and present, is undoubtedly related to their sporting ability, but also to their capacity to embody these elements of the local imaginary. One of SSC Napoli's most symbolic figures who combined spectacle and football, in all senses of these words, was Attila Sallustro, the star of the team from 1925 to 1935. Skillful and entertaining, nicknamed "the greyhound of football", Sallustro divided his passion between football and Lucy D'Albert, a diva from the New Theatre, whom he married at the end of his career. Of the other past glories, the fans particularly remember those who best symbolise one of the facets of the local style: in the 50s, Pesaola ('el Petisso'), a cheeky and whimsical Argentine; Vinicio ('the lion'), a Brazilian who bewildered the opposition, going on to become the manager of the team in the 70s, promising all-out football at a time when the sweeper system dominated the Italian game; in the 70s there were other skillful attackers: South Americans Jarbas, nicknamed Cane, Altafini and Sivori ('el Cabezon'). Symptomatically, other footballers, equally effective but less spectacular, occupy an inferior position in local legends. For example, Jeppson, a vigorous Swede, who played tennis and did gymnastics, who was transferred to Naples in 1953 for a record-breaking fee - "he was admired but not loved" by the Neapolitan fans, as G. Palumbo said.

In recent years the undisputed popularity of Maradona has been based on the quality of his sporting deeds, yet he would not have known such glory if there was no parallel between Maradona's style and that of the city: skillful, cunning, a joker, loving dramatic scenes, and always to be found with family and friends. Maradona found it difficult to adapt to Barcelona's 'geometric game' - where they have always preferred the Northern European players to South American

- and the somewhat mannered lifestyle appreciated in the Catalan capital. In Naples his success, sporting and symbolic, has instead been fully realised, scarcely overshadowed - on this point the fans opinions differ - by recent scandals. The identification is such that he willingly acknowledges Italian origins, certified, so they say, by his spitefulness, recalling the urchins - 'scugnizzi' - from the back streets of the city.

Forms and styles of support

The style of play appreciated on the pitch corresponds to a style of support which itself carries signs of the local culture. The Neapolitan support can be neither characterised by the breadth of the spectacle in the stadium, nor the blows exchanged in the confrontation of adversaries, but rather by its lyrical expression, for its capacity for self-mockery, its sense of parody and for an extraordinary mix of tradition and modernity in its forms of support.

The many slogans that can be read on the banners that are displayed in the stadium and in the streets distinguish themselves through a grandiloquent lyricism, now and then revealing an amused complicity in front of the enormity of the metaphors that are brought forth: "Naples, raise your eyes and look at the sky: it's the only thing greater than you"; "The immensity of the sky is not enough to express our love for you"; "The blues, you're Beethoven's Tenth"; "After God, Naples"; "Long Live the South"; "Children of the sun snatch the championship from the children of the cold".

For a foreign observer used to the typically self congratulating slogans that adorn stadiums and cities, these self-mocking slogans seem all the more original, marking an ironic culture of failure and self-pity. The irony of a pure joy expressed when a fan writes on the walls of the city: "If this is a dream don't wake me". The jocular bitterness, when another sticks a poster in the window of his hovel, saying: "The dream is now reality", thinking, without doubt, that reality has not become a dream. But above all the ability to turn one's own insults to ultimately reply to the stigmatisers. Responding to "Welcome to Italy", displayed by fans from Northern teams when they receive the Neapolitans, they reply: "Milan, Turin, Verona is this Italy? It's better being Africans!" Furthermore, "Better to win as country bumpkins than lose with Berlusconi." The symbol of this cheeky response - which clearly does not exclude the strong parochial pride - is the very symbol that the team was given in 1926: the donkey, the ass. On the circumstances of this paradoxical choice for honouring a city, various stories abound: following a disappointing championship a fan may have compared the squad to a donkey; according to a contrary explanation, a manufacturer of fireworks had arrived in Rome with his donkey for the 'Sunshine Derby', Naples having won the Derby, Ascarelli would have chosen this humble animal as a symbol of his squad. The Neapolitans remain strongly attached to this emblem which has been officially replaced for some years, to the annoyance of the fans, by a puppet of Saint Gennaro(1) with a much more modern appearance. Beaten, treated with disrespect, accused of all the wrongs, the donkey represents well the image that others use to allude to the Neapolitans, and which they themselves mockingly adopted. On the night of the championship victory, an effigy of the donkey, accustomed to pulling peasant carts, was carried triumphantly on a allegorical chariot - an ironic image of changing fortunes.

Beyond these stylistic traits the Neapolitan fans are characterised by their capacity to employ, in a more or less parodic fashion, the diverse aspects of local folklore, past and present.

The practises of fans attempting to escape the spell of bad luck and tip the scales in their favour, in that game in which the use of the feet and the role played by the referee are uncertain factors, draw abundantly from the 'official' or marginal tables of belief. Few are the fans who would not travel around carrying sacred images; some pray before the match. Yet modern sport is essentially secular, football is a field where the preferred rituals are magic and spells: supporters carry good luck charms, brandish horns to cast disgrace on others and protect their side; some put on underwear in team colours, others always deposit tickets and banknotes on the same side.

Before an important match the fans attempt to evade initiatives to stir envy and unleash the 'evil eye': arrogantly flaunting the certainty of bringing back the National and European Championship. Berlusconi did not attract envy and defeat. For the ethnographer these practices are excellent fields to investigate creeds; the sincerity of the fans that conscientiously respect them, does not exclude a critical distance, and often assume a humorous aspect: "It's not true, but we believe" can be read on the placard of a vendor of lucky charms. Here, as in many other places, the adoption of distance from a ritual is still part of the ritual.

This ambiguous mass of principles, respected in a more or less fervent or parodic fashion, characterises many episodes in the championship celebrations that appropriate, in certain aspects, other traditional rituals. Parody exploded when, on the day before the championship victory, one supporter organised the sale of an abundance of Berlusconi's tears, which included a certificate of inauthenticity; or in the 'Our Father' in which Maradona replaced the Lord: "Our Maradona, who descends onto the field, we have sanctified your name, Naples is your crown. Do not lead us into temptation but lead us to the championship. Amen."

It is without doubt in the funeral rituals that these parodic and carnivalesque elements are most clearly asserted: the chapel mass erected in the Forcella district to the memory of Berlusconi, countless funeral processions with the colours of the rival team carried on shoulders through the city. The cult of idols assumed the classical form of the religious festival: the effigies of Maradona taking the place of Saint Gennaro and Saint Antonio, or have been associated with those of Our Lady of the Arc. Some fans even built a bust of 'Saint Gennarmando' associating the name of their patron saint with that of Maradona. The cult of the dead - another conspicuous dimension of the popular passion - has not been forgotten in this *mise en scéne,* which mobilises the symbolic resources of local culture: "What have you missed"; "In homage to the fans who have not had the pleasure of being here today".

Complete spectacles, the championship celebration and, to a lesser extent, the great meetings of the championship are privileged moments of affirmation, or even of resurrection, of the traditional forms of festival and artistic expression. On the occasion of the two championship victories, the allegoric chariots which, in other times, lead the great pomp of the Piedigrotta procession, were returned to action: the traditional puppets replaced by models of the players, for example, one of Maradona giving a blood transfusion to a terrified Gullit. On the occasion of the last championship victory, a 100 metre battery of fireworks - an appropriate symbol of the colourful and chaotic city - was installed in Santa Lucia, as is done in September when the festa of the Virgin of Catena is celebrated. And, finally - does it need to be underlined? - various slogans and hymns which celebrate the squad are derived from the repertoire of Neapolitan songs. *'Maradona innamorato' ('Maradona in love'),* is an adaptation of a song by Sergio Caputo about Garibaldi; the famous *'E me diciste si na sera e maggio,'* (*'And you told me yes on a night in May'*) - the 'must' of the celebratory slogans in the 1987 championship - comes from the famous *'Maggio si tu!'* (*'You are May'*) composed in 1913 by E. A. Morio (cfr. G. Cesarini, 1987).

Clearly the support in the stadium and, to a greater extent, the celebrations on the occasion of the championship victories present themselves as a *mise en scéne* of a more or less parodic re-adaptation of traditional local culture. However, it would be wrong to close our observations here, with the risk of falling into folklore and a kind of bucolic ethnology. The fans, here as in other places, are also perfectly inscribed within a most vibrant modernity. The tunes and the rhythms of the encouragements are at the same time marked by international hit melodies, by Italian songs, by slogans used in the demonstration, more than Neapolitan songs; the names which ultra groups give themselves, the emblems that they display (Che Guevara, for example) do not reflect a direct symbolic affinity with local culture. The 'Commando Ultra' which occupies the centre of the B 'curva' [end] in the San Paolo stadium is in this sense closer to a firm than the more traditional brotherhood: managing its capital of six thousand followers, making preparations for professional banners, sponsoring its own emblem, publishing a magazine with a 10,000 print run, producing a weekly TV programme ('One hour with the B Curva'), perform their shows in the most modern way, through the workings of the media. The charismatic leader of the 'Commando', Palummella, nicknamed this because he jumps from one tier of the stadium to another, embodies (in exemplary fashion) the fusion between tradition and modernity. He prays before a match, collects sacred images from which he will never be parted, and has his bathroom painted in blue and white. In the television programme which he enthusiastically presents, he evokes, with his calls to mobilisation, a popular leader of former times, and is accompanied by a poet and a singer.... This is the actualisation of tradition. However, at the same time, Palummella cultivates the 'clean look' of a successful manager, runs the office of his fan club like that of an enterprise, has socially elevated himself thanks to these activities and carries himself like a star in his dealings with the media, embodying one of the major elements of modernity: the visible consecration of the individual.

So both in the stadium and in the streets (with the festivities that accompanied championships), one may see, though in various proportions, the conjunction of modern and traditional cultural traits and forms that combined in the celebration of a derided identity.

Meanings and destiny

Beyond the scenic, ludic and festival culture which predisposes Naples to become inflamed by the spectacle of football, what is at the bottom of this extraordinary passion, what sense do the fans make of the ups and downs of the team?

It is typical of a fallen city, nostalgic for its great past and today derided by strangers, to fervently support the team which represents them. In this sense, Naples has a notable affinity with other cities in crisis, like Marseilles or Liverpool. A few figures give an idea of the passion for the team in the Parthenopean city: more than 70,000 season ticket holders in 1975, a happy year, when in April more than 10,000 Neapolitans travelled to Turin for a decisive championship match; more than 67,000 season ticket holders in the 1984-85 season when Maradona made his debut; more than a million products with a value of about £30,000,000 sold during each championship celebration. And, beyond these figures, second to none in Italy, the ubiquity of the fervour in this city, which translates into the azure colours the edges of the roads, walls and traffic signs of the lower class districts; or, moreover, the exceptional density of the supporter clubs in Naples' urban and provincial web.

The Italian Association Napoli Club certainly does not hold the record number of members: 96,000 made up of 526 clubs (in comparison the prestigious Juventus of Turin holds more than double), yet the concentration of the former is in the major part in Campania, while Juventus counts only 15% of its supporters clubs in Piemonte. Naples clings tightly to its identity while for others it is dispersed. In the network of supporters clubs the club has altogether few friends (Bologna, Genova, Cesena, Perugia, Ascoli, Empoli) and provokes, as is well known, the most virulent slogans when its team plays in the North of Italy: "The Neapolitans along with the Jews", "No to vivisection, use the Neapolitans", "Neapolitans help the environment, get a wash" - could all recently be read on the Milan supporters' banners.

In the face of this stigmatisation, the Neapolitan responses are marked by various types of self-valorisation and denunciation, which

97

may vary according to the circumstances, the adversary and the ideological tendency of the group of fans: the exaltation of the sun against the greyness of the North, the vindication of the civility of the city as opposed to Northern profiteering ("Naples champion of football, culture and civilisation", "Civilisation cannot be bought"). Who is the more civilised? This old evolutionary question seems to impassion Italians from North to South; the affirmation of liberty against the domination of captains of industry ("Juventus supporters working for the boss", "Black Juventus 'sucking peas' from the Agnelli family"); or, moreover, the revolt of virtue against the plot fostered by a corrupt North ("Against Freemasons, cheats, exploiters, mercenaries and racists, the Neapolitans invite the Blues to fight hard without fear" could be read in one of the last issues of *Napulissimo*, the Ultra commando magazine). If the fans have their own poets, they even have their own philosophers, who elevate the squad to a symbol of the subaltern social strata, stripped by the industrial powers of the North.

However, let us not fall into the sanctification of the Neapolitan supporters against the brutal practices of the Northern clubs. On the one hand they shout bloody insults when matched with Juventus (chanting "Brussels, Liverpool" to invoke the memory of the Heysel drama); on the other hand, if the Neapolitan public won the 1986-87 prize for fair play that was, above all, the consequence of the voluntary policy of the sporting society who, with support from leaders of Naples Club and Commando Ultra, adopted a policy of controlling and directing the crowd in the stadium. In previous times, uproar, brawls and rows, ground invasions punctuate here, as elsewhere, the most important matches.

A second type of response to the discredit hurled on the city, has been to assemble a brilliant and cosmopolitan team of celebrated athletes. Recruiting Krol, Dirceu, Maradona, Careca, etc., making them Naples, isn't a symbolic proof of the power of attachment of an unjustly despised city - challenging the contempt through its fame? The composition of its team, over the last twenty years, may be interpreted, for all that as a sign of a profound shift in the representation of its destiny. Up until the 70s they signed Northern players, the symbols of a prosperous Italy which they turned to. "Nobody is prophet in his own country" was said to illustrate the vision of an irremediable dependent destiny. The actual squad, composed of many Southern players (Ferrara, De Napoli, Mauro, etc.), surrounded by great international stars, represented a vision of a free and optimistic response to the city's destiny.

Defeat or victory against a Northern squad are taken as a contest of differences similar to a philosophical debate. Defeat is often attributed to the bad luck which plagues the city, to the partisan decisions by the referee, undoubtedly bribed, to the good fortune which always favours the adversary, to a fate which cannot be avoided. "Games are made, the match is fixed, the dog bites the poor", following the popular saying. According to this point of view "the last championship", won thanks to a throw of the dice, "is only the fortune deserved after much bad luck and many injustices" one fan announced. Victory, essentially the championship, is like a clamorous revenge deserved under a tenacious curse and, for some, an omen of a new future ("No night is long enough to stop the sun shining...and we're rising"). Finally, the roles are reversed; the dominated becomes the dominator ("Naples the champions, pride of the nation"), dismissing those who usually dismiss them ("Naples the champions, fuck the nation"; "You won the championship for fucking the Northerners"); the weak rule the powerful: Berlusconi is invited to work as a car parking attendant and other Milanese to serve like lads in the stable of the donkey, which is carried in triumph. Is this carnivalesque inversion of usual roles a reassuring herald, or even a compensatory illusion? Is it possible that a great footballing victory initiates a renewal of confidence in the city. The president of a supporters' club affirmed this with conviction on the night of the last championship victory. But no approach permits us to seriously assess the effects of these collective emotions on the reality of the city. Yet it seems uncertain that these celebrations, and more generally, the passion for football, distil real problems and brutalise the masses. Fervour and joy do not necessarily in themselves entail illusion; here football catalyses a derided identity and in this sense does not represent a sedating opiate, and does not mask, any more than in other places, the gravity of everyday problems. The Neapolitans are not, any more than others, 'cultural idiots' blind before their practices and incapable of critical distance.

Territories

The scene of the sporting spectacle, the stadium, is also the scene of a spectacle of a spectacle, offered by its public. In its form and scale this space is one of the few which a society, in keeping with modern times, can give imaginary shape to both its unity and its diversity. In this sense the footballing encounter constitutes an exceptional event in the spectacularisation of social relations. Two aspects require particular attention in the San Paolo stadium: the contrast between the two ends, A and B, where admission is the same price; the affirmation, mediated through writings on banners that circle the terrace, of the importance of neighbourhood as a basic structure of support.

At the centre of the A end, the Blue Tigers, numbering 1,900 members, are generally youngsters from the poor industrial suburbs in the east of the city. Their headquarters are in Barra, where on Tuesday and Thursday they meet in preparation for Sunday's match with a programme which varies depending on the importance of the match, the strength of the adversary, and the need to organise travel. The charismatic leader of the Blue Tigers, Bombo, a man of about 40, is the leading spirit of the group - almost a lay preacher who would devote himself into the ministry of his club, keeping a watchful eye over often wayward youths. The style of support in the A end, which has many youngsters from the local neighbourhood, is constructed in the image of this culture of a youth club in a craftsman's parish: unruly, facetious, exhibiting home-made emblems and banners with whatever means they have available.

The Blue Tigers do not like the Commando Ultra, who occupy the centre of the B end, who have an elegant and strict style and, as previously mentioned, number 6,000 youngsters, the vast majority resident in the city, from all social classes, amongst which a good number are secondary school and university students. In this way the A and B ends constitute two clearly represented territories, each characterised by a unique style of support. Yet in both cases, the organisations run beyond sporting commitment: if necessary Bombo lets youngsters in difficulty stay in the headquarters of the Blue Tigers; the Ultra magazine *Napulissimo* reports not only football, in the strict sense, but also follows politics and city news.

Many of the official Naples supporters' clubs, that is to say those recognised by SSC Napoli, decorate the stadium following a protocol which requires meticulous collective organisation; in effect the banners of the various clubs never occupy the same space during the championship, guaranteeing each absolute parity. An inspector assigned by the Associazione Italiana Napoli Club checks, with a plan of the appropriate points, on the proper arrangement of the banners. The stadium, it can be seen, is considered by the fans as a space which belongs to them which they manage, each in their own territory, following their proper rules.

The Neapolitan supporters' clubs from the city and provinces today undoubtedly constitute the basic structure of sociability between male neighbours. Each must make plans from independent premises and will gather at least 50 members, with local houses which have at their disposal leisure facilities (games, libraries, etc.). The local club offers pensioners and the unemployed the possibility of recreation, sometimes organising other activities unconnected to the sport: outings and family excursions, for example. In short they symbolise and actualise the fundamental unities of affiliation which districts and neighbourhoods continue to represent.

There are few events which can be deemed to be 'complete social events' - following Marcel Mauss rather than some of his commentators - "phenomena which in some cases mobilise the totality of a society and its institutions." The championship celebrations undoubtedly belong to this order, a total spectacle in which various constitutive elements of Neapolitan life and imagination are embodied: the underground economy, which almost entirely provides the materials for the festa (unlike most other footballing societies SSC Napoli does not manage supporters' trade); a style and unique cultural form, put into action or adapted to the circumstances; an extraordinary capacity for parody; the importance of the districts, the real units of the festa's organisation; the celebration of an identity torn between two contradictory symbols: fireworks and the ass.

Notes

1.   Saint Gennaro is the patron saint of Naples.

Bibliography

Cesarini, G., (1987), 'E Campione fa rima con canzone', *Il Mattino*, June 13.

Da Matta, R., (1982), 'Notes sur le football brésilien' *Le Debat*, No. 19.

Vovelle, M., (1982), *Idéologies et mentalités*, Maspero, Paris.

8 'Allez l'O.M., forza Juve': The passion for football in Marseille and Turin

Christian Bromberger with Alain Hayot and Jean-Marc Mariottini
Translated by Justin O'Connor

Translator's introduction

> Afterwards, she was the first to offer a bitter, sarcastic analysis of the orgiastic character of people's religious devotion week after week and month after month - to the rite of carnival. Exactly the same sort of tribal witchcraft, she would say with revolutionary contempt, as the soccer rituals in which the disinherited expended their combative energy and sense of revolt, practising spells and enchantments to win from the gods of every possible world the death of the opposing halfback, completely unaware of the Establishment, which wanted to keep them in a state of ecstatic enthusiasm, condemned to unreality. (Umberto Eco, *Foucault's Pendulum*)

The Unit for Law and Popular Culture in its Working Papers series 1990-92 initially published writings of Christian Bromberger. This collaborative piece first appeared as 'Allez l'Om! Forza Juve. La Passion du Football à Marseille et à Turin', *Terrain*, 8, pp.8-41.

The article comes from an anthropological tradition very different from that of British Cultural Studies within which so much of the work on football in Britain is situated. This tradition, which radicalised itself in the 60s and 70s under the diverse influences of such as E. P. Thompson, Raymond Williams, Stuart Hall and those around New Left Review, is concerned with a particular 'way of life' that was deeply riven by class difference. The history and specificity of this cultural configuration, and its consequences with regard to working class politics and the peculiar nature of the British state, have formed the basis of a thirty year debate within the British (or, more specifically, English) left that has deeply marked Cultural Studies. This tradition has been concerned with the points at which one 'way of life' has come in conflict with another, or the configuration of domination, evasion and sociopolitical 'compromise' that has stalked British popular culture since Richard Hoggart and his book *The Uses of Literacy*, first published in 1957.

Bromberger et al come from a gallic tradition which asks very different questions of its subject. We can hear echoes of Durkheim rolling beneath the text, with is a neo-Kantian question, "How is society possible?" Bromberger et al certainly deal with issues of class in this piece, but it is symptomatic that this is done in terms of their articulation and distribution within the space of the public. The text uses the word *public* as others would use the word*crowd*; the crowd or le foule have a resonance in both countries that links them to the mob ('*mobile vulgas*' - the common people on the move), to the 'swinish multitude' (Burke), to mindless group behaviour, the abandonment of individuality and acts of criminal and civic violence.[Editor's note: See the most recent use of this in Bill Buford's 'Amongst the Thugs']. Bromberger et al's *public* is certainly overwhelmingly 'popular' [which is used where others would talk about 'working class' - I have translated it thus] but it is not restricted to one class and one 'way of life'.

This concern with 'society as a whole', and the representation of this society in the public space of the stadium, takes us back towards the roots of sociology in the late 19th century; and at times it is in danger of falling into the sort of functionalism of which its early North American practitioners were often guilty. But it demands that we think popular culture in terms of a public rather than a 'working class'. The end results of this approach may be disputed, but it certainly raises interesting questions for the study of popular culture at a time when so much political debate is concerned with issues of *citizenship*. At the very least it directs us outside 'cultural studies' towards other politico-cultural configurations.

The article also raises the question of myth and ritual in contemporary society. We find less of a concern with ritual as the means of social and political 'resistance' than with, firstly, the expression and comprehension of life-histories, of one's 'destiny', as the authors call it; and secondly, the articulation and representation of 'sociability' (the social bond as it is felt and lived in specific situations) in its complex and conflicting whole. This does not necessarily mean conservatism or an abandonment of 'politics'; perhaps these questions lead us to another confrontation with the Anglo-Saxon world's (both right and left) loss of a 'language of community'.

The lines of a critical political response to this article could already be found in the Chapter by Alessandro Portelli. Both Chapters deal with the same material of myth and ritual in Mediterranean soccer culture, and both act as fruitful (implicit) critiques of the other. Portelli's notion of football as 'rich versus poor' rather than 'workers versus capitalists' takes us into a more sophisticated version of the critique contained in the Eco quotation above. Any revolt on the terraces is doomed to failure because it is couched in terms of feudal class relations rather than capitalist ones. It represents an eternal circle of fate in which submission follows revolt, and social injustice is blamed on a crippling sense of supernatural destiny.

Parts of this article are specifically aimed at the notion that the football spectacle is part of a ruling class strategy for working class containment, something which Portelli argues with greater or lesser reservations. But the bulk of the text is concerned to look more closely at this ritual, this myth making, which is 'half parodic, half dramatic', which is secular but washed through by the sacred, which is 'lived rather than said'. Portelli's paper ends with a piece of 'folk wisdom' inscribed in Sardinian ritual games, where the winner does not take all, but leaves some for the others. This is the culture of poverty. But it also represents a painful awareness that 'we live in a world of limited goods'. That 'pre-modern' (for Portelli therefore 'feudal') wisdom is used as a critique of the 'modernist' capitalism points us to some of the more nuanced, complex and perhaps more fruitful ways of seeing contemporary popular spectacles - ones marked, as Bromberger et al put it, "by uncertainly and renewal, those two figures of modernity".

Marco, Marseille, the North, the South

"The days coming up to a big O.M. match, I'm all tensed up, like I'm ill. It gets me a week, sometimes fifteen days before a decisive match. For example, before Lyon - O.M. in 1984", a match where Marseille's victory meant the team's promotion to the first division after four years of 'purgatory', "I couldn't think of anything else, at home like at work. A week before leaving for Lyon I dressed in the O.M. colours: I would only wear blue underpants and blue socks. I try hard not to be superstitious, to control my emotions, but I never can. When I'm going towards the stadium, four or five hours before the match, I start to tremble with nerves and it's difficult for me to control myself." Leader of Commando Ultra,(1) which groups the most ardent young O.M. supporters, Marco nevertheless directs, with great calm and authority, the demonstrations of support for his favourite team, programmed in minute detail in advance: chants to the rhythm of drums, songs, letting off multicoloured flares when the team come out onto the pitch, unfurling the immense blue and white banner, releasing balloons, also in club colours, etc. When the match has finished the accessories must be packed away, an assessment made of the conduct of the troops ("too much indiscipline today...the flares weren't coordinated"), lessons drawn that could improve the team support for the next confrontations. Victory or defeat, joy or suffering, Marco remains 'tensed up' during the night following the match; he tries in vain to sleep, reliving the match, the moments of joy, the dramas that succeeded one another during that weekly one and a half hours which gives rhythm to his life.

The passion for football and for O.M. doesn't just occupy the days and the dreams of Marco; it forms the frame against which the milestones of his existence are marked out. Son of a Sicilian immigrant, well integrated into his adoptive city, Marco owes to his father "his love for the ball", the stadium and Marseille - three terms equivalent in his books. With him, like with most of the supporters, the interest in football is a case of family tradition and an identification fusing him to the city - so much the stronger for an immigrant, or son of an immigrant, in that it can symbolise the satisfaction of a successful insertion.(2) A tragic event played a decisive role for Marco in his vocation for his career as supporter; as an adolescent he lost one of his uncles in an accident. This uncle, he tells us, watched over him "like a brother" and had contributed strongly to his religious education, taking him to mass every Sunday. Faced with what appeared to him as an injustice of fate, Marco lost his faith. But a new fervour rapidly took the place of his religious sentiments; it was, in effect, the year which followed the death of his uncle that he began his real passion for football - for O.M. but also for Juventus of Turin, the leading light of the Italian league, which rallies much of the support of the emigrants from the peninsula. In spring 1984, Marco married, the same day of O.M.'s victory over Thonon, which officially consecrated the promotion to the first division (the date of the marriage had been fixed deliberately to coincide with this event). On the day Marco had himself photographed on a car painted in O.M. colours, in front of Marseille town hall; it was, for him, one of the clearest memories of this ceremony. Now aged 25, Marco sings his son to sleep with songs sung by the Juventus Tifosi(3) to encourage the team, melodies which he and his mates try to popularise among the O.M. supporters, to enrich a choral tradition much poorer in France than it is in Italy.

Until the end of the 1985-86 season the Ultras occupied a well defined space in the North End (*virage* = curve or bend) of the stadium, forming the noisiest and best organised group amongst a young public coming mostly from the working class districts to the north of the Marseille conglomeration. In effect, the distribution of the public in the stadium reflects, roughly, the social geography of the city (we will analyse later the mechanisms of this territorialisation). The tumultuous supporters of the North End are traditionally opposed to the wealthier, more family orientated, older and more peaceful public of the South End, who come from the suburbs and the central districts of the city. At the beginning of the 1986-87 season, Marco and his mates decided to move to the South End and to establish their territory.

This migration within the space of the stadium was the object of bitter discussions among the Ultras and was experienced by some as an uprooting: "That did me in. I'm from the Rose - an area to the North of Marseille - and since I was small I've been coming to the North End. Since the start of the season something's not been right." Francois, who had gone to the South with bitterness, henceforth kept himself to the margins of the hard core of the Commando. Marco was the principle architect and defender of this move: "In the South End you can organise better, it's less cramped, the public are more disciplined and anyway, we must break down the barriers between the North and the South, give a more unanimous image to the stadium and to the city." In fact, for Marco, this transition from North to South symbolises, above all, the ideal route that had been laid down for him, a route to which, for the most part, he has conformed. Born in a working class district of the city, he currently lives in the south; married, settled down somewhat, he now feels hardly any affinities with the young public from the working class suburbs who occupy the North End. His suggestion displays a profound desire for recognition and advancement, a desire he has partially satisfied by his activities as leader of the Commandos: from anonymous spectator he has become, with his mates, an object of spectacle, recognised by his confederates but also by the officials of the club, interviewed by journalists and...ethnographers. "Look how far we've come", he remarked proudly at half-time in the O.M. - Paris-Saint-Germain match, stating that the Ultra group which could count 12 devotees at its beginning in 1983 now constituted an organisation of 600-plus members.

Marco's destiny, since his adolescence, is undoubtedly exceptional, in that it represents a perfect osmosis between the principal steps of his personal life and the great events which have marked out the history of his favourite club or the group of supporters which he leads. It does, however, offer an ideal resumé, extreme though it may be, of the values, the stakes, the behaviours involved in the passion for football and the unrelenting attendance at the stadium: the emotional effervescence translated into an intense corporal participation; the identification with a city in an atmosphere of ritualised war (banners [*étendards* = standards] in club colours, the presence of 'commandos' to support the team); the affirmation of social identities in the spectacular space of the stadium; the sociability of peer groups, reinforced, match after match, by meetings on the terraces; the symbolisation of the dramas, joys, the ups and downs of existence (relegation, promotion, victory, defeat); and, for some, a fervour drenched with religiosity, attempting to tame fate by a profusion of propitiary attitudes and symbols.

Turin, La Maratona, La Filadelfia, Scarlet and Black

Whilst O.M. is the only professional club in Marseille and the local region, in Turin, as with many European and Mediterranean cities, the exclusive favours of the supporters are shared by two clubs: F.C. Torino (Toro) and Juventus (Juve). The Tifosi of Toro and Juve represent, grosso modo, two distinct social and cultural universes.

Toro is for the locals, an old deep-rooted proletariat, an autochthonic population that leans on the past glory of the city; its president, S. Rossi, industrialist and 'self-made man' himself originates from one of the city's working class quarters. The 'grenat' [garnet] passion (the dominating colour of the club) is deeply rooted in a celebration of the past. Before, and immediately after, the war Toro were one of the leading teams of the Italian championship; in 1948 they won the Scudetto(4) for the sixth time, but a tragic incident put an end to this golden epoch. On the May 4, 1949 the team plane crashed onto the Superga Hill, just outside Turin; every year since, Toro supporters make a pilgrimage to the site of the drama. On this day all the supporters clubs place a wreath under the plaque and attend a commemorative mass. In 1976, F.C. Torino, after a thirty year eclipse, won the championship; the Superga pilgrimage that year was *una cosa incredible;* ten thousand people turned up at the basilica which dominates the hill and which was lit up for the occasion.

Juve represents another universe. To the nostalgia for a glorious past and the uncertainty of the present symbolised by Toro, it opposes the arrogance of a team which is both victorious (it has won everything from the national championship to the European cups) and rich (its capital in terms of players was valued at £9 million in 1985), and whose renown spreads, year after year, throughout Italy and the world; in 1985 one could count 1,166 Juventus clubs, 1,124 in Italy and 32 abroad (the figures for 1986 showed an increase of 100 clubs and a steady increase in Europe, Africa and Asia). Juve owes its power to the solidity of its infrastructure; the club is a subsidiary of Fiat and was managed directly, between 1923-1935, and again between 1947-1962, by the Agnelli family, which holds presidency of the firm. Since then 'The Avvocato' has delegated his powers, but continues to jealously watch over the destinies of the team. The club *bianconero* (black and white) undoubtedly owes its renown to the scale of its recent successes, but its emblematic force also reflects the industrial phenomenon which underlies it, and which has burst beyond the bounds of local barriers and parochialisms. The principal forces of support for Juve do not come from the native population; they are essentially the Fiat workers; immigrants from Southern

Italy (according to the census of 1981, 55% of migrants installed in Piedmont were born in the Mezzogiorno (the south); the non-Turinese regional population: students, whose horizons go beyond those of the city; and the millions of Tifosi who have travelled through Italy and across the globe, and for whom Juve represents the very model of success. Thus, to roughly characterise things, Toro (which evokes the name and power of the city) and Juve (which effaces references to Turin) oppose each other as the local to the universal, the past to the future, bad luck to good fortune...*Quando tutti tradiranno solo mio rimarremo fedeli!!!* (When all betray, we alone remain faithful), says a slogan of the *Legione Granata* [the Garnet Legion], one of the groups of Toro Ultras.

Twice a year the Derby(5) between F.C. Torino and Juventus of Turin constitutes one of the summits of the Italian championship; on this occasion the two huge ends of the Stadio Communale make up two clearly symbolised territories; *la Maratona* is the fief of the Toro supporters, *la Filadelfia* that of the tifoseria bianconera. At each end [*virage* = curve] the groups of supporters spread themselves out from the centre to the edges, according to their respective importance and following an agreed protocol; three hours before the match starts, the troops are in place shouting chants and slogans - to the glory of their favoured team and derogating the opposing team. Gestures, speeches, hymns, the deployment of banners, the letting off of balloons...all are minutely orchestrated within each group by a *capo-tifo* (chief supporter) also known as a *carismatico*. The actions of the end as a whole are regulated by a choreographer; the one that directs the tifoseria granata (reputedly the most beautiful in Italy) is a specialist, let us note in passing, in the restoration of church frescoes. From one end to the other fly insults, half-parodic, half-dramatic, shouted at the top of the voice or written on the banners; this joust, spoken and written, is organised in terms of a crescendo, offences becoming ever more wounding; when the Juve supporters show a banner *"Grand Toro, ti preghiamo: si prendi l'aero, te lo pagiamo moi"* ("Grand Toro, we beg you: if you take the plane we'll pay", a parodic evocation of the Superga tragedy), the Torino Tifosi reply immediately: *"Animali, con voi Bruxelles e stao troppo onesta"* ("Animals, Brussels was too good for you", a parodic evocation of the Heysel tragedy). To set such a spectacle going on the terraces demands a detailed organisation and a quite significant expenditure; the 'Black and White supporters'(6) - one of the principle Ultra groups supporting Juve - claim to have spent 11 million Lire (£5,500) for the choreography of their *magica curva* (magical end) on the occasion of the second Derby of the 1985-86 season.

In terms of football culture and of the cult of football, Latin society is far in advance of French society: a widespread understanding, amongst the (masculine) population, of the systems and tactics of the game; four daily newspapers exclusively given over to football (only one in France) and a whole bunch of specialist magazines; an average first division gate of 36,000 (10,000 in France); a flourishing *mercatifo* (supporters' market), offering to the fans a profusion of emblematic objects (scarfs, pens, jerseys, cuff-links, stickers, etc.)(7) But it is above all in the demonstrations of support for the teams that the differences - qualitative and quantitative - between the two traditions are most apparent: the emotional effervescence, the tension, the theatricalisation of the passions, the variety of magico-religious practices performed to influence destiny - these are all without comparison in France. The excellent films of P. Demont (*Les fous du Stade* - The Madmen of the Stadium) and of D. Segre (*Ragazzi di Stadio* - Kids of the Stadium), dedicated to the Tifosi of Juve, furnish some remarkable examples of this infatuation and frenzied fervour; four days before a decisive fixture some supporter had put a black and white scarf around the neck of a statue of Christ, which had pride of place in his room: "I would have no fear of dying for Juventus" he comments, "the most beautiful death I could think of would be during a Juventus match." D. Segre, for his part, shows us the detailed preparations, as the Derby approaches, of the Juventini on some waste ground near the Stadio Communale: making crosses and devil masks...which are to be brandished during the match to defy and to dishonour the enemy, bringing down evil on them and proclaiming the superiority of their own team, protecting them against misfortune. One could add other examples, observed during the games, which testify to the atmosphere of intense religiosity which permeates the preparation and progression of the great Italian football matches: prayers, propitiary scattering of salt behind the goal, sometimes the sacrifice of a cock before the game.... "L'enfant Jesus," we are told by 'Mamma Juve', a retired teacher who, before each game offers a cake, lovingly prepared, to the players - "is without the slightest doubt juventino".

To begin the analysis of the forms and significations of the popular infatuation with clubs and football games via an overview of the summits - emotional and symbolic - simultaneously both opens and closes our route. We are thrown straightaway into a universe loaded with meaning, where images of life and death, warfare, sacrifice and religious ritual jostle with each other. And it is true that the evocation of the supporters' emblematic figures, their beliefs, their speech, their behaviour, lead us directly down this path. It may perhaps be objected that it is a question here of marginal cases and practices, an ethnologists' paradise but hardly reflecting the attitudes of the majority of the spectators. This argument has little weight. Marco, the *Leoni de la Maratona* (Toro Ultras), the *Fedelessimi* of Juve offer, in a compressed and dramatic manner, that which is lived, and sometimes thought, in a euphemistic and minor mode, by the mass of spectators assembled in the stadium. The 'levelling down' [*denivellement*] involved in joining in, fervour, knowledge - are these not traits common to all ritual? But to confine ourselves to these heights, where the horizon of grand symbols can be seen more clearly, does this not risk seeing only the most dazzling fragments and missing the totality of the edifice which underpins them? Fundamentally, the correct approach does not so much consist in analysing symbolic expressions in their generality - the sacred, warfare, and so on - but to render intelligible, in the specificity, the processes and the mediations which make of this particular terrain - the football field and the stadium - a privileged space for the affirmation of a certain number of values. Consequently the questions become more precise and more intermingled. Why does football, more than any other sport, provoke fervour and infatuation? Do the properties of the game and of the spectacle predispose themselves to symbolic investments - and with what mechanisms? If it is indeed a question here of ritual, what are its distinctive traits, and what are the traits it displays in common with other ceremonial forms?

Football today: A universal referent

The social and spatial diffusion of football as both practice and spectacle derives from a series of factors - extraludic, let us say - which have been well analysed, in all their diversity, by certain British and German historians and sociologists (E. Dunning, E. J. Hobsbawn, C. P. Korr,[8] Tony Mason, R. Lindner and H. T. Breuer[9].

Let us recall the essential here. It was from within the Public Schools in the 1860s that the Football Association gained autonomy from Rugby and began to progressively codify itself. From the start it was a question of an aristocratic sporting practise profoundly marked by the spirit of amateurism. But within 20 years the practise and the spectacle of football was to become one of the symbols of working class culture, on the same level as the pub, fish and chips and the flat cap. Symbolising this rapid popularisation was the victory in the 1883 cup final of the working class team Blackburn Olympic over Eton. To the elitist ideal of amateurism, of the game for the game's sake, the 'honourable defeat', was opposed a radically different ethic, valorising competition and professionalism, and seen as a means of social promotion. The first professional league championship took place in 1888. Most of the teams were works' teams, created by the workers themselves or on the initiative of paternalistic bosses intending the promotion of social hygiene and the spirit of solidarity. From then on, football became strictly associated with the industrial world, with the culture of the factory, the big city and the life of the local pub (discussing the match and celebrating the victories).

The diffusion of football in the various other European countries largely followed a scenario similar - though with great differences in the time-scale and the number of players and supporters - to that of England: a practise at first aristocratic and unpaid becoming a popular leisure activity, a central point of attraction for the labouring population of a factory, a district or a big industrial city. Juventus of Turin, founded in 1897, was originally a student and cosmopolitan club before becoming, as we have seen, a factory team, directed from 1923 by the same boss as Fiat. It was at this time that the professional league championship emerged in Italy, and the main industrial cities built themselves big stadiums - stadia reflecting the infatuation for the spectacle but also the architectural ambitions (amongst others) of the fascist epoch. Olympique de Marseille was created in 1898 on the initiative - according to the club itself - "of a number of young people of the Marseille bourgeoisie, fresh from their studies in Great Britain".(10) The first premises of the club were those of a 'cercle', the traditional form of Mediterranean sociability.(11) But it had to wait until 1924, the date of the first victory of O.M. in the French Cup, before the city really identified itself with its team. The ties became stronger with the creation of the professional league championship in 1932, and the construction, in

113

1938, of the Stade-Vélodrome - which rapidly became the symbol of the club, even though it did not belong to it (in Marseille you do not say, "I am going to the stadium" but "I'm going to l'O.M."). More generally, the diffusion of playing and watching football in France, as in most of the countries of Europe, has followed the distribution pattern of the great urban and industrial centres; in Germany, almost all the great clubs are concentrated in the Rhur;(12) in France, the star teams of the 30s to the 70s were mostly all representatives of working class cities: Sochaux and Peugeot, Roubaix and the textile industry, Lens and the miners, Metz and metalworking, Saint-Etienne and manufacturing, etc. The breeding-grounds for professional players were quasi-exclusively in the mining regions and the industrial suburbs. Is it necessary to underline the fact that, today, the infatuation with watching and playing football is extremely socially and geographically diversified. On whatever scale one measures it (regional, national, international), one finds the extraordinary progression and diffusion of the *amour foot* - to use an express of J. Bureau.(13) In France, the number of registered players went from 759,000 in 1971 to 1,606,000 in 1982; the rare inquiries conducted on the stadium public (in Nantes, Rennes, Saint-Etienne, Paris,(14) and by us, in Marseille) make it clear that, contrary to a still well entrenched notion, the spectators come from diverse sectors of the population and reflect the sociological physiognomy of a city and region. The same indications of social diversity occurs in respect to the social backgrounds of professional players; they no longer, with rare exceptions, come from the slums of the working class suburbs, but most often are sons of players at the lower levels (this body of specialists can thus be seen to have begun to constitute themselves as an autonomous micro-society). Another testimony to a wider social and spatial diffusion is the more equal distribution of star clubs: the leading lights of the league are no longer concentrated in the industrial North.

At the international level, the International Federation of Football Associations (F.I.F.A.) can be justly proud of being able to count in its ranks more nation members than the United Nations. Competitions are today organised in accordance with a principle of segmentation and agglomeration which directly reflects the great divisions of society at the global level (from regional and local championships to world championship, passing through national, continental and intercontinental stages) - thus giving to the spectators, with each confrontation, an expressive support to the symbolisation of the various facets of their identity (local, professional, regional, national). Such as it is today, football thus appears as a sort of universal referent, one of the rare (even the only) elements of a world-wide masculine culture, understood by all, transcending regional and generational distinctions; only an isolated few (of which the U.S.) still escape its grip. Moreover, football has become, in everyday interaction, a conventional theme of discussion, feeding the phatic function of language, as defined by Malinowski, and then Jacobson.(15)

Why has football, more than any other sporting or ludic practice, diffused so rapidly and generated such infatuation? The answer is not simple, but we can deal straight away with two types of explanations, one based on the arbitrariness of sporting tastes(16) and the other denying all the structural qualities of the game and confining itself to manipulations in the social field. The first makes imitation the driving force: innovations - sporting amongst others - begin on high and gradually become commonplace as they trickle downwards; the poor countries copy the rich countries, the East copies the West, the North, the South, etc. So be it! But nothing in this schema enables us to understand why football became popular when other sporting activities and spectacles remained aristocratic. The second explanation, widespread within a certain macrosociology in the 60s and 70s,(17) sees in the popularity of football - and other mass sports - the result of a plot, a trick, on an international scale, by the traffickers of the opium of the people. Sport-practice, and worse, sport-spectacle - 'ideological apparatuses of the state' - were encouraged in order to turn the oppressed classes away from the class struggle with their bosses, and to encourage an intellectual brutalisation and depoliticisation of the people. Against this entirely manipulatory and manichean vision of social facts, it could be argued that football can be both an opium (such was, for example, the case in Mexico at the time of the 1970 World Cup(18)) and a powerful catalyst of social, regional and national identities, normally ridiculed or despised (one recalls, for example, the demonstrations of the Lorraine metalworks, supporters of F.C. Metz, at the time of the club's victory in the French Cup in 1984 or, in a more general fashion, football in the role of 'cultural cement' amongst the working classes of Northern Europe). Moreover, we may say that this 'explanation', like the proceeding one, confines itself to the most general terms;

there is nothing in detail about the attraction of large numbers to one sport in particular, an attraction which cannot be explained by a simple play of influences on an amorphous and purely receptive mass.

On the margins of these general theories we will argue that the popularity of football, amongst other sports, rests largely on properties specific to the game. Not that there is some 'natural' predisposition for football to occupy the premier rank amongst sports; but in considering the qualities - athletic, ludic, dramatic - set in motion by this sporting practise and spectacle, one can see that:

1. This sport offers an exemplary condensation of the ethos that models the modern, urban and industrial world - of which it is, in its actual organised and codified form, the product.

2. In contrast to other team sports involving contact and competition (such as basketball, handball or rugby), with which it shares a number of structural affinities, it presents a range of singular characteristics which have been powerful stimulants to its popularisation. Now it is precisely these specific attributes which constitute the mediating elements, the points of crossover between the sporting field and the symbolic and ritual fields, within which football is inscribed.

Like other team sports, football symbolises, in its actual organisation, the salient characteristics of industrial society: division of labour and tasks; an equality, at least theoretically, of chances (championships and cups are founded on this principle); competition, performance, promotion, relegation.... The spatial configuration of the game favours the concentration of large crowds within a closed stadium and surrounding the pitch. We do not need to emphasise that sports which take place in more reduced spaces (ping-pong) do not lend themselves to such mass gatherings, which are up to the measure of the phenomena of collective identity in urban and industrial life. The stadium also offers itself as a stratified space, where one can see better or worse depending on where you sit or stand, and thus one can inscribe oneself within, and read off in an instant, the social differentiations which mark the city.

These characteristics, with a grand scale necessary for this century, combine with other properties which confer a singular, unique place within the field of sport to football. [Translator's note: Based on the work of C. Pociello,(19) Bromberger claims that the skills necessary to play football are varied and unrestricted to any particular athletic type]. Everyone can find on this terrain, material with which he can express - if he plays - or recognise - if he is a spectator - the qualities intrinsic to the cultural universe in which he participates.(20)

Football's popularity also relates to the simplicity of spatial requirements.(21) [Unlike many other team sports it does not require complex minimal givens such as a grass pitch (rugby) or an ice-rink].(22) It also requires minimal equipment: a ball, or a substitute ball....[It does not need expensive contraptions, just players. They can play in anything, and only need jerseys to become more sophisticated. They do not need expensive protective clothing as in other sports. It can even be played or practised alone, with individual skills playing a role within it]. Football is also distinguished by the simplicity and immutability of its rules: [each goal counts for one point; the number of restrictions is limited; the ball can flow in all directions and there is no restricted zone; only the off-side rule casts a shadow of complexity; the 17 rules of the game, fixed in 1863 have had a relative stability].

One can also add that the popularity of football, as practice but above all as spectacle, rests on the range of its dramatic qualities, on the scale of the great genres of theatrical representation which have fascinated the West. It faithfully respects the classical trilogy; unity of place, of time, of action - a factor favouring the phenomenon of 'communion' between the spectators and the players, the former following the whole of the match, contrary to what happens in road cycling, for example. But the dramatic force of football derives above all from the considerable place occupied by chance, by the incertitude as to the outcome of most matches. Those who do the pools or bet, week after week, know through bitter experience the difficulty of forecasting. To what does the singular incertitude of this type of confrontation owe itself? Not just to the relative equality of the competitors, but also to the technical complexity of a game founded on the abnormal(23) utilisation of the foot, the head and the body. [The technical difficulty of ball control with the feet(24) contributes to the uncertainty of the outcome. Also the role of the referee, who has to make an instant decision. Equally, such chance things as the shape of the crossbar, round or square, whose different deflections have determined the course of many a match].

117

This evocation of the properties of football and the foundations of its popularity is not simply an introductory necessity, an obliging concession to history and techniques, before getting down to the essential. "The individual does not 'go hunting'", wrote M. Mauss, "he goes hunting rabbits",(25) thereby emphasising that each type of synergetic practice predisposes - by virtue of the nature of the quarry, the techniques employed, etc.(26) - to specific symbolic investments. The same goes for the sports we are interested in here. Between research into the general functions and significations of the football phenomenon, at the whim of superficially suggestive analogies, and an analysis which flattens out the object, seeing the spectators as no more than expressions of the social, let us look more closely at how a club or a match, by their own distinct properties, become objects of identification, symbolisation and ritualisation.

An exceptional melting-pot of identifications

By the diversity of qualities that it requires and exhibits, football is focus for an extraordinary variety of identificatory possibilities, modulating according to the specific habitus of the different categories of spectators: identification, of course, with a city, a region, with a firm or company in terms of the style of the team one supports; a preferential identification with such and such type of player according to the qualities (force, finesse, organisational sense...) that are valued in ones cultural universe and professional practise; the identification of the team or club with an ideal image of collective life; identification of the drama which constitutes the match with the experiences - happy or unhappy - of ones own personal life.

Need we underline that the success of a local team is one of the rare objects of consensus in modern urban societies? Thus, in Marseille, the grant given by the city to O.M. was voted - unheard of event! - unanimously by the local council.

For the spectators, the process of bonding to a city and to a team follows a complex route, varying according to their geographical and professional position. Amongst the mass of the public [le public populaire] the nodal points for the constitution of supporters' groups, affiliated or not to an organisation, are the local bars. It is there that one meets up before and after a match. Marc, aged 25, son of a self-employed immigrant mason from Italy, is a coach builder in a working class area of the north-east of Marseille, Saint-Marthe. He is interested in his local team, whose stadium lies next to the Ricard factory, but his real passion is for O.M. Until his recent engagement, he used to go to the stadium with a dozen mates, for the most part sons of workers 'de chez Ricard'. The meeting point, three or four hours before the match begins, was precisely the 'club' [cercle - see above] that the celebrated pastis-maker, basing himself on the traditional forms of southern sociability, built for his workers. From there, Marc and his mates formed a loud cortege of cars and mopeds going towards the stadium; they went to the North End, above the scoreboard, a highly symbolic space, where the young and turbulent public from the North of the city congregate. Since his life has settled down, Marc has migrated - according to a process we have already encountered - towards the South End, where he watches the match, sometimes with his fiancee, sometimes with a friend.

The identification with the city follows a segmentary logic, defining itself via a consensual inclusion against urban poles, especially the closest to it, which appears as a menace to their regional leadership, and against the capital, perceived as haughty, arrogant and over-bearing. In Marseille the passion for O.M. goes alongside sentiments of marked hostility towards Toulon, but above all against Paris, the fat city, seen as the home of 'anti-Marseille racism'. Beyond this union around the city team, identifications differ according to the histories of the various individuals. Placing O.M. above all, Marc, of Italian origin, supports Juventus without reserve when they play Bordeaux in the European Cup, but is fully behind the French team when it meets Italy in the World Cup, even though his father leans to the latter. Both of them are united in their support for Latin teams against those of Northern Europe. Thus the graduated competitions provide support for the expression of a number of complementary and contradictory identities.

Figures of collective identity: The style and composition of the team

If the supporters identify so intensely with their city's, their factory's or their national team, it is because this team is perceived, through its playing style, as a symbol of a specific mode of collective existence, and not as a simple sign (arbitrary) of a common belonging. The 'style' of the team does not always correspond to the real practise of

119

the players - who change year after year, obeying different tactics depending on the manager, fashion, etc. - but to a stereotyped image, rooted in tradition, that the collectivity gives to itself and wishes to give to others. Thus style is part of a 'mentalité' or a 'collective imaginary' in the sense used by M. Vovelle,(28) not so much the way in which men live, but the manner in which it pleases them to recount their way of life. To win is, without doubt, to affirm ones superiority, but it is also to experience the joy of imposing your own style, your own mark to the detriment of the others. The victories of the French team were thus regularly perceived as celebrations of the 'genius' of a people, which distinguishes itself by its vivacity, its creativity, its intelligence, all characteristics of 'champagne football', of the game 'a la francaise'.

The styles of O.M. and Juventus are strongly opposed, each reflecting a particular vision of the world, of mankind, of the city. O.M., and thus Marseille, signal themselves in terms of their taste for panache, for the fantastic, for the spectacular; the motto of the club is 'straight to goal'. It is true that this stereotypical image reflects and partially moulds the destiny of the team; O.M. is more than anything a cup team (it has won it 9 times) rather than a championship team. The championship is a long-distance race which demands calculation, regularity and discipline, all qualities foreign to the local style. The management must take into account this image of the city's true culture, tenaciously held on to by the supporters. M. Hidalgo tells us that he has recruited or held on to spectacular players in the current team(Sliskovic, Papin, Bell, Diallo), partly as a response to his expectation. In a large survey we did on 1,000 persons at the O.M. - Paris-Saint-Germain match (December 1985), it was the above players who occupied the top of the publics' list. Bell, a Cameroon, nicknamed 'the black panther', is an unpredictable goalkeeper, who loves to run outside the area and other spectacular gestures. Diallo is a fast Senegalese winger(29) who loves to make the most disconcerting dribbles, though they are not always effective.... In the popular memory it is the explosive (such as Skoblar) or quick-turning (Magnusson) strikers who have left the deepest traces, whilst a talented, but sober, defender such as Bosquier - for a long time holder of the most caps for France - is today almost forgotten.(30)

Juventus' style is the mirror image of that of O.M. Here, it is true, that it is not a question of the ideal culture of a city, but of a company, rigorously organised. The 'Juventus style', a model invented by E. Agnelli, president of Fiat and of the club from the 20s to the 50s, is symbolised by the three S': Simplicita, Senieta, Sobrietta (Simplicity, Seriousness, Sobriety) which brings to mind one of the company mottoes. This motto is completed by an adage which it pleased E. Agnelli to repeat on his way to success: 'Una cosa fatta bene puo essere ancora fatta meglio' (Something done well can be done better'). The functioning of the club and its style of play largely reflect this model of rigour. Here there is no scandal - when the Italian calcio sees so many - amongst the players, who are asked to be careful in their statements and behaviour. They are asked to wear a tie when they travel as a group, to avoid all polemics within, or on the subject of, the club and not to respond to speculative press questions. A stable family life must, if possible, complete the good brand image. Occasionally the club will suggest the marriage of a player whose bachelorhood seems too prolonged. In the logic of the company spirit, those who have faithfully served the group image will be recompensed at the end of their career: they are given a position within the club, or a Fiat concession, greatly sought after. The playing style of the team, broadly speaking, goes along with this ethic. Tactical simplicity, defensive rigour, all to a single objective: the result. The important thing here is not to provide a beautiful spectacle, to score the maximum number of goals, but to win. The case of Platini is instructive in this respect. An adept of the 'French game', the captain of France became, after his transfer to Juventus, an ardent propagandist of Turin realism.

The make-up of the local team is often perceived and conceived of as an ideal reflection of the population for which it is the standard-bearer. Next to the international stars of high standing (Boniek, Laudrup, Platini) - symbols of sporting success, of the global reputation of the club and, more indirectly, related to the promotion of the company (the recruitment of Boniek was not completely foreign to the commercial politics Fiat was conducting in Poland) - the Juventus team regularly counts within its ranks players from the South, as does the company itself. Yesterday Anastasi, Causio, more recently Brio, Caricola, Mauro.... This last - nicknamed by some of the more astute observers, 'il popolo della Juve' ('the people of Juventus') - appears as a figure both emblematic and caricatural of the destiny of the immigrants from the South who come to find their fortune in Turin. Born in Catanzaro, his father having died, he supports his mother and brothers who have stayed at home. Symptomatically, there is no player from Turin in the team - Turin is playing a minor role, as we have seen, in the image and imaginary propagated and condensed by the club.

The composition of the O.M. team has been balanced, throughout its history, between two extremes, symbolising the contradictions constituting the identity of the city. On the one hand, there is the appeal to local players, on the other, a more valued formula - the buying of foreign stars. In one period, between 1981 and 1984, the city really identified itself with a team composed almost exclusively of local players, when the 'minots'(31) from the club's own recruitment ladder, got O.M. back into the first division. 286,000 went to watch O.M. at the Stade-Vélodrome in 1983-84, "an average of 16,000 per match. Never seen before in the second division."(32) For some, the heroic adventure of the 'youngsters' symbolised an ideal formula: "To defend with the faith and the courage indispensable to a club and a city, one must love it, and the most simple way to do that is to be born there". The popularity of these young players derives largely from their local origins, which everybody likes to recall: "Caminiti comes from Saint-Antoine, de Falco from Canet, Flos from Saint-Marthe, Anigo from Saint-Louis..." all quarters in the North of the conurbation, real fiefs of Marseillais patriotism. But this type of figure, the representation of the self by self, the object of a passing consensus, is effaced, in the history of Marseille football, by the opposing formula - the representation of self by the Other. Undoubtedly, there always needs to be one or two local players in the team, a sort of moral insurance, a guarantee of social identity. (In the mid-80s, in a team completely restructured, this role was held by Jose Anigo and two other 'historic youngsters'). But the ones who have always received most favours have been, incontestably, the foreign stars, who, after having given a public declaration of the 'adoption' (declarations placing a high value on Marseille, an ostentatious pilgrimage to Notre-Dame de la Garde), are charged with the mission of 'bringing honour to the club'. From its beginning, but above all from the time it became professional in 1932, O.M. have followed a policy of recruiting foreign talents - manifested in the "association of players from central Europe and of players from North Africa" forming "a spectacular team."(33) From this first period of professionalism (1932 to the war) older supporters have kept lively memories of the

Hungarians Eisenhoffer and (above all) Kohut; of the 'black pearl' Ben Barek, from North Africa. The post-war teams saw the emergence of the Swede, Anderson, then later the Brazilians Paulo Cesar and Jairzinho, and - beating all records(34) - the Swedish Magnusson and the Yugoslav Skoblar, both members of the double-winning team of 1972. It is remarkable that the French players, who have played a major role in the success of the club - Crut and Boyer before the war, Dard and Scotti after, and in the last 20 years, Bonnel, Bosquier, Carnus, Tresor - all are much less present in the memory of the supporters. One could argue that the foreign stars were, for the most part, attackers, and that it is to this that they owe their greater popularity in a city that loves spectacular football. But this does not fully explain it: for a start, one can count amongst the 'forgotten' a number of French players who counted amongst the leading goal-scorers of the club(35) (Zatelli, Dard, Pironti, Robin...); and again, it is a goalkeeper - foreign - who now is the supporters' favourite. In fact, despite equal talents, a foreign player invariably possesses a superior aura to that of an indigenous player. To what does this fascination with foreign players relate? What does it say to us, what does it express about the identity of the city?

Mediterranean city-port, the Phoenician city was characterised by its cosmopolitan population. The foreigner has a double image. On the one hand, devalued, that of the poor immigrant, arriving en masse to earn a livelihood in the port, in industry or in commerce. On the other hand, there is the image of the foreigner coming from the sea, founding the city.(36) A pioneer, bearer of material and symbolic riches, bringer of glory and prosperity for the city, he is capable of hoisting high the image of the 'golden city unjustly despised'. It is in this second register that the figure of the foreign star plays on the imagination of Marseille, a symbol of an ideal cosmopolitanism of the city, where the presence of the Other is to be a source of wealth and honour, not conflicts and stigmatisation. Does not the extraordinary welcome reserved for Bernard Tapie by the O.M. public and, more generally, by the Marseille population derive, at least in part, from this imaginary dimension? Without doubt, the arrival of a businessman was perceived by the supporters as a promise of renewal and success; here the important thing is to win. But the popularity of Tapie, without doubt, is owed to the qualities he likes to show, recalling those of other foreign 'saviours'. He himself is an adventurer, starting off with nothing, ambitious, and with a highly developed sense of spectacle and play. The three Rs (Réve, Risque, Rire - Dream, Risk, Laugh) which make up his motto - counterpoint to the Agnelli family's three S' - do they not also bring together the stereotypes that the Marseillais like to recognise in themselves? Let us add here that, like in many Mediterranean societies, the clever foreigner, a new man, dispenser of honour, can create more unanimity by the fact that he escapes, by his very foreignness, the traditional partisan cliques.

The 'cult' of the foreign star - in actual fact a trait common to several cities of the north-western Mediterranean - is much less widespread in Northern Europe. At one and the same time it forms part of the Mediterranean sense of defiance and honour, and of a singular history. To attach the best to you, by ruse if necessary, to celebrate your own identity via others - that is at the same time to affirm your supremacy, the force of your attraction, and it is also to repeat, in an ideal fashion, a history moulded by powerful migratory movements.

The players: Emblematic figures of social identities

If the team as a whole offers, across its style and composition, an expressive support to the affirmation of a collective identity, each player gains more or less favour amongst the public according to the specific qualities that he brings to the game. Infatuation for a team is thus both an object of consensus and a means of differentiation. Each category of spectators identifies preferentially with such and such a player, a function of sporting characteristics which appear as metaphors for one's social and professional universe. Large scale surveys taken at Marseille and Turin have shown - beyond common preferences for the incontestable stars - very clear variations in the popularity leagues amongst the different social categories of supporters. At Turin, in 1984-5, a lot of the youth and workers preferred the centre-forward Boniek - the 'mad horse', charging and aggressive, a 'scrapper' who spared no energy on the pitch - to Platini, the strategist, director of the players and the game, calculating and avoiding useless gestures - the favourite above all of the executives and managers. At Marseille, Jose Anogo - an outside back, son of the northern districts, always 'getting his hands dirty' ['Mouillant le Maillot' - 'wetting his jersey'], going in for often brutal, physical contact - gets the best popularity points amongst the workers and the office workers, and amongst the youth who stand in the North End of the stadium; Jacky Bonnevay - the sweeper, captain during the 1985-6 season, known for his sobriety, the seriousness of his game and his tactical sense - is more valued by industrial and commercial directors, the small businessmen and self-employed artisans, and medium and higher executives, than by the manual and office workers. Significantly, it is on the east side of the stadium, where the self-employed and middle management stand that this 'petit patron' ['small boss'], with a great sense of organisation, gets his best score. Amongst the glorious veterans it is Skoblar and Magnusson who stand out most in the memory and hearts of the supporters. The Yugoslav was a resolute centre-half, a 'big mouth', 'knowing how to get respect' and to 'impose' himself on the opponent's defence (he did not hesitate, so one is told, to elbow his opposite number in the stomach, or to spit in his face!); the Swede was an extraordinary dribbler, preferring to avoid physical contact, his game all finesse. The two players, symbols of success, have remained very popular amongst all sectors of the public. But, symptomatically, Skoblar gained the best score amongst the working classes (especially the office workers), Magnusson amongst the middle and higher executives.

Thus the preference for such and such a player modulates according to the social class of the supporter. Amongst the middle and higher executives, tactical finesse and strategies of evasion are most valued, whereas amongst the working classes it is about virility, the use of the body, giving your all - each of these traits of distinct styles of life.(37) "Sack him! Look at how fat he is, glassback!" These are common insults on the popular terraces where physical effort is appreciated, a valuation common to the game and to their daily life.

Football: A career model, a social model

When one conducts in depth interviews with supporters, sooner or later the conversation turns to comparisons between the working of the club, the team, the training...and the world of work. "It's like in my job...", "when I was in the army...", "It's a bit like in my company...". The football team is thus perceived - implicitly or explicitly - as an ideal metaphor for the collective universe in which one participates, and functions symbolically as an interweaving of the, often contradictory, projects proper to ones life in society.

Mr. G. is a retired college teacher who lives in Gap, in the Hautes-Alpes. His passion for O.M. and Marseille, where he did his military service, has not diminished since 1932. Not only has he regularly attended the match since then, but he has written, now and again, to the president of the club to give him advice or criticism. At the Stade-Vélodrome, "his place since way back" is the south-eastern corner. There he meets his 'colleagues'(38) some of which are young people to whom he gives advice and recommendations on their student careers or jobhunting. Upon the football team, this old teacher, animated by an ideal of the 'Hussars of the Republic'(39) projects a vision entirely pedagogical. The team is like a class, with studious and hardworking pupils, those who could do better with a good teacher (i.e. trainer) and the incorrigible idlers who create a bad spirit. His worst memory: D. Six, an international winger, with a great talent but pig-headed: "A real idler, not conscientious at all, not taking a single step to get the ball!" And in the 1985-86 O.M. team he didn't take to B. Zenier either, an ex-international also, but who "never made the full effort." On the other hand, he had fond memories of the 'minots'; young lads educated all at the same time within the club's training centre, unequally gifted perhaps, but loyal and sincere and listening to their masters.[...](40)

The football team - by the diversity of its virtues (solidarity, sense of duty and competition, discipline, responsibility) which, at least theoretically, mould it - thus offers a backdrop for the most varied projections; for the convinced military man, the club must be organised along disciplinary lines; inversely, for the youth it represents a group of mates where enthusiasm goes along with a sense of complicity ("Champion! He put it in with his hand and the referee noticed nothing!"). Let us stop and concentrate on a particular vision of the team and the club, one that its holders have the means of putting into effect - that of managing directors and big industrial bosses. We have underlined above the role played by big industrialists in the development of football clubs, conceived by them as one of the means of the social management of the workforce in the paternalist, hygienist and moralist tradition - ultimately they are conceived as symbols of the organisation of work. On this last level, however, in the last few years, we see a profound metamorphosis of the schema which fashions teams and clubs. To the paternalist model

- hierarchical and disciplinary, incarnated, in France, by F.C. Sochaux(41) tied to Peugeot, and, in Italy, on a much bigger scale altogether, by Juventus of Turin - is today opposed a very different conception of team spirit; symbolised at Marseille by Bernard Tapie, at Paris by J. L. Lagardere, and at Milan by Silvio Berlusconi, those condottieri of modern management. Henceforth it is a question of treating clubs like merchandise, promoted by marketing professionals, rather than as associations managed, to a greater or lesser extent, by unpaid volunteers. But the realisation of financial profit is not - far from it - the sole objective pursued (J. L. Lagardere's R. C. Paris team, the most expensive in France, often play in front of a few hundred spectators!) The clubs are, in fact, promoted to the rank of symbols of a social project on the scale of the times: "I have responsibility for a huge industrial group", declared J. L. Lagardere to *Libération*, January 23, 1986, "and in these difficult times of technological and economic competition, I know that the strongest assets are willpower, the ferocious acceptance of competition at the highest level and team spirit. In short, I am certain that the example of sport is the key to success for companies at war." In the same article Bernard Tapie went further: "The alliance of sport and industry sets in motion an image with a double virtue: that of communicating on the exterior and the interior. In the interior of an industrial group there is an identification with sportspeople when they are winning." And he declared, at the time of his enthronement at O.M. on 12 April: "We must take the company spirit into the heart of sport." At the same time, "the sponsor must feel the effects of his sponsorship in the heart of the company". The team and the club are henceforth thought of in terms of an ideal image of a company, based on participation and consensual relations, where the personnel are closely bound to its declared objectives - the very condition of success.

The football team thus presents itself as a symbol with a very high degree of hermenuetic plasticity, onto which individuals project, as a function of their life history, the most varied images of the ideal organisation of collective life (from a school class to the most competitive industrial group).

A symbolisation of the dramas of life

In effect a match, a competition spread across the annual cycle, offers a symbolic resume of the dramas and steps which mark out life: an alternation of victories and defeats; of promotions and relegations; the intervention - aleatory and exclusive - of luck and ill luck; the arbitration of a justice - sometimes favourable, sometimes unfavourable - which decides the fate of the 'good' ('us') against the 'bad' ('the others'). Thus the comments that follow a defeat reveal a vision of the world much more profound than simple sporting disillusionment. "We didn't have a chance....It's always like that", "We were the best but the referee was against us". The outcome of the match is thus perceived in terms of destiny, as shown by A. M. Cirese in analysing other types of game.(42) In a world where goods and riches are finite in quantity, the condition of access to happiness is the unhappiness of others. And, according to a conception deeply rooted in the popular classes, happiness falls always to the rich, to the powerful, those that fate has favoured. A proverb from southern Italy admirably sums up this ludico-mataphysical vision of the world: 'The die is cast, the match is rigged and the dog bites the poor'.(43) This pessimistic view of football and life emerges from numerous interviews with Torino supporters, whose team, as we have seen, is accustomed to defeat, when its rival, Juventus, is regularly showered in glory. "When we loose we suffer twice, firstly because of Toro's defeat, and then because of the victory of Juve. And most of the time it is like that. Them, they have money, power, but we, we have a just cause and, as often happens, this just cause is disappointed. Me, when I was little, I preferred, in Westerns, the Indians to the cowboys. Toro and Juve, it's the same thing". In such a context the referee's justice is perceived as an evil trick, always, as in life, on the side of the powerful. "The Juventus players are on first-name terms ['ils tutoient'] with the ref!" This palliness, reserved for the 'happy few', was the object of a bitter polemic at the time of the last derby. Thus a football competition is sometimes seen in terms of an ideal progress (when victory follows victory), sometimes like a destiny stripped bare.

An expressive theatricalisation of social relations

Place of spectacle of a practise, the stadium is also place of a spectacle of a spectacle - that presented by the public. In its amplitude and in its form this space is one of the few where a modern society can give itself a material image of its unity and its differentiations. Let us enter the Stade-Vélodrome, Marseille, on December 12, 1985, when O.M. 'welcomed' Paris-Saint-Germain, the league leaders. Who came to watch the match? How did the different categories of spectators divide up within the enclosed space? How did they differentiate themselves by their behaviour?

60% of spectators lived in Marseille, 20% came from industrial zones situated within a 50km radius of the city: the mining area of Gardanne, La Ciotat, but above all the swamp region of Berre, where there are large petrochemical and metalworking complexes, built in the 50s and 60s, drawing many workers from Marseille; for these 'exiles' 'going to l'O.M.' constitutes a sort of pilgrimage, a return to origins.(44) The attractions of the club do not fade at the borders of the Bouches-des-Rhone (88% of spectators reside there); a sizable minority of the faithful come from Vaucluse, Var, Alpes des Haute-Provence - in short, all the departments that constitute ancient Provence. Broken down into socio-professional categories, the Marseille public broadly reflects the profile of the active masculine population of the city. On the terraces higher management, the liberal professions, company directors, artisan and retailers, are more or less similarly represented as in the city. There is a slight under-representation of intermediary professions (middle management) and workers; a clear over-representation of office and service sector workers. The tenacious image of a predominantly proletarian public, clearly then, must be nuanced. Must we conclude that the football match is no longer a popular spectacle? According to the evidence, no. On the one hand, manual and office workers form 70% of the active masculine population in the stadium, that is to say, a higher proportion than in the city (62%); on the other, the 'match de ballon', as they call it in Marseille, is without doubt the spectacle - sporting or otherwise - which draws in the highest percentage of workers.

Broken down by residential origin, the public in the stadium presents a faithful copy of the spatial structure of the city. The different districts are represented in proportion to their respective demographic importance (though with a slight over-representation of the 'nice areas' of the city, those in the south). In short, the support for O.M. is, spatially and socially, a generalised phenomenon. Only differences of sex and age are very clearly marked when one compares the composition of the public and the profile of the

Marseilles population. 96% of spectators are men (as a comparison the public of the Stadio Communale in Turin has slightly more women - 19%): 62% are aged 15-39 (against 37% in the city); 30% aged 40-59 (against 23.5%); 4% more than 60 (against 21%).

The distribution of spectators in the stadium does not reflect the simple mechanisms of segregation by price of ticket (varying from one to seven) but is established according to a complex combination of criteria (age, profession, district). If one could say that as a whole, the structure of the city projects itself on that of the stadium, one must also take account of the multiplicity of social micro-networks which mark out territories at the heart of the bigger ensembles formed by the terraces, the ends, the sides, etc. Let us make a rapid tour of the stadium, hopefully being able to discern the equilibriums and the more unexpected variations of this distribution.

Although the prices are very similar, the east and west sides, and the north and south ends, form clearly distinguished sociological universes. The west side is the most prestigious; it is there that one finds higher management and the inhabitants of the 8th district, the most chic in the city. In its centre, the 224 places of the official (or presidential) tribune are distributed according to a strict hierarchy between those with political power (mayors, deputy-mayors, etc.) and those with sporting or economic power (club sponsors, but also large companies who have reserved seats on a seasonal basis for deserving employees or clients they wish to entertain). The spectators on the east side do not like those on the west; they find them unenthusiastic, 'less marseillais': "On Jean Bouin (i.e. the west side) they talk 'pointu ' (that is, with a Parisian accent, the supreme insult in Marseille). It is true that the east side appears as the refuge of the 'real' Marseille. It is here that the largest proportion of artisans, retailers, small bosses and middle management gather. It is a question of an older population than the rest of the stadium (46% from 40-59, as opposed to an average of 30% in the public as a whole). Here they like to wear caps, that token of maturity amongst the retailers, artisans and skilled workers (we have counted twice as many caps in the east side than in the west).

Another big division - already mentioned in connection with our interviews with Marc and Marco - is that between the north and south ends. On the one end collects a young public (81% from 15-39) with a high proportion of workers and schoolkids, with a majority from the city's northern districts and suburbs; on the other, an older

130

public (55% only are 15-39), in which white collar workers are more represented than the blue collar, coming mostly from the suburbs to the south of the city. The 'south' is much less passionate and faithful than the 'north'; there, 25% of the supporters come to every match, on the north, 42%; there, 39% only go occasionally to the match, here on the north, only 17%. One can see that these two territories are strongly symbolised; a supporter from the north will accept with great reluctance, his exile to the south. More significantly, in the 1985-86 season, for most matches, the management of the stadium forbade access to the *'populaires nord'* - the seats behind the goal only a few metres from the pitch; it was from there that all sorts of rubbish was thrown in the direction of the referee or the other team's players. One would have thought that this turbulent public from the northern *'populaires'* would have quickly installed themselves in the southern *'populaires'*, equally close to the pitch and remaining open. They did nothing of the sort. These young supporters went back onto the main terraces, situated at a respectable from the pitch but still part of their territory.

The macro-spaces designated by the morphology of the stadium are further differentiated into smaller units, grouping members of preconstituted networks; habitues of the same bar, work-mates or friends from the same school, members of a firm whose places are paid or partially paid by the firm.... Here, on the east side, 85 dockers find themselves socialising together after working together; there, on the north-east bend, 69 Social Security workers. On the South End, a group of pied-noirs (ex-colonials), coming from all corners of the department, constitute a micro-territory....

Each important step on the supporter's biographical path is translated, as we have already seen, into a differentiated manner of occupying the space of the stadium. A young man from the northern districts would commence his 'career' under the score-board of the North End; engaged or married, he would install himself on the South End; becoming self-employed or going into retail, he would go to the east side. Thus, by the end of his life perhaps he could have made the full tour of the stadium.... The differences between the types of public are not expressed solely in terms of territoriality. Each large category of supporter displays specific behaviours. They arrive late on the west side, two or three hours before the match on the North End. July 26, 1985 - 7 o'clock. An hour and a half before the start of the O.M. - Nice match, the first encounter of the season. One can count 16 people (out of 224 places) in the official tribune, 3,000 (out of 5,000) on the North End. In general you go to the stadium with your friends (this is the case for 60% of spectators) but arrival as a group is an obligatory rite in the ends, and less frequent on the sides where the public is more familial: 40% of spectators on the sides come with the family, but only 25% on the North End. But above all, corporal attitudes are clearly contrasted from one group to another. Individualised bodies in the numbered places on the side, bodies melted into a mass on the ends; festive atmosphere, an intense corporal participation on the ends, more discrete demonstrations on the sides, more spectacle than festival. Sometimes the supporters at the ends boo those on the sides, judging them stilted and unenthusiastic. A space of consensus, the stadium is also the locus of a recognition and expression of differences and oppositions - contestations which once again give the lie to the verdicts of a certain macrosociology on the mystificatory functions of sporting spectacles and on the homogeneity of the behaviour of crowds.

These oppositions are again reflected in the profiles of different supporters' associations. There are three in Marseille: the Central Club of O.M. supporters, run by a bar owner, brings together members coming mostly from the popular milieu; O.M. Animation, enthusiastic members, but not wishing "to be confused with those bringing banners"; The Association des Supporters de l'O.M. - the official name of the Commando Ultra - is made up of youth from all social classes. The social world of clubs organises itself according to the principle of segmentation; rivalries for recruitment of members; polemics on the ways and means of showing support for the team; antagonism at the very heart of O.M.'s Directive Committee - but finally there is consensus on the defence of the common good. A remarkable trait is that only the Ultras meet in the stadium, whilst the members of the other associations remain dispersed during the match. Put otherwise, at Marseille, the spectators divide themselves up into the space primarily by sociological affinity. At Turin the football world imposes its own hierarchies to a far greater extent. On the ends, the grouping principle is not district or profession, but membership of such and such a supporters' association. These separate out from the centre to the edges of the end according to their relative importance. Thus, instead of a differentiation based on extra-sporting characteristics there is a hierarchy founded on the level of fanaticism and demonstrative force. This autonomisation of the society of supporters in respect to society as such is one illustration, amongst others, of how the sporting spectacle in Italy is subject to a very high degree of ritualisation.

Where it is a question of war, life, death and sex

An exceptional interweaving of identifications, a unique occasion for the theatricalisation of social relations, the football match offers - by its dramatic texture, its antagonistic characteristics and its instrumental strategy - a privileged field for the affirmation of a certain number of values; values which the supporters express through its rigorously ritualised forms (the result of an apprenticeship and not a spontaneous manifestation).

A contact sport - where defence alternates with attack, according to a strategy studied beforehand on the blackboard - football offers the support, by means of a mimetic participation, for the expression of antagonisms (local, regional, national) and warlike values. If one can say that the match takes on all the characteristics of ritualised war, this is not simply to echo technical-journalistic comment on the preparation and progression of the match (where the military metaphor is wilfully drawn out: the 'conquest' of the ball, the 'centre of retreat, the implacable weapon of modern football', 'commando' action, 'general mobilisation' before an important confrontation just before the 'winter truce', etc.). On the contrary, the statement is founded on the examination of the behaviours, half-parodic, half-dramatic, of the supporters; their emblematic accessories (banners in club colours), their drums and fanfares, sometimes their clothing (combat fatigues), their slogans and their cries. To an injured player the Tifosi of the other camp chant in chorus: *"Devi morire!"* In the same circumstances, one can hear on the terraces of the Stade-Vélodrome of Marseille: *"Achéve-le! Coupe-le! Casse-le!"* (roughly, "have him put down"). During Juventus/Torino Derbies the supporters have been seen to exchange, via inscriptions on their banners, promises of death and vengeance. The Ultras are the most expressive choruses of this symbolic war; organised in 'commandos' - which in Italy freely name themselves *'Legione'*, *'Brigatta'*, *'Falenge d'assalto'* - they exhibit and collect provocative emblems (skulls, targets with a silhouette of an opposing supporter on it, etc.). Their major feat is to capture the opposing banner and to expose the trophy for all to see. Every bit as much as these loud and spectacular demonstrations (this peculiarity is precisely one of the principle motivations of the Ultra groups, who collect, just as much as they do the emblems of the club, the press cutting and photographs dedicated to them),(45) the spatial organisation of the game and spectacle; the configuration of the international institutions, guardians of the laws and coordinators of the big competitions; the constitution amongst the clubs of networks of allies and enemies - all evoke, in both patent and latent fashion, these warlike dimensions.

To the 'spectators' who occupy the side of the stadium are opposed, as we have seen, the 'true supporters' installed at the ends, who 'push' or pull their team along the axis of the game. By their territorial position in the stadium the supporters thus appear as a force of support, whilst the public on the sides occupy a territory removed from the 'spaces of truth' ['*espaces de verite*'] and confrontation. Despite the incertitudes of the toss,(46) the teams that win it always begin the match from the half where the bulk of their supporters are concentrated (one can verify the frequency of this territorial choice at Marseille where the team start the match on the north where they feel 'pushed' by a particularly demonstrative rearguard). In such a context the concept of 'neutrality' gains its full meaning; in the choice of ground for the final phase of the big competitions, and in the location of the international football bodies (Switzerland). The European Football Union has its seat in Berne, the International Federation in Zurich. Who says war says 'allies', 'traitors' and 'mercenaries'. The clubs - and especially the supporters' clubs - who participate in the Italian league are organised into two great, mutually antagonistic networks of alliance. Juventus of Turin is 'allied' to Sampadoria of Genoa, to Atlanta of Bergamo, etc., enemy teams for F.C. Torino, who have good relations with Verona, Florence, etc., enemies of Juventus. During a confrontation between two enemy teams the supporters fix themselves on their respective territories, square up to each other, defy each other, mutually responding. They exhibit not just the colours of their own club but also those of its allies, the enemies of the adverse team. Thus, at the time of the Juve/Torino Derby the Tifosi of Toro dress in grenat (their own colour), but also in violet (the colour of Florence), and yellow and blue (Verona) - thus organising a sumptuous spectacle of defiance, reminding the adversary of the capital sum of enmity that he has raised across the country. Inversely, when two allied teams meet, the Tifosi of the two clubs do a tour of the stadium, carrying their banners, to symbolise the perennial nature of their union beyond the difference of the day. This system of complex segmentarity finds further expression in the support the Ultra groups bring to allied teams who make transfers within their region. In such a context, players who go from one network to another are perceived as 'traitors' and must give to the team to which they have rallied, public assurances of their sincerity. A. Serena, a centre-forward for Juve, recounted bitterly how he had to give up most of his old friendships when he transferred from Torino to the neighbouring club and enemy par excellence. If players do not adopt these traditional enmities, which are the supporter's afffairs, after all, nevertheless they take scrupulous account of them in their public rites of interaction.

Over this warlike symbolism - which expresses suffering, tension or jubilation - is superimposed a sacrificial symbolism, a variation, half-parodic, half-dramatic also, on life and death. During certain encounters, at the beginning of the match the supporters exhibit a coffin in the colours of the rival club; on big occasions the newspaper announcement sections carry notice of the deceased of the opposite team, etc. The expected outcome of the match entails, in a substitutive and mimetic mode, the adversary being put to death - this death sometimes proclaimed from the terraces to the tunes of the bullfight. 'Sacrifice' of an emissary victim; why? We have no exegetic tradition to enlighten us on the function of this 'ritual'...but to feel the extraordinary jubilation of the supporters after a victory, the rediscovered unanimity after the tensions, the conflicts over such and such a player, it could be suggested, following R. Girard,(47) that the reconciliation of the community with itself is one of the major functions of this sacrificial manifestation; one which - and we return to this - presents all the appearances of a religious ceremony without it being possible to discern the figures of sacredness or transcendence.

A practise and spectacle almost exclusively masculine (only a few women, on the margins of conventional femininity, go, on their own initiative, to the stadium), football is still - no matter what the Rugby men think - a privileged terrain for the affirmation, even the exasperation, of virile values. The insults to the players, the referee, the opposing club - all play on the register of sexuality; including gestures of defiance and condemnation (raised arms, the horns...).

Durkheim and Mauss, had they frequented the stadia Marseille, Turin or elsewhere, would have been struck by the simplicity of the forms of human classification of the context of a football match. On the other side, the greats, the 'we'[on] ("We have won! We are the best! We were robbed by the ref!"); on the other, the 'enculés', the buggers, a generic term covering all Others (the opposing team, the referee, the journalists from the capital, etc.). There is not a match where this qualifier does not resound, attached to the name of a player, the other team or the referee, as if it was an obligatory rite. Similarly, inscriptions stigmatising the Others attack primarily their lack of virility. ("*P.S.G.: Petits Soutien-gorges*" ['small bras' (sic)]; "*O.M. te Bez*" ["O.M. fucks you" - Bez is also the name of Bordeaux's president].

Comments on the performance, and attempts to express the emotions experienced during the game, are nearly always accompanied by sexual comparisons or metaphors. Descriptions of goals - something we can understand without rushing to our arsenal of psychoanalytic weapons - are variations, direct or indirect, more or less elliptical, on the theme of orgasm - and not just for the spectators; all the players we interviewed described these privileged moments in terms of '*jouissance*' [ecstasy/moment of ejaculation]. A lack of goals and defeat are experienced in terms of frustration. A comment during a match in 1986, when O.M. were losing to Toulouse: "It would have been better to go to the restaurant; I might have been able to get off with Claudine!" When the team loses, the most ardent supporters accuse the spectators and the players lacking virility: "I don't believe it, they've all become soft cunts!" [*c...molles*].

To what, at bottom, does it relate, this exasperation of virility within the enclosed stadium, this sexual disqualification of the adversary, the Other - reduced to the rank of a '*Mademoiselle*'? Playing football, even to a limited extent, has become, in our societies, a quasi-obligatory step on the road leading towards adult virility. More than 90% of the spectators interviewed by us at Marseille played, or had played, football - even if only in the school playground. Using round objects of different sizes seems to clearly mark out a masculine destiny, to the extent that one can call to a player who you do not like: "Go back to playing marbles!" The stadium thus appears as a place where the masculine identity is played and replayed - according to a fixed periodicity and by means of mimetic participation - in the mode of defiance. The exasperation of virile values during the match is only, at bottom, the price paid for the 'condition' of men in our societies. Whilst the feminine destiny is separated into successive and irreversible segments (a mother of a family does not skip, unless it is to teach her daughter, nor get impassioned about hopscotch), the masculine destiny can be seen perpetually unachieved - according to the expression of D. Fabre - always having to test itself, to prove itself. The sexual disqualification of the Other in the space of the stadium is - as, in a different way, is hunting(48) - one of the means by which this virility proves and reaffirms itself. Feelings of belonging, warlike and virile values, sacrificial drama - all these are put into play in a football match, and expressed through an intense corporal and sensoral participation; something which makes the sporting spectacle unique in relation to other forms of representation. Rigorously codified gestures accompany each phase of the match (raising the arms and clenching the fists at the announcement of the team sheet, jumping and raising the arms to celebrate a goal, etc.); coloured visual symbols (flags, banners, multicoloured balloons, scarfs, etc.) are exhibited according to a precise sequence of events: before the match, the entrance of the players, a goal.... A similar codification regulates the vocal and audible participation (slogans, hymns, chants, whistles, use of musical instruments, rattles and claxons), which amongst the Ultra groups are subject to a meticulous programming. The melodic, rhythmic and instrumental forms used to support a team are characterised by their banality (there exists an international supporters' vocal culture) and by a number of highly significant traits which single out each regional or national tradition: bells waved and shaken in the Swiss areas, slogans chanted to the tunes of Verdi in Turin, etc. More fundamentally, this minimal vocal and choral culture, which forms the audible background of a football match, appears as the concretion of an extraordinarily varied repertoire: slogans from May 1968, whose rhythms provide the basis of some chants: "'Qui c'est les plus forts, les plus forts, c'est l'O.M." ["Who are the most strong, the most strong, it's l'O.M."], after the fashion of "Ce n'est qu'un début, continuons le combat!" [It is only a beginning, let us continue the fight"]; religious chants; operatic arias; folk songs; pop music; national anthems (they sang the Marseillaise at Turin to encourage Platini), etc. This stratification of heterogeneous genres, is this not the mark of folklore - that "undigested agglomeration of all conceptions of the world and of life, succeeding one after the other", according to Gramsci's definition(49) - in its most contemporary version? In any case, the football match is one of those rare occasions on which we see expressed, collectively, those minimal elements of a common culture which seal the unity and community of feeling of the public.

The football match, a kind of religious ritual?

At this point in the analysis one could be tempted to place the football match nearer to a great religious ceremony, following the lines suggestively sketched out by Stemme, Brettanini and Mastrolonardo and, more recently, Auge.(50) Do we have here a real homology or merely a simple metaphorical game which interferes with, rather than enlightens, the analysis of the phenomenon? All the ingredients of a ceremony - at least as conceived in traditional Christian practice - seem to be present in this type of sporting encounter: the 'faithful' who express their emotional effervescence according to a rigorous codification of gesture (one stands up and sits down at precisely determined moments of the match...) and voice; 'brotherhoods' group together the most fervent (supporters associations); 'officiants' charged with the execution of the sacrifice, with which the 'faithful' commune; an organisation, the club, which is rigorously hierarchical, as with ecclesiastical organisations; laws pertaining to all (the XVII Laws of the Game: capitals are always used when referring to them), watched over, with respect and authority, by the International Board; a closed space consecrated to the 'cult' - the stadium, and, at its centre, the pitch, inviolable by any other than the 'officiants'; a regular 'liturgical' calender which culminates at certain times of the annual cycle (this regularity is remarkable in Italy where the match, and it alone, has always taken place on a Sunday afternoon); a theatricalisation of social relations within the enclosure of the stadium, similar to the highly regulated distribution of different social groups during important religious ceremonies; the obligatory presence, during these great 'celebrations' of those holding power in society; the expectation of the 'sacrifice', consecrating, in mimetic mode, the victory of the goodies over the baddies. Good over Evil, of 'us' over 'the others' (and, in the case of defeat, the maledictions against the forces of evil who have disturbed the workings and desired outcome of the ceremony: the referee, the wind, the rain

138

which made the turf slippy, the officiants lacking fervour and conviction, etc.).

We could push this analogy much further in revealing other significant isomorphisms: the differential mechanisms of the idolisation of players (those who like Platini, those who like Boniek...) which recall the social, regional and professional specialisations in the cults of the saints; the existence of a 'special language' and a corresponding culture which is possessed in full only by true initiates (those who know what a 'remise en pivot' is, or an 'aile de pigeon'..., those who can distinguish between 'penalty' and a 'direct free-kick', even more, those who know the whole menu of tactical combinations, or Law XI - the off-side rule - in all its nuances...); a hierarchy of individuals, in this world apart, operating to different laws than within civil society; each is placed in respect of his proximity to the major officiants (he who knows Platini or some other big player occupies, in this referential field, a position much more prestigious than he who, though occupying a far superior social status, does not know him...); the tension between the universalist ambitions of the practice and the spectacle (rigorously defined in the rules) and the local particularisms which come to be grafted on to them - such as, in Latin countries, the off-the-pitch celebrations of the players after a great goal, which brings forth calls to order from the official (we can find here the equivalent of the complex relations between official religion and popular religion); but above all, the sequential framework of the match which, whether looking at the practice or the spectacle, recalls that of a religious ritual. Let us be more precise.

Before a big match - before most matches - the players have a custom of 'retreat' (the term itself is revealing), far from the madding crowd, whether in some green spot in the surrounding countryside or in a hotel in the town; in Marseille and Turin, as in most Mediterranean countries, women are strictly excluded from this period of contemplation; they are seen to threaten verbal and physical disorder. The retreat without women appears as a ritual element par excellence, where symbolic reason is more important than practical reason. G. Banide, O.M.'s trainer, one of the best technicians in French football, is not fooled: "What do you do before a match, especially if it is important? De-dramatise the event so that the players go into it with the maximum possible degree of relaxation. A 'retreat', on the contrary, only accentuates the drama.

As for sexual abstinence, allow me to be sceptical about its efficacy: they have calculated that making love once corresponds to the effort used by an athlete during a 40 metres hurdles; it's nothing." This parallel with the jumping of obstacles is also suggestive! We can note, however, in order to underline the relativity of the practical efficacy of the woman-free retreat, that it is a predominantly Mediterranean 'custom'. In Northern Europe the wives of the players frequently participate in these 'country retreats' without any apparent effects on the team (as the results show). Other episodes in the preparation and progress of the match are characterised by a high degree of ritualisation (fixed sequences and a symbolic depth). It is thus with the meal before the match (always the same dishes), with the arrival as a group at the stadium at a fixed time (an hour and a half before the kick-off), in the changing rooms where each players sticks invariably to the same rites (*cf. infra*), the entry on to the pitch in a straight line, the ritual parade in the centre whilst the teams are presented. During the match, gestures and attitudes appear strictly codified, fruits of a symbolic apprenticeship. Such is the case with the embraces which invariably follow a goal. A. Serena said to us, with a perspicacity wholly ethnographic: "*E uno fatto culturale!*" He recalls that when he started, in the minor team of Venice, he felt a great personal joy when he scored a goal but felt no need to hug his team mates. It was on the orders of his trainer that he conformed to the practise, since then it has become a habit. Although, contrary to a religious ritual, the scenario of the match is unforeseeable, it nevertheless divides itself up into a relatively fixed temporal sequence: half-time, of course, but also phases of greater or lesser intensity (if one can go by the experience of referees,(51) it is the ten minutes opening and closing each half which generally constitute the most dramatic heights of the match). Finally, amongst the recurrent element marking out the event, we can mention the 'examination of conscience' (an expression equally revealing) to which the players give themselves over during the night following the match, and which disturbs their sleep. "I don't know a single player". J. F. Domergue, an international full-back from O.M., told us, "who finds it easy to sleep after a match. The lads, during the night, replay the match."

For the supporters, the pre-match, the match and the post-match, also divide up into a relatively fixed rhythmic schema, coloured by the importance and progress of each match. The example of Marco, presented in the opening pages of the text, furnish us with a striking illustration. The 'liturgical' week begins two days after the preceding match: discussions on the composition of the team, recalling past encounters - these mark out, in a form of crescendo, the days which proceed the match. The night or morning before are concerned with the preparation of the emblems; the meeting is at a fixed point, always the same, from where they go down to the stadium. For the most fervent this pre-match stage is marked by tension and contemplation; they eat nothing, or very little before the match (this fast recalls another, that imposed before communion). In the stadium, as we have seen, the demonstrations of support are conducted according to a relatively invariable scenario (this tendency is much clearer in Italy than it is in France): the pre-match exhibition of the emblems and execution of chants, according to an order fixed by the capo-tifo; nervousness, and codified gestures when the team comes out of the tunnel and onto the pitch, followed by stereotypical attitudes of outrage and exultation during the progress of the match. After the game the groups of supporters meet at a fixed spot on the square in front of the stadium, where they begin discussions which stretch out endlessly over several hours in bars or restaurants. For the most fervent the night will be agitated, punctuated by dreams and nightmares, according to the outcome of the drama.

One could object that if a football match presents all the appearances of a religious ritual (rupture with the everyday, specific spatio-temporal location, the regular and codified nature of the practices, emotional effervescence expressed through agreed conventional means, symbolic density, the presentation of good and evil, et.), it does, however, lack an element essential to found the validity of such a comparison: the belief in the active presence of supernatural beings or forces. In fact, football appears as a universe which is a refuge for, and creative of, magico-religious practices; a place where there is a belief - again half-parodic, half-fervent - in symbolic efficacy. The sheer number of habits of this nature is all the more remarkable in that nothing has predisposed football, in its history as a sport, to be the depository of such investments - as opposed, for example, to sports in the Far East, which are inscribed within a rich religious tradition, or an athleticism which has had its theologians (such as P. de Coubertin). Players and supporters - one can talk here of a homology of behaviours even though they do not have the same field of application - use diverse procedures, springing from a personal or borrowed from official religion, in order to tame fate and master the aleatory. In the first case, these rites are most often founded on the principle of analogy, or, to use the terminology of J. G. Frazer, on the law of similitude ("an effect is similar to its cause") and on that or the virtue of contact, the law of contagion, according to the same author's expression ("two things which have been in contact at a certain moment continue to act on one another even when this contact has ceased").(52) Amongst the players, the choice of equipment and place are thus marked by the sign of fetishism: a jersey or a pair of shorts which have inaugurated a run of wins will be worn systematically right through a season, even a career. Zoff, coach for Lazio and old Juve and Italy keeper, wore the same pair of shorts all through the season, to the point of causing indignation amongst the federation's medical hygienists! But this propitiary vigilance is exercised above all - unsurprisingly - in the choice and preparation of boots: "When I was young", J-F. Domergue tells us, "I polished my boots at home. Then, one day, I forgot to do it and I had to polish them in the changing room. That day I scored my first goal. Since then I always polish my shoes in the changing room." Amongst the current O.M. players it is undoubtedly A. Giresse who has pushed furthest the law of similitude: "I have a room, a cellar, at home, where I lay them all out. I have around 50-60. Each boot has its history. I know all the games that each boot has played, and often I take account of this...I've said to myself: 'I'll take these boots because they've already done a 0-0'...and really, it's worked....On the contrary, with another pair, I played twice with them and got injured twice, so, I don't wear them anymore." Other players always lace the right boot before the left boot, or even bang the soles on the goalpost before the match, to mollify fate. Choice of place is also regulated by the same laws: occupying the same place in the bus on the way to the stadium, and in the changing room; the custom, as we have seen, of beginning the match from the same end (ready to reverse this practice if fate has shown itself to be unfavourable). Other habits bear further witness to the same fetishistic vigilance: not shaving during a cup run (the Samson complex), pinning up a photo of your opposite number in the days leading up to an important match, etc.

The most fervent supporters bring the same attention, as we have seen at the beginning of the text, to their choice of clothes, even their underwear. Some of them do not go anywhere without a club emblem (scarf, pen, programme, medallion...), and transform their private universe into a sort of domestic altar, where they conserve the precious relics of their attendance (match tickets especially) and witnesses to their presence next to their idols (autographs, photos). In such a context of veneration, one great feat - rich in grace? - is to approach and touch a player, after several hours waiting outside the changing rooms - a virtue of contact which recalls that attributed, in popular religion, to the act of touching, or kissing the statue or relics of a saint. For the rest, as we have noted, many of the practices used to tame fate are borrowed from the ranks - official or marginal - of the Catholic religion: signs of the cross, pilgrimages, prayers, sacrifices, etc., whilst others spring from a folklore specific on two accounts: they apply to objects proper to sporting competition (boots, jerseys, emblematic colours, etc.); and they are the fruit of a personal magic which is not planned, not the object of any explicit apprenticeship, but which, by a quasi-identical repetition, is transformed into a collective phenomenon. [Translator's note:Touching the 'This is Anfield' sign at Liverpool, for example.]

One could object, finally - and this objection is widespread - that the notions of 'communion' between officiants and audience, which commentators make so much use of, is most illusory. Now, all religious ritual is founded, in theory at least, on a community of intention between the two groups. In fact, two matches with different objectives and different stakes take place in the enclosure of the stadium. One opposes supporters from different cities, and for whom the team is a symbolisation of their collective identity, the other opposes players of a high level, transferred through the years from one club to another, for whom the reference to the city is minor and who dedicate themselves to competition within the closed field of a professional football career. But on closer examination the situation appears more complex. For one part, both seek victory; for another consciousness of 'communion' is very clearly coloured by the social and geographical origin of the players. One can thus set a local player, long-time supporter, often of modest social background, who feels that he is carrying the values of the city when he is defending the colours of the club, against the international star, whose claims to be attached to the local area are purely superficial, if, indeed, he makes such claims at all.

Let us compare the comments of Mauro and Platini during the 1986 Juventus/Torino Derby. The former thanked the Tifosi: "At the most

143

critical moment of the match, the *curva* (the Filadelfia end) woke up. That was decisive because the game was bogged down and we didn't know how it was going to turn out. I made two successful runs because I was pushed by the crowd [public]." Platini is much more detached: "I'm not from Turin. The Derby for me was a match like any other. But I was happy about the victory, for all those who had come to sing Juve's De Profundis." Finally, this disparity in the stakes for the officiant and the audience, does this not mark religious rituals, when one considers them as they are and not what they claim to be? Feast days and pilgrimages are not conceived and lived in the same way by those celebrating and the 'faithful' (but, it is true, in the football match, fervour changes camp, so to speak, being stronger amongst the audience than amongst the officiants).

At this point, the analogy between the football match and the religious ritual in its deepest sense, borrowed from an ethnology done elsewhere - involving a break with the everyday, regular and codified behaviours, symbolic density, beliefs - may seem to have been established and the category of religious ritual impose itself, not by reference to its general and invariable functions and significations, but as a descriptive tool capable of grasping behaviours, the framework of events and the symbolic stakes in the relatively exhaustive manner.

However, two stumbling blocs appear if we follow this path, limiting the wider implications of a too reductive analogy and inviting us to seek out more analytically specific categories:

This ritual does not present itself, does not name itself, does not categorise itself as ritual. To use the words of V. Turner,(53) used in another context, one can find there many operative dimensions (officiants, audience, sequence of codified actions, well-defined spatio-temporal framework, emotions expressed through conventional means, etc.) but no exegetic dimensions (an explicit mythical or symbolic configuration which gives an account of the organisation of sequences, the meaning of emotions, and of which the ritual would be the manifestation). Here it is the ethnologist who is responsible, through an intellectual operation, for the process of ritualisation which escapes the consciousness of the participants. In other words, to use the opposition introduced by K. L. Pike,(54) football would be a ritual from an 'etic' point of view - that of an outside observer - but not from an 'emic' point of view

- that of the participants.

Moreover, the constitutive dimensions of the great religious rituals are lacking here: their strict repetition within a sequential framework, the permanence of idols - which are renewed, in the world of football, at an ever accelerating pace, to the point where a player adulated a few years ago is now hardly even looked at ("Afterwards, he was nothing" a supporter said to us) - but above all, as we have alluded to above, it lacks a representation of the world, transcendence, the beyond, salvation.

Stating these differences demands that we rethink the category of ritual as applied to football, and in terms which, as is necessary in ethnology, go forwards rather than backwards from the lessons of the fieldwork. It is a question here of a ritual without exegesis, that "does rather than says",(55) "thinks itself in the heads of men without their knowing" ['se pense dans la tête des hommes et a leur insu"](56) consecrating collective identities in a manner fitted to the contemporary world - marked by uncertainty and renewal, those two figures of modernity. This ritual can, with good reason, be considered as a 'total social fact', if we understand by that, with M. Mauss - and not with certain of his successors who have banalised the concept - "a phenomenon which, in certain cases, sets in motion the totality of society and its institutions." The long route we have traced from the local bar to great industrial concerns; from the stadium, where a society gives itself as spectacle to itself, to the dim realms where emblems are fervently prepared; from north to south, workers to management, young to old, men to women, good to evil - all this bears witness to the diversity of values and institutions which this type of 'sporting' encounter puts into play. Support for an extraordinary range of possible identifications, an exceptional occasion for the expression of social relations, in their most contradictory aspects, the football match is today the ritualised event par excellence, where a collectivity mobilises and theatricalises its social and symbolic resources.

Notes

1.   *Ultra:* a group of the most extreme and demonstrative young supporters. The phenomenon was born in Italy during the 70s. The 1983 *Commando Ultra* of O.M. was based on the Italian model.

2.   In symptomatic fashion, North African immigrants (especially first generation) are underrepresented in the stadium with respect to the city. According to a large scale survey done by us (and to which we will make frequent reference in this text), they form 8-10% of the Marseille population but only 5% of the O.M. public.

3.   *Tifosi:* supporters, from tifo, support; a term which forms the base of many derivations and composites: *tifoseria:* given to the groups of supporters as a whole; *mercatifo:* marker for supporters, etc.

4.   *Scudetto:* shield, a warlike symbol of championship victory.

5.   [In English in the original.]

6.   [In English in the original.]

7.   The official Juve catalogue offers no less than 86 items (as a comparison, that of the main O.M. supporter's club lists around 40). A mail order service for *oggetti di culto* ('cult objects') has been in operation since the beginning of 1985; it deals on average, with 250 orders a day, and has an annual turnover between two and three thousand million Lire. (*La Repubblica,* December 11, 1985, p.31).

8.   E. Dunning, 'The Development of Modern Football', in E. Dunning (ed.), *The Sociology of Sport,* (1971), London, Frank Cass; C. P. Korr, 'West Ham United Football Club and the Beginnings of the Professional Football in East London, 1895-1914', *Journal of Contemporary History,* 13,2, (1978); and above all, T. Mason, *Association Football and English Society (1863-1915),* (1980), Brighton, Harvester Press.

9. R. Lindner and H. T. Breuer, *Sind doch nicht alles Beckenbauers*, (1982), Frankfurt, Syndikat.

10. L. Grimaud and A. Pecheral, *La Grande Histoire de l'O.M.*, (1984), Paris, R. Laffont.

11. [A 'circle' was a social club for bourgeois notables]. For a profile of this institution in the 19th century see M. Agulhon, *Le Cercle dans la France Bourgeoise*, (1977), Paris, A. Colin. *(Cahiers des Annales, 36)*.

12. See R. Lindner and H. T. Breuer, op cit.

13. 'L'Amour Foot', *Autrement*, No. 80, May 1986 (issue edited by J. Bureau).

14. [Sources unpublished with C. Bromberger]. For the public of the Parc des Princes, Paris see 'Le Foot a Paris', *L'Equipe Magazine*, No. 305, November 29, 1986.

15. B. Malinowski understands by phatic communication "all those remarks (which) serve to create and maintain a situation, an atmosphere of sociability." 'The Problem of Meaning in Language', in C. Ogden and I. Richard (ed.) *The Meaning of Meaning*, (1923), London, pp.313 sq., and R. Jacobson, *Essays in General Linguistics*.

16. We have borrowed this expression from C. Pociello in the overall study he made of sporting practises: 'La Force, l'Energie, la Grace, les Réflexes. Le Jeu Complex des Dispositions Culturelles et Sportives', in C. Pociello (ed.), *Sports et Societe: Approche Socio-culturelle des Pratiques*, (1983), Paris, Vigot. Pociello demonstrates that nothing is less arbitrary than one's taste in sport.

17. Particularly representative of this tendency: J. M. Brohm, *Critiques du Sport*, (1976), Paris, C. Nourgois; and G. Vinnai, *Fussballsport als Ideologie*, (1970), Frankfurt.

18. But even here it is a question of an opium that sends us only

half to sleep, and can even wake one up, since the inhabitants of the slum towns run through the streets shouting, "We want haricots, not goals!"

19.   C. Pociello, op cit, p.87.

20.   R. Cailois, *Les Jeux et les Hommes*, (1985), Paris, Gallimard. (New Edition).

21.   For the spread of rugby in France see C. Pociello, *Le Rugby ou la Guerre des Styles*, (1983), Paris, A. M. Metailie.

22.   C. Pociello, op cit, p.87.

23.   Certainly, all sporting gestures are subject to an apprenticeship and not just a maximisation of natural potentials; but football is without doubt one of the sports which demands the most 'cultivated' gestures; cf. G. Boulogne, 'L'Apprentissage de Football', *L'Entraineur Francais*, No. 1822, December 1982: "Football is not a natural game; football is a difficult technical game."

24.   A. Leroi-Gourhan, *Le Geste et la Parole, Technique et Langage*, (1964), Paris, A. Michel, p.119.

25.   M. Mauss, *Manuel d'Ethnographie*, (1967), Paris, Payot, p.58.

26.   On the correspondence between types of synergetic technique and types of symbolic configurations, see C. Bromberger and G. Lenclud, 'La Chasse et la Gueillette Aujourd'hui. Un Champ de Recherche Anthropologique', *Etudes Rurales*, 87-88, July-December, 1982, pp.20-21.

27.   With only two exceptions, all the headquarters of the O.M. Central Supporters' Club sections are in bars. One could find similarly in Turin, where only the most important Juventus Clubs have their own premises...which include a bar.

28.   M. Vovelle, *Ideologies et Mentalités*, (1982), Paris, Maspero, (see especially the introductory chapter). For the game as

representation of a society and its style, see the very judicious remarks of C. Geertz on Balinese cock-fights: "For a Balinese, attending and taking part in the cock-fights is a form of sentimental education. He learns there the 'feel' and the ethos of his culture and its particular sensibility." ('Jeu d'Enfer. Notes sur le Combat de Coqs Balinais', in C. Geertz, *Bali. Interprétation d'une Culture*, (1983), Paris, Gallimard, p.211. For football, the notes by R. de Matta on the style of the Brazilian game present evidence of a similar type of correspondence.(R. de Matta, 'Notes sur le Futebol Bresilien', *Le Débat*, 19, February, 1982, pp.68-76).

29.   On the importance of, and representations of, foreign stars at Marseille, see above.

30.   The fact that we are dealing with a defender is not enough to explain this effacement from the popular memory; we will see below that even great French attackers have been forgotten.

31.   *Minots:* in the regional dialect, young boys.

32.   L. Grimaud and A. Pécheral, op cit, p.321.

33.   R. Meunier, 'Naissance du Football a Marseille', *Histoire des Implantations Régionales et Locales*, (1986), Paris, I.N.S.E.P., p.55.

34.   In the 'Hit-Parade' of old players, the two of them won 73% of supporters votes.

35.   The list of great achievements, drawn up by L. Grimaud and A. Pécheral (op cit) tells us that these four players occupy the 5th, 6th, 7th and 8th places in the best goalscorer list 1932-1984.

36.   Must we repeat that, according to legend, the city was founded by Protis, a Phoenician sailor, who married Gyptis, the daughter of the local king? The medallion that some of the O.M. supporters wear has a picture of this founding couple.

37.   On this homology, see the remarks of C. Pociello, 'La Force,

l'Energie...', op cit, pp.189-190.

38.   In the regional dialect *colleagues* is used to mean friends [camarades].

39.   [In French Third Republic and the school-teachers, strongly republican, were given this title because of their role in the struggle against aristocratic and clerical 'reation'].

40.   [This section has been slightly edited in order to leave out some of the minutae of the recent O.M. team].

41.   The F.C. Sochaux training school provides one of the hardest footballing apprenticeships in France; the team's style of play reflects this disciplinary model: they appreciate 'no-nonsense football' ['le football au carré].

42.   See, in particular, A. M. Cirese, 'Essai d'Analyse d'un Jeu Cérémonial de Premier Mai en Sardaigne: 'Cantare Su Maju', (1974), Paris, p.169.

43.   Cited by A. M. Cirese, op cit.

44.   Significantly, of all the sections of the Central Club of O.M. supporters, it is Marignane's which has the most members.

45.   The concern for visibility amongst the Ultras has been well analysed by A. Ehrenberg, 'La Rage de Paraitre', in L'Amour Foot, *Autrement*, No. 80, May 1986, pp.148-158.

46.   [Toss: in English in the original].

47.   R. Girard, *La Violence et le Sacré*, (1972), Paris, Grasset.

48.   On hunting as a means of articulating the ages of masculine life in our societies, see 'La Chasse et la Cueillete Aujourd'hui', *Etudes Rurales*, No. 87-88, July-December, 1982.

49.   A. Gramsci, *Letteratura e Vita nazionale*, (1975), Rome, Editori Riuniti, p.288.

50. F. Stemme, 'Football et Societe', in *Les 25 ans de i'U.E.F.A.*, (1981), Berne, pp.269-276); A. Bettanini et P. Mastroloardo, *La Partita di Calcio. Un Linguaggio Giocata*, (1971), Genoa, SAGEP, (especially the chapter 'La Partita come Cerimonia'); M. Auge, 'Football. De l'Histoire Sociale a l'Anthropologie Religieuse', *Le Debat*, February 1982, pp.59-67.

51. See C. Caron, P. Schwinte, *L'Arbitrage du Football*, (1971), Paris, Salvator.

52. J. G. Frazer, *The Golden Bough*, [p.41 in French edition].

53. V. W. Turner, *Les Tambours d'Affliction*, (1972), Paris, Gallimard.

54. K. L. Pike, *Language in Relation to a Unified Theory of the Structure of Human Behaviour*, (1954-1960), Gendale, Summer Institute of Linguistics.

55. The conclusions to which we have come have received both confirmation and, at the same time, refinement in a remarkable article by J. Pitt-Rivers, 'La Revanche du Rituel dans l'Europe Contemporaine', *Annuaire de l'Ecole Practique des Hautes Etudes*, (Ve section, Sciences Religieuses), Vol. XCIII, 1984-1985 (1986), pp.41-60), the article from which this quote is drawn.

56. C. Levi-Strauss, *The Raw and the Cooked*, (cited by Pitt-Rivers, op cit, p.55).

9 Soccer casuals as cultural intermediaries

Richard Guilianotti

Introduction

Over the last fifteen years or so, the critical social and political sciences have experienced a gradual movement away from modern models of social stratification and reproduction, towards a greater examination of the consumption of cultural practices and symbols. Theories of postmodernity, with European post-structuralists at the fore, have made the most telling contribution here, with numerous protocols issued for 'new language' and 'new research' (cf. *Marxism Today*, any edition 1990), to theorise the significance of the New Times in which the West, and latterly the old Second World, are held to be now ensconced.

For all these edicts, and their correlative support for the triumph of ontology over epistemology (Boyne, 1990, p. 281), very little effort has been discernible in grounding the new theory through examination of particular social groups and practices. This lacuna has allowed the more brazen proponents of postmodernism *qua credo* to continue re-identifying the presence and mechanics of postmodern culture within their own social strata, while the not insignificant remainder, Baudrillard's (1983a) 'silent majorities', appear unworthy of sustained examination.(1)

In this Chapter I offer a modest contribution to the grounding of one feature of contemporary cultural theories, that of 'the new cultural intermediaries'. I extract this concept from the symbolically privileged grouping in which it is perennially identified, and relocate it within the vanguard youth subcultural(2) grouping of Scotland in the 80s, the Aberdeen Soccer Casuals (hereon, the ASC). The ASC's cultural-political efficacy as intermediaries, in de facto opening up cultural codes and spaces for wider public appropriation, is examined diachronically, contextualised within their unique Scottish cultural milieu, and evaluated according to Habermas's three-fold hierarchy of cognitive interests.

I should mention at the outset that in examining a 'soccer hooligan' formation (such as the ASC) according to its objectively symbolic and cultural-political (rather than transparently violent) dimensions, I refute any claims that this value-neutral stance can be construed as the reading of a 'native'. As Feldman (1991, p.79) shows, anthropological definitions of violence may be more illuminating than empiricist, policy-orientated sociological offerings:

> Violence can transgress systems of classification and produce discontinuity within a symbolic order by effecting a slippage between systems of restricted designation and the 'opened' domains of material and reference. Violence alters the residual character of the system of material reference and detaches this domain from the domestications, the conventions of the symbolic order.

Equally, the subculture that both encloses and underpins some forms of violent conduct may be taken to represent a subaltern social grouping targeting this activity, both immediately and indirectly, against competing groupings in control of these various symbolic orders. The research for this Chapter was undertaken through participant observation study and interviewing of various groupings of Aberdeen Soccer Casuals. It was funded by the Economic and Social Research Council.

'Dinna mak a fila us': The new hegemony of designer aggro

To be a casual, as a Dunfermline exponent blankly explained in court, "you wear a certain type of clothing, go the football, look for trouble with the opposing fans or the opposing casuals" (*Dunfermline Press*, July 23, 1991). Stylistically, casuals wear designer sports and leisurewear, ranging from Armani suits or jeans, to ZX600 trainers, Fila tracksuits to Farrah cords. This apotheosis of *haute bourgeois* fashion has not by itself engendered a casual gender apartheid - hence Scotland's 'casual quines', 'casualettes', or 'gobblers'

(Giulianotti, 1991c) - but separating the sexes is the males' relatively (and variably) instrumental pursuit of violence within soccer contexts. This quest for liminal and violent sublimation of the collective denotes a marked continuity with earlier soccer subcultures in Scotland (see Murray, 1984; Moorhouse, 1984; Walker, 1990) and Britain in general (see Armstrong, 1992; Dunning et al, 1988; Robins, 1984). Yet, the casual paraologics of expensive attire and flailing limbs is both symbolically and physically striking. The symbiosis of instrumentalism and *bien pensant* style in official and academic discourses on casuals is such that these two features become self-referencing. Some academic commentators have chanced upon a reductionist decoding of the 'style', rendering it synonymous with 80s political hegemony.[3] Thatcherism's praxis, of melding centrifugal interests under the banner of an instrumental 'individualism', procures a double-edged self-parody of the working class 'for itself':

> Hence Britain's newest youth subculture, the 'casuals', whose aggressive, stylistic celebration of leisure goods and 'life-style' conceals both continuing dole queues and continuing 'hooliganism' - the street-corner menace now comes from such nice, clean-cut, Tory-looking boys and girls. (Frith, 1988, p.471).

Conversely, official discourses on the casual fashion view the bourgeois style as a simple ruse to alleviate police suspicions when entering the opposition's 'end'. Thus, the style's instrumentalism is considered its kernel quality: a higher hooligan stage of the Weberian *zweckrational*, using a premeditated means towards a violent, autotelic end.

> I don't call them casuals - they're just well dressed criminals, with their £80 trainers and designer sweaters. They never wear anything to identify them with a particular club (Scottish Head of British Transport Police, *The Sunday Post*, November 12, 1989).

Casual instrumentalism in official discourses acquired a reified mantle for the former's Scottish variant, given the contrived success of the Criminal Justice (Scotland) Act 1980 in removing 'normal' hooliganism by criminalising its affective etiology: drinking or drunkenness at soccer matches (Giulianotti, 1991b). However, this compatibility of designer style and instrumental hooliganism becomes problematic, at the point where the latter is popularly signified by the former, as in official discourses themselves. In the mid-80s, effective Scottish police escorting and corralling of casual gangs produced a challenge to the identified 'trendies' concerning their major focus of identity: style or violence. Where violence was considered by some casuals as essential, the response was pure realpolitik. Embracing the anti-fashion of their stylistic nemesis, the archetypal trainspotter, to usurp these policing strategies, prominent hooligans set in short lived vogue a casual adornment of cheap parka jackets, plastic shoes, downmarket slacks, even NHS spectacles (with sticky tape an optional extra). This project atrophied when it failed to generate subcultural appeal, allowing police to concentrate on individuals already marked out as 'leader' figures.(4) Yet, the very inception of this 'dressing down' denotes the 'moment' when the social interdependencies of discrete hooliganism discourses - official and subcultural - have their boundaries collapsed, into the instrumentalist narratives of the former within the practices of the latter. Today, the very term 'casual' is somewhat hackneyed, and very irregularly used within the leading 'post-casual' Scottish hooligan formations; most prefer to speak about rival 'boys' clustered into 'mobs'.(5) However, I will continue to use this term in order to highlight the separate subcultural identity which the 'casual' represents, both objectively and affectively, to that of earlier Scottish hooligan subcultures.

Sociological explanations of 70s British hooligan subcultures - on the symbolic anthropology of the 'sacred' pitch being defiled by invasion, the 'taking of Ends', the metonymic victories over opponents - have been widely documented and recapitulated, and I do not propose to rehearse them here (see Taylor, 1971, p. 156; Clarke, 1978; Marsh, 1978; Williams, 1991). Suffice it to mention that Scottish casuals are specious in discarding their forebears' ritualistic displays of team loyalty, and mocking the fandom of those swathed in team colours.(6) This departure from prior soccer subcultural practises must be balanced by recognising general continuities and discursive overlaps within the two hooligan epistemes. Casuals retain a more ambivalent relationship towards using the props of *prima facie* 'affective' hooliganism, particularly with regard to drinking, than their official instrumental habitus would otherwise allow (Giulianotti, 1991b). Although 'service trains' on match days no longer sell alcohol on match days, the tendency of the top casual mobs to travel by bus ensures early morning raids on off-licences, and flouting of the laws that these vehicles be 'dry'. In addition, the geographical marginality of Aberdeen relative to the Scottish central belt, the locus of the majority of major Scottish sides, continues to ensure that when travelling to away matches, Aberdeen casuals spend longer drinking before matches than their southern counterparts.

Perhaps the best elementary insight into the casual gang habitus is contained within the names of the gangs themselves. British gang names tend to appeal to two distinctive symbols of identity: locally, with regard to the *sui generis* significations of club or town/city culture; or macro-subculturally, with regard to the practices and values of the movement as contributing to what was the dominant nationwide youth style for the early 80s (Hills, 1991; Redhead and McLaughlin, 1985; Redhead 1986).(7) Thus, for the first order, we have in Scotland alone the Capital City Service (Hibernian F.C. from Edinburgh); the Fair City Firm (St. Johnstone from Perth); and the late Her Majesty's Service (Rangers from Glasgow) which references the club's dense Unionist baggage. The Carnegie Soccer Service offer civic veneration of Dunfermline's most famous and philanthropic son; and, the Inverkeithing casuals are named Divit Station Trendies, the first word denoting the type of dwelling first built in the town centuries back. Conversely, of the second order, there is Rangers' current formation, the Inter-City Firm, which has borrowed its *nom de plume* from West Ham hooligans;(8) and, the Mainline Service Crew again ascendant in Perth, and referencing the railway mode of transport favoured by the subculture generally.

Given this nominal dialectic of continuity and change, where does 'Aberdeen Soccer Casuals' reside on the continuum? Jay Allan (1989, p.85), an ex-'top boy' within the gang, states in his autobiography that during these halcyon days the ASC were "by far the oldest, biggest and best organised." On the final point, there may be some contestation, as Allan's book is regularly an exercise in self-promotion, and also attracts quizzical responses from his coterie over the accuracy of its detail. By the same token, there is little doubt about the vintage of the movement. The 'moment' of its emergence in the very early 80s confirmed its *avant garde* status relative to more foetal Scottish casual siblings, and thereby facilitated a greater potentiality of agency for the ASC's self-definition. However, the socio-historical aporias within the ASC's title would indicate that this agency collapsed upon emission. I would suggest that, without presaging the argument, 'Aberdeen Soccer Casuals' connotes neither an affective appeal to localist tradition, nor a metonymic development of the incipient casual 'imagined community'. Rather, the title delineates a conservative 'claim to membership' of the 'soccer casual' style sweeping through England. It suggests a greater preponderance with denying the movement's peripheral geo-cultural locus in the midst of an incipient national subculture in England. Yet, there are excellent historical and cultural-political reasons for this elementary subcultural self-enervation, and these resonate beyond the football arena. Before examining these factors, it is necessary to outline the ASC's objective project as 'cultural intermediaries' within a subcultural setting.

The new balance of cultural intermediaries

The term 'cultural intermediaries' is derived from Bourdieu (1984), and pertains to those involved in the 'production, marketing and dissemination of symbolic goods' (Featherstone, 1991, p.5). Featherstone (1991, p.35) goes on to state that theories of postmodernity are predicated sociologically upon the 'new cultural intermediaries', whose rapid expansion 'has involved a widening of the range of legitimate cultural goods and the breaking down of some of the old symbolic hierarchies.' Bourdieu (1984) locates this new entity within the 'new petit bourgeoisie', transmitting or appending meaning to cultural significations before wider consumption. Featherstone's (1991, p.19) stratification of this grouping is more informative, being "those in media, design fashion, advertising, and 'para' intellectual information occupations."

Removing the stratification of this grouping, it is possible to substitute the New Age intelligentsia for a youth cultural formation, in this instance the ASC. In doing so, I seek to test both the claims of some writers on the social breadth of the post-modern experience, as beyond their own primary groups; and, to explore the extent to which the emancipatory project of a prominent and creative Scottish movement may be derailed by the structural inequalities bequeathed it by modernity.(9) On this latter point, there is the association

158

between late modernist (Gramscian Marxist) and post-modernist (post-Gramscian) analyses of youth (sub)cultures, within the overall configuration of youth cultural politics. A post-Gramscian dimension in youth cultural studies has, for some time, been developing in the disparate works of Hebdige (1979; 1988), Willis (1990), Fiske (1989a; 1989b), Grossberg (1988), and Redhead (1986; 1990; 1991) *inter alia*. The academic and geographic distinctions of these authors are elided by a general commitment to advancing the study of critical cultural politics, a field first genuinely mapped out by Stuart Hall and the Birmingham Centre for Contemporary Cultural Studies (hereon, CCCS) during the 70s (see particularly Hall et al, 1976).

The structural or superstructural Marxism of the CCCS - depending on its variable syntheses of Marcuse, Althusser and Gramsci - ensured a strong political inflection in its reading of youth cultural productions. These productions were taken to represent the operative subculture's 'spectacular' circumvention of 'repressive desublimation' enforced upon it by the hegemonic 'dominant culture'.(10) Within the imaginary, subcultural practices have been taken to reclaim rather romantically and 'magically' an old and traditional working class *communitas* (cf. Cohen, 1972; Taylor, 1989). Inevitably, such subcultural projects are deemed to atrophy as the dominant culture consumes (or 'recuperates') these productions, defusing their inherent sub-political purchase, and diffusing these styles across a wide and commercialised class strata. Punk, skinhead, mod, and black subcultural identities, for example, can all be interpreted as recuperated for wider appropriation via the cannibal activities of earlier cultural intermediaries (e.g. especially the young bourgeoisie located within the market responsive 'counter culture'). The grain of truth in the CCCS' argument is that these commercial interlocutors operate according to the popular assumption that youth culture is essentially the site of the avant garde now and the stylistic norm tomorrow. A 'metaphor for social change', the neoteric vibrancy of postwar British youth remains the discursive referent for hawking new commodities to the older public.

Since the late 70s, post-Gramscian perspectives, assisted by the emergent disciplines of semiotics and post-structuralist analysis, have turned to examine the *consumption* side of youth cultural practice.(11) Through such conceptions as the "grounded aesthetic" (Willis, 1990, pp.21-4), "ironic nihilism" (Grossberg, 1988, p.41), the pleasurable "will to knowledge" (Fiske, 1989b, p.161) and the "post-political" (Redhead, 1990, pp.91-107), we may arrive at the vertiginous statement: "'Authentic' subcultures were produced by subcultural theories, not the other way around" (Redhead, 1990, p.25). The analytical purchase of this narrative is the common denominator of agency and enablement recognised within youth cultural practices, the capacity of individuals, groups and social formations to operate as cultural intermediaries for themselves, appropriating and recoding symbols of *privileged* styles, practices and spaces for *further* colonisation by wider social groupings. But some, restraint is also required here. It is not the case that by uncovering the construction of knowledge about a social category (such as a subculture) in this way, the objective validity of the category is simultaneously nullified. Nor is it the case that, in dealing with Marxian theories of subcultures, such as the Birmingham School's, we must consider the entire analysis to be discredited or 'inauthentic', if we disagree with the analyses' inherent identification of an emancipatory teleology within these youth subcultural 'styles' (e.g. the reclaiming of community). Ironically, to follow this method of analysis would be to stress incongruously the role of Crusoe-like production (of 'authentic'/'reality-congruent' theoretical meta-narratives) over social cognizant consumption (of selected theory segments in molecular, hybrid forms). In general, it may be stated that 'experience' is measured by the failure of some social groups to reproduce themselves as 'new cultural intermediaries', in collapsing old symbolic hierarchies diachronically. Before turning to examine the utility of the ASC in illustrating this point, there are two further matters which must be dealt with: the objective means of evaluating the formation's merits or failures, and the siting of its activities within the over-stratified domain of Scottish cultural politics.

I evaluate the ASC's efficacy in redefining the boundaries of Scottish youth cultural spaces and practices according to Habermas's (1978) objective hierarchy of cognitive interests. These interests' 'quasi-transcendental' status indicates an ontological equilibrium on his part, with regard to their teleological potency and social immanence, a balance which may translate for some as equivocation:

Habermas does not pin down the precise epistemological status of these interests, or even the status of the claim that these three primary interests exist. Clearly he wants to avoid two extremes: that they are merely contingent empirical interests,

160

or that they are rooted in a transcendental ego outside of and beyond human history. (Bernstein, 1976, p.220).

Nevertheless, within this context, Habermas's cognitive interests remain a colourful and intelligible prism through which to view and critically evaluate the cornucopia of ASC practices in socio-historical relation to Aberdeen, Scottish and British cultures and subcultures. Habermas's three interests are, in ascending order of importance:

i) The empirical-analytic: this possesses a technical 'constitutive interest', premised upon the objectivist and descriptive precepts of the natural sciences. In this sense, a youth subculture's success as a cultural intermediary is measured according to universal (non-negotiable) and nominal variables, such as the numbers identifying or involved with the formation, according to young peoples' dress style or participation in violence at soccer grounds.

ii) The historical-hermeneutic: this possesses a practical 'constitutive interest', premised upon the interpretive and intersubjective precepts of the social and cultural sciences. In terms of youth culture, this secondary interest is evinced through shared codes of style and argot, the presentation of a collective self in public. The ASC's members efficacy as cultural intermediaries here is measured by reworking the meanings of subculturally privileged codes and styles for broader public appropriation.

iii) The critical sciences: this consists of a self-reflective interest, leading to political emancipation, breaking from 'ideologically frozen relations of dependence' (Habermas, 1978, p.310). In youth culture (as a subset of culture generally), the third cognitive interest exposes the mystified dependency of one group upon another (expressed interactively through 'distorted communication'). Discursive spaces open for youth cultural formations to fight these reified inequalities, by redefining the symbols and practices of those with superior economic and cultural capital. As cultural intermediaries success is measured historically according to the effective, 'transcendental' challenge that one formation may signify against another, whether this is expressed in explicit or symbolic terms.

161

Evaluation of the ASC as cultural intermediaries via these three cognitive interests is viewed here as fundamentally flavoured by the movement's Scottish locus. The epicentre of the quandary appears to be the irresolved matter of Scottish cultural identity. Informed sociologists of Scotland appear unwilling to confront the implications of this vogue for national self-analysis, preferring instead to dismiss it as given to discursive essentialising (McCrone, 1989) or as a futile endeavour to adhere the hopelessly fragmented (Bruce in *The Glasgow Herald*, August 31, 1991) - a thesis which Nairn jestingly christens 'Fragmentosis Calendonica' *(The Scotsman*, September, 1991). Little wonder English commentators feel able to get away with collapsing 'identity' questions *per se* into those of 'stereotypes' and 'tribalism' to traduce the whole debate. The net effect of this curious discursive taciturnity has been the virtual relegation of the issue to the forum of popular media. A recent exchange in *The Scotsman* between the two Scottish cultural 'heavyweights' - Tom Nairn and Pat Kane - illuminated the two major and involved discourses focusing upon Scottish cultural production, mediation and consumption. Nairn, a dour modernist historian, upholds the materialist argument of Scottish dependency upon England, reproduced culturally since the Union; Kane, a self-styled SNP 'visionary' with political pretensions and post-modernist predilections, perceives a new sense of agency within Scottish culture that borders on the voluntarist, particularly within the young. Ignoring either of these discourses would be to do the 'Scottish cultural identity' question a disservice, to the point of its misrepresentation. More germanely here, the debate produces an important heuristic for evaluating the ASC's utility as cultural intermediaries, and one which I will seek to intermediate. In short, the ASC may be viewed, at various points along a trajectory, as studiously mirroring English subcultural practice within 'North Britain', or eking out cultural spaces and practices which symbolically challenge the cultural hegemony and hierarchies emanating from south of the border. Should the dialectic be resolved in favour of the latter reading, such an eventuality would be rendered all the more remarkable for the reason that the subculture itself emerged within a city the abject exemplar of Scottish cultural dependency.

Scottish culture: Intrinsically Jekyll and Hyde?

According to Nairn (1981), Scotland's signature of the 1707 Act of Union effectively abdicated any claim the new 'hinterland' might have purveyed for a genuine 'high culture', with a modern 'nationalist' purchase as its definitive constituent. Henceforth, what has passed for positive cultural production in Scotland comprises either a valedictory eulogy for days of chivalrous freedom and gallantry (e.g. the work, life and times of Sir Walter Scott); or, an excoriation of the Scottish psyche's self-abusing, schizoid character (e.g. Robert Louis Stevenson's Jekyll and Hyde) - the Caledonian antisyzygy. Administering Freudian discourse to a Marxist diagnosis, Nairn professes that Scottish culture is eminently neurotic, lacking the capacity to offer any self-critical or emancipatory reading of its stateless predicament; like some fabulous and meretricious beast, it colludes in marking its identity as an autonomous civic 'body' without any indigenous sovereign 'head'. In this sense, the 'repressive desublimation' of Scottish culture is located in its relations of acquiescence and dependence with England, the *sine qua non* of the British State. Rather homologously, Scottish low culture represents an even more bizarre prostitution of political celibacy: Kailyardism (small-town pithy stories)(12) and Tartanry(13) are the sugary residues of an excessive diet upon *kitsch*, devoid of even sub-political currency. Soccer, and less than vicarious contests with the English, remain key valency points for the transmission of this 'vast, tartan monster':

> ...it is something else to be with it (e.g.) in a London pub on International night, or in the crowd at the annual Military Tattoo in front of Edinburgh Castle. How intolerably vulgar! What unbearable, crass, mindless philistinism! One knows that *Kitsch* is a large constituent of mass popular culture in every land: but this is ridiculous. (Nairn, 1981, p.162).(14)

Aberdeen appears to be a microcosmic archetype of Nairn's bete noire, the Kailyard in its full, hologrammatical design. Lacking the politico-demographic relevance to have spawned a respectable historical text, the city is intelligible to old inhabitants and visitors alike through a couthy, anti-political meta-narrative. Aberdeen is assigned the role of quintessential market town; though aspiring to exude an aura of urbane detachment from its mechanistic environs, the 'Silver City's staple industries have always been fishing and farming. This fiscal tranquillity was electrified by the early 70s discovery and mining of North Sea oil (to the extent that house prices quadrupled inside the first three '(Barber) boom' years (Payne, 1975), but the (live)stock referents for the North-East ontology remain. Consistent with Nairn, the North-East of Scotland is historically devoid of any autonomous 'high culture', though its most acclaimed writer, Grassic Gibbon (*Grey Granite*), did bitingly expose the acerbic, indigenous gossip culture.(15) Aberdeen has pursued a monocentric cultivation of public cultural institutions: one theatre, music hall, art gallery, university, soccer team. Even the texture of Aberdeen is uniformly granite. The cult of Balmoralism and Royal Deeside, instituted by Queen Victoria, constitutes the city's principle linkage to aristocratic practice and culture. This neatly submerges the latent, historically radical tradition of an Episcopalian city concertedly disinclined to sign the Covenant before the collapse of the Stuart Rebellion, 1745 and Culloden (Chapman and Dobson, 1949, p.9).(16)

Also in line with Nairn, low culture produce remains a source of civic pride. Aberdeen's finest contribution to the popular arts might have been the inter-war vaudeville performer Harry Gordon, while its musical metonym 'The Northern Lights' was penned by a Rochdale lass n'er acquainted with aurora borealis. On the football front, the local team, founded in 1903, have always played at home in a ground whose name, Pittodrie, is derived from the Celtic for 'place of manure' (Leatherdale, 1986, p.1; Webster, 1990, p.11). There the bonnetted 'death instinct' has traditionally transfixed local patrons, notorious for their silences, cynicism and dark depredations of home players.(17) In the hour of the team's greatest achievement, victory in the 1983 European Cup-Winners' Cup Final, an affected self-composure retained favour short on fervour. Local lyricist Jack Webster reports a near telepathic exchange between club chairman (Dick Donald) and captain (adopted son, Willie Miller) at the post-match 'carnival':

Without breaking stride or diverting from the business of shovelling on a slice of ham, some salad and tatties, the doughty Dick said: "Well well, Willie, its been quite a night." To which the inscrutable Willie replied: "Ay, so it has." Two

164

unflappable men of sterling (sic) character had surely said it all. (Webster, 1990, p.228).

Axiomatically, Aberdeen's post-war youth cultures inherited this self-abusing weltanschauung. Fortunately for them the intrinsically Scottish obsession with sanitary presentation of self in public (as a produce of the 'gossip culture') was camouflaged by the more subculturally acceptable ethos of 'style', which also drew attention to the Goffmanesque examination of dramaturgical minutiae. The best theoretical conception of this orientation which I am aware of is Arthur W. Frank's (1991) 'communicative body'. Here, the body represents a vessel of disclosure, expressive and, being related to the presence of the other, is sociologically dyadic. Frank looks forward to a positive, stylised actuation of this corporeality, offering by way of illustration the performative act of dance. However, where the communicative body's ontology is articulated through the micropolitics of non-disclosure (Scottish culture over-determined by youth subcultural 'style'), the effect is to infuse with negativity his empowering reading.

Characteristically, in relation to the emission sites of national youth subcultural forms, Aberdeen lagged well behind in terms of importation. By the 'moment' of arrival in the city (most easily mediated through the local cinema halls),(18) subcultural styles had by necessity encroached upon the field of recuperation, and survived beyond their natural 'lifecycle' in hypostatised form.(19) Numerically significant but two-dimensional groupings of Aberdonian Teds survived into the 60s, Mods into the late 60s, Rockers throughout the 70s (becoming progressively more middle-class in the process). It was only in 1973 that the city's judiciary felt compelled to adopt an alarmist approach for dealing with the late 60s 'folk devil' of Skinheads (known locally as the Crew), asserting that in their fighting with the Rockers (the Half-Breeds) "this hooligan element is becoming distressing to the citizens of Aberdeen" (*The Aberdeen Press & Journal*, February 7, 1973).

The naming and practices of local gangs attested to another site of subcultural dependency: Glasgow. Robins (1984, pp.41-4) argues that the patina of 'hardness' and 'violence' coating Glasgow's criminal subcultures from the inter-war years onwards, was mediated throughout Britain, and most perspicuously consumed by post-war youth subcultures, particularly those following soccer teams. The aesthetics of spray-painting, and the formal demarcation of gang groupings into senior and junior siblings, e.g. The Toll and The Young Toll, are the main subcultural artifacts of the West of Scotland influence, and Aberdeen was equally well colonised by the 60s and 70s.(20) Legends still circulate in the city of fights between Glaswegian 'teams' who had travelled north to quell the reputation of emergent Aberdeen subcultures, such as the Crew or its precursor 'the Tory Boys'. Yet, with the early 70s collapse of the two-estate alliance that had founded the Crew a decade earlier - an implosion effected by the pressure of the first generation of youth subcultures emerging in the city's post-war housing estates - Aberdeen's youth subculture fragmented along longeveal eco-social lines (Giulianotti, 1989b). Overall, the inter-relations of Aberdonian, Scottish and British cultures and subcultures, within the Nairnian imaginary, may be depicted as illustrated in Plate 1 opposite.

Rather belatedly, perhaps, Strathclyde has produced the most strident exponent of Scottish youth cultural self-enablement, in the figure of Pat Kane. One of Kane's most pertinent and intrinsically post-modernist criticisms concerns the unthinking retention of the old modernist dichotomy of High and Low Culture when deciphering the contemporary cultural politics of any nation. Kane himself is a 'pop musician' and 'thinker' on record as aspiring to the position of Minister for Culture in an independent Scotland, circa 21st Century.(21) In his opening criticism of Nairn's theses during their recent exchange, Kane enquires:

> "football nationalism" - the behaviour of our fans in the World Cup both convivial and outward-looking? Aren't Scots - particularly young ones - enabled by Scottish popular culture a lot more than they're disabled these days, in pop music, television, literature? (*The Scotsman*, March 2, 1991).

In his first remark, Kane conflates the self-conscious representations of Scottish fan behaviour with the actual affect behind this behaviour, a distinction whose interplay I have examined elsewhere for the same phenomenon (Giulianotti, 1991a). Nairn's response to the argument behind the second question is more salient. Drawing a cultural fault-line between the Scottish identity of 'ethnicity as ethnicety' and his more sanguine 'paralysis of the will', Nairn states:

It's down to history alone: the byproduct of retaining a national civil society and institutions with no political state. But of course this history has now endured long enough - almost three centuries - to affect culture profoundly, and to foster a simulacrum of nation character. (*The Scotsman*, March 9, 1991).

Kane finally responds with a replication of earlier points, made none the more persuasive by his manifest application of privileged epistemology: "the people will seize the time, Tome, I'm sure of it" (*The Scotsman*, March 9, 1991). Disappointingly, in doing so, he allows himself to become ensnared in a hoary debate on the Scottish cultural psyche, and its sceptibility to a post-modern Scottish state, rather than retaining focus on his initial 'agency' grouping, Scottish youth. Presumably, Kane had premised his new "purposive sense of agency" on some recent, material development in the youth culture of Scotland, which points the way towards some degree or form of cultural or subcultural emancipation from established symbolic orders. As noted by way of this Chapter's *raison d'etre*, the ASC were undoubtedly a vanguard formation within the dominant subculture of 80s Scotland, the casual style. Is it the case that this grouping constitutes one genuine cultural intermediary in the Scottish sense, challenging the established symbolic hierarchies, at least upon a subcultural plateau, pertaining to either England or, from the peripheral viewpoint of North-East Scotland, Strathclyde?

A crucial issue which must be remembered is that we are dealing with a subculture which has one of its two definitive characteristics (the relatively instrumental pursuit of autotelic soccer-related violence) consensually rejected by the hegemonic power blocs at all structural levels. In this stark light, the ASC's transformative potential within cultural politics must be essentially handicapped at the very outset, a fact over-determined by their intransigent micro-cultural locus within Aberdeen. Consequently, a refocusing of the movement's objective, symbolic aspirations is required: success as cultural intermediaries in Aberdeen rather than Scotland *per se* becomes the most perspicuous issue under assessment.

Having grounded the movement's genesis within the context of Aberdonian/Scottish culture (modernist or post-modernist), and introduced the three 'quasi-transcendental' cognitive interests of Habermas to evaluate the practices and symbols, the genealogy of the ASC is now introduced. The three time groupings cover the periods 1981-85, 1985-88, and 1988-present. In chronicling the ASC's history according to culture, cognitive interest and time, I will also apply other sub-categories to his analytical matrix: space, the other and the body. The analysis of space will appeal to three dimensions of ASC activity in core-periphery terms:

i) Internally, according to the core loci of city centre and home soccer ground, and the peripheral city locales (post-war satellite housing estates).

ii) Externally, in relation to ASC travel to focal concerns in Scotland/Britain; primarily matches, but including other cultural festivals.

iii) Figuratively, referring to the ASC's relationship to the core spaces of Scotland/Britain, finally indicating the extent to which the ASC have succeeded in representing Aberdeen as a less peripheral social space than in the past.

Other groups are also important, representing the 'objects' against which the ASC, as a collectivity of subjective actors, define themselves; the maintenance and occasional collapse of these boundaries will be assessed longitudinally.

The centrality of the body has already been alluded to; its cultural-political importance is only really pertinent during the final period of 1988-92, and the examination of how the ASC can discard the langue of the communicative body for a diametrically opposite one, that of the mirroring body.

1981-85: Try and Kappa that

The first casuals in Aberdeen consciously emerged on October 31, 1981, when a precocious trio donned Pringles for an interminable 0-0 home draw versus Dundee United. Empirically, this was an event immediately resonant of the casuals' movement beyond the city's sub-political pedigree of youth subcultural lag, as this group represented the first casuals in Scotland. The ASC's subsequent emergence germinated a chronology of rival casual gangs in

Motherwell, Dundee, Edinburgh, Perth, and Glasgow. Within eighteen months of the ASC's establishment, most youth formations from the city's upper-working class post-war housing estates, with one noteworthy exception, had demonstrated equal self-absorption in banding together under the aegis of a new mediary.(22) This was another sub-political first for the city, since never before had this breadth of intersubjective harmony between the city's youth subcultures been forged, portending as it did a final emancipation from the inter-estate rivalries of the recent past.(23) Operating in a sporting context in which Scottish soccer violence had been hypostatised into an affective, sectarian mundaneness, the ASC, through an active corporeality of violence and style, embodied a new subcultural challenge to Glaswegian hegemonies of violence. Coterminously, the casual style - of Ellesse, Benetton, Tacchini, Lacoste, Patrick, Kappa, Fila, etc. - signified a semiotic artillery entirely homologous with the domestic and European successes of Aberdeen Football Club.(24) The successes of the football side on the park, and of its 'soccer crew' off it, were commonly confirmed at the expense of the Old Firm and its supporters. These material challenges were reflected more obscenely still by the nascent, indigenous awareness of the city's privileged industrial and commercial definition abroad: the 'Houston of Europe' as it enjoyed considering itself (Smith, 1989, p.1), most agreeably in contrast to the de-industrialising central belt of Scotland. The Scottish unemployment rate for 1981 was 14.4%, more than double the Aberdeen rate (7.1%), but still less than the Glasgow equivalent (15.8%) (*Economic Gazette*, December 1981). Technically, the most omnipresent casual accoutrement, the Pringle jersey, was not out with the physical or financial reach of most prospective 'trendies' Those at the more disadvantaged end of Aberdeen's socioeconomic spectrum could still utilise the bludgeoning casual black market to attain stylistic ingress to this dynamic new subculture. Ironically, the vast majority of casual attire was obtained during football and 'shopping' excursions to the central belt and beyond. Two established shops in Aberdeen proved particularly responsive to stocking casual attire as it became fashionable in the south. These head-starts were themselves facilitated only by employment and kinship associations between the young market and the forward looking outfitters.(25)

Upon more expansive terrain, it may be stated that the ASC also assisted in deconstructing the objective interdependency of

Glaswegian hardness and English subcultural 'styles', by-passing the former in order to soak in and synchronise with the revivification of the latter. Whilst Aberdeen youth cast off the financially incongruous entropy of late 70s subcultures during the period 1981-85, youth in Scotland's central belt stagnated within the stylistically subaltern and atavistic 'moments' of punk, skinhead, mod, ska: a marriage to an obsolete decade over-determined by the 'wear the colours' fandom surrounding the Old Firm football culture. This sub-political component of the early casual project is neatly identified by one commentator critical of the response to it from those within the established symbolic hierarchies of Scottish soccer:

> Scotland's casual gangs are undoubtedly a new-firm. Much of the disbelief and anger that surrounds casual violence is premised on the fact that it refuses to follow the traditional rules of the football fanaticism of the past. Rangers and Celtic do not command the level of fear that they had in years gone by.... (Cosgrove, 1991, p.136).

Indeed, at this juncture, Scottish casual subcultures also corresponded with their English counterparts, in mediating a more aleatory use of identity and group conflict. They did not await a 'repressive desublimation' of the subculture, across broad structural categories of class and gerontology. Rather, their emancipatory interest was located at more molecular levels: not the magical recovery of parental community, but the group prosecution of 'number one' status, through the corporeal and within the subculture *per se*. The drive to be 'number one' represents the hermeneutic link between these *prima facie* warring factions. In this sense, the 'number one' status constitutes an 'ideal speech situation' in which subcultural discourse and action is actually dominated, or 'distorted' in Habermasian terms, in the act of seizing control of the symbolic order, in violent and stylistic terms. This status is publicly assigned through compelling subcultural recognition from casual rivals, the 'significant others', and claimed by the communicative action of 'running' the opposition, or enscribing actual violence upon the other. The numinous and quasi-transcendental quality of a collective participation in interpersonal violence is brilliantly captured by Feldman, as the legitimation and authorisation of power "where it takes place, in a zone of particularity from which all generalities and universal claims of domination flow"; "a metonym of doing, the simultaneous site of origin and effect." (Feldman, 1991, p.3). Briefly stated, the ASC - the first casual formation in Scotland - initiated and mediated the collapse of one, 'done', symbolic hierarchy of hooliganism (Old Firm and soccer-dominated) with its replacement by another hooligan 'regime of signification' (largely outside Glasgow and dominated by macro-subcultural style). In 1985, this recourse to England for stylistic developments in casual identity, was symbolically re-examined as Aberdeen casuals initiated and dominated the violence between rival fans at the 1985 Scotland v. England match, both inside and outside Hampden Park.

The ASC played a critical role in mediating to wider publics the accessibility of two important geo-cultural leisure spaces. Firstly, the formation actuated the instrumental hooligan discourse - of positioning one's 'mob' in as close a proximity to the opposition as was viable - by seeking to 'penetrate' the rival fans' end, the Beach End, at the ASC home ground. Ironically, for long-standing Aberdeen fans within the formation, this could have been interpreted as a 'magical recovery of community' - but only in a strictly football sense. For the Beach End had been the traditional 'Dons' End', until 1979-80 when disgruntled home fans were relocated to the traditional 'away end', to minimise clashes outside the ground. After several successful (re)incursions of the Beach End, by the 1983-4 season the local police had responded effectively, being able to identify the generic semiotics of this new hooligan identity. In turn, this precipitated the reproduction of hooligan spaces initially institutionalised by ground segregation of the early 1970s: the ASC shifted into the stand adjacent to the away fans' end. In doing so, this area began to emerge as the setting for the most participatory section of the home support, and further policing measures were introduced outside the ground to ensure home fans did not have access to roads used by departing visitors.

Secondly, at this juncture the city centre was becoming an important symbolic space for bands of prospective trendies from the city's satellite housing estates. On quiet midweek evenings, over one hundred casuals or fellow travellers would pour into the core city spaces, abandoned by their parental group only a couple of hours before. Certainly, the intersubjective unification of rival estates according to this time-space dimension was never unanimous. Each micro-collectivity mapped out its own specified domains, in shop

171

doorways, street corners and customary walks. Yet, by 1983 an inchoate core group of casuals had clustered on the premise of this identity, in contrast to previous, locale-based ones. At the weekends, following matches or otherwise, the casual style assisted in transforming the collective habitus of those within key leisure spaces, most of which were alcohol related. Dominating the city centre in a technical/numeric and hermeneutic/symbolically *avant garde* sense, the casuals were a catalytic force in de-differentiating(26) the formal (nightclub) and informal (pub) bifurcation of established working class leisure identities. In an emancipatory sense, this collapsed the high/low semiotics of bodywear into an intermediary 'smart, but casual' syncretics where the old symbolic hierarchy no longer resided. Thus, casual style mapped out an intermediary social-leisure space within the coterminously ascendant 'lounges' that relaxed the nightclub stance on attire, but retained the stylised significations of 'night-out-ness' through negotiated standards of self-presentation with the clientele. ASC pre-eminence within the city centre was typically perceived as a direct challenge to the spatial freedom of older subcultures. Major battles ensued with 'bikers' who had claimed the adjoining Beach Boulevard as their own; prominent figures within gangs which rejected the ASC's dualist protocol of inter-estate rapprochement and stylistic revivification engaged in regular fights with the new subcultural vanguard.

Counterpoising this litany of furious agency, Aberdeen's casuals betrayed a curious and obtuse self-absorption with their new self-empowerment, a cultural elixir minus historical referent. Elements of the old Scottish neuroticism cast a Hyde-like shadow over their emancipatory achievements. Firstly, empirically and hermeneutically, the formation's style reproduced a strong dependency upon the south, albeit in a newly synchronised setting.(27) Thus, when word filtered through that Pringles were *passe* in London, anyone spotted sporting one in the North-East was subjected to a gambit of social deprecation. The 'dominating body'(28) of Aberdeen casual style thus displayed an incestual synthesis of macro-subcultural and micro-cultural deference to the symbolic leadership of others. Deference to the south also had its self-parodic consequences. When the macro-casual style introduced deerstalker hats as requisite headwear, the ASC simply reproduced this mode and acceded to localist claims to symbolic emancipation from the kudos accorded gentrified rural Scottish fashion. Secondly, the

Aberdeen casuals were more than aware of the paltry subcultural legacy of the city. This unease was most explicitly conveyed inter-subjectively. Cockney argot and accents were regularly preferred when interacting with those from 'home' or previously rival housing estates. This suggested that full sublimation of the casual ontology would be out with the formation's reach, so long as its affiliates continued to structure this within subculturally regressive Aberdonian discourses.

1985-88: The thick end of the wedge

During this period, the semiotics of the ASC style gradually underwent recuperation into the broader social spectrum, as assisted by the latter's redifferentiation. Three external and one internal (subcultural) levels of cultural capital are identifiable as the sites at which this 'diffusion and defusion' process occurred:

i) The upper strata of casual attire was now networked to a wider, indigenous audience through the new vector points of Burberry, Benetton, Austin Reed and other branches of high fashion chains appearing in the city. Previously, it had been up to casuals on stealing trips in the central belt to explore what Phil Cohen (1972) might have called the 'upward option' of this style. Thus, the role of mediating this attire to a wider populace passed from casuals (emphasising semiotic appropriation) to retailers (emphasising property consumption).

ii) The middle strata of casual attire, particularly sports-orientated items, passed from the youth subculture to established chain stores feeding upon the leisure boom of the 80s. These retailers including Olympus, Intersport, but also new (ill-fated) ones such as Next; the definitive features of this strata are an eagerness to showcase 'house' names, but within a price range discrete from the upper strata above.

iii) At the base of the stylistic spectrum are sited the High Street stores, which expanded their clothing remits during this period into promotion of sportswear bearing corporate insignia: British Home Stores, Littlewoods and more recently, Woolworth's.

Unlike the upper and middle strata, the resultant abattoir of self-presentation emanating from here was rarely re-reappropriated by casuals. Yet this lower level still furthered the broader transition of stylised leisurewear from *haute bourgeois* refuge to subcultural weapon to public sector utility.

Within the casual macro-subculture, the ASC's symbolic concessions to the south were re-encountered through following the latter's jettison of designer logos in favour of more understated and up-market menswear, such as Armani and Ralph Lauren. Two pragmatic reasons - one empirical, the other more cultural-political - would suggest that this transition was essential to the reproduction of any casual formation. Superficially, it was evident that striding around in a stylistic billboard, several years after its first adornment, was a somewhat anachronistic pastime. The casual predilection for quality attire was now solidly embedded within youth consciousness, and no longer demanded such dazzling confirmation. Secondly, and more problematically, wider diffusion of casual style significations as chic promoted a nascent, antithetical grouping, the post-1985 'trendies'. This sub-subculture represented both a symbolic challenge to the ASC's reproduction, and a sub-political challenge through its disengagement from the fray.

'Trendies' had nominally been synonymous with the 'casuals' during the formative years of the subculture *qua* well-dressed football hooligans. However, in the latter half of the decade, and unlike other mobs such as Hibs and Celtic,(29) the Aberdeen casuals failed to evolve their own 'baby crew'. In effect, what would have been their junior cohorts *mutatis mutandis*, actually became a simulacra of the soccer casual, through their disinclination to ground style in soccer-related violence. The style itself which the young 'trendies' pursued consisted mainly of the meretricious, sporting brand names now frowned upon by the wider casual subculture. Genuine (or self-identified 'authentic') casuals preferred to discard their more eye-catching trainers for appropriation by trendies, rather than risk being aligned with these non-combatants by peers or, worse still, other casual mobs now seriously challenging the ASC's 'number one' status.

The emergence of the 'trendies' during this period, and the coterminous reappropriation of casual semiotics at the supply/commercialised side, assisted in a narrowing of focus upon

174

the Scottish dimension to preserve ASC discourses of pre-eminence. The advantage which the ASC accrued in disengaging from English association for retaining status in Scotland was more than over-determined by the effects of Scottish police successes in the monitoring, stewarding and control of casual gangs. Numerically and interactively, the declining Scottish presence of the ASC was significantly camouflaged by the ubiquity of police measures in and around Scottish grounds. Hibs casuals and latterly Rangers casuals were capable of mounting symbolic challenges to the Aberdeen casuals' pre-eminence which the police were more successful in repelling.

The 'other-relatedness' of the formation deteriorated, as the ASC practised inter-subjectively what Baudrillard (1983) terms the *eminence grise*, the art of making the other disappear. In the manner of the valedictory identified by Nairn as structuring the politics of paralysis, Aberdeen casuals ruminated on the golden years of before, as enhanced by caricatured, yellowing pictures of their more mature opponents. Discursively, other casual gangs were dismissed, as unable to obtain the subcultural alchemy which the ASC had mined one epoch previously. Yet equally, the others were chided for experiencing the technical and hermeneutic youth cultural support outside Aberdeen which the ASC no longer commanded at home, as though these later projects were regressive or atavistic. This denial of presence was not reflected in an objective sense at both the empirical and sub-political level, as the ASC's own symbolic hegemony was challenged by rival casual formations. Where such challenges were encountered a ready variety of auxiliary hypotheses were lurking to explain an ignominious result against the young pretenders. Most of these refutations were premised on the argument that these opponents had not entertained the real 'A/deen Blagging Crew' - but much of the latter no longer existed. Only in very exceptional circumstances were the ASC able to muster two hundred away from home, and very rarely did this translate into collectivisation. A clear empirical and intersubjective decline from the days of five hundred plus, this also necessarily impinged upon the reproduction of the ASC's privileged status in the casual symbolic hierarchy *inter alia*.

This refocusing upon more parochial, localist and Scottish concerns was confirmed in spatial terms. The ASC underwent a gradual haemorrhage to the peripheral post-war housing estates from whence they had sprung, retreating from the triple pressures of being unable to control styles, public leisure spaces, and personal biographies. As non-fighting trendies came to dominate numerically the city centre, displacing the Aberdeen casuals from their prior habitat, many older casuals deserted the claim to avant garde status for the predictable, routine reproduction of working class culture in the home estates. For this group, casual style now represented little more than a temporary emancipation for urban Kitsch. The introspective 'local', with its darts, pool and bookie culture, replaced the pioneering mobility and activity of four years earlier. Over-determining this transition, capital controllers of major city centre leisure spaces further marginalised ASC presence, with 'no jeans or trainers' posted outside many major nightclubs and discos at weekends. Through reconstructing the 'formal/informal' dichotomy of high/low recreation spaces, the ASC were penalised through compression into 'exploring the downward option', the 'late licence' lounges hanging onto the coat-tails of the 80s nightclub boom. Thirdly, many early casuals simply considered their emancipatory experiment with the *avant garde* to have stylistically actuated their 'true selves'; settling for a reification of the body politic, this essentialism was conveyed through adornment of threadbare Tacchini tops in 1986, or wedge haircuts circa 1983. Aberdeen building site workers in their early twenties were the best dressed tradesmen in Scotland. No further 'progress' in Casual style was necessary or viable: history ended here.

In relation to English soccer casual experiences, the Scottish geo-cultural locus of the ASC enabled the latter to distance itself from the former, a distinction that was, ironically, contrary to the 'catch-up' cultural politics of the formation circa 1982. Disengagement from the south allowed the formation to avoid re-appraisal of football hooliganism at the subcultural[30] and political levels,[31] following the Heysel riot and the Luton v. Millwall match in 1985. The resultant repressive deconstruction of English soccer subcultures - enacted by the judicial-administrative coalition of right-wing, proactive forces ('dry' Tories, law-and-order police chiefs, tabloid and broadsheet press) - culminated in a litany of 'dawn raids' which were ultimately futile in court (Armstrong and Hobbs, 1992). Apart from two theatrical, judicial-political measures against the ASC in 1985-6 - one an abortive anti-casual Private Members bill, the other the jailing of eight casuals - the ASC escaped the sensationalist coverage of soccer hooliganism in the south. There can be little doubt that this restraint was premised upon wider popular cultural politics. The perceived success of the Criminal Justice (Scotland) Act, 1980, has been well entrained into official and popular discourses on the Scottish soccer fan. Deep-seated anxieties about a belated inclusion of Scotland in the post-Heysel global ban on English fans and teams(32) proved unfounded. Scottish fans have since shown themselves to be particularly adept in successfully defining themselves succinctly abroad, specifically against the 'hooligan' English (Giulianotti, 1991a). This syntactical type of self-understanding, within the field of Scotland's most important popular cultural pursuit, still owed much to the alienating cultural arrogance of English football administrators.(33) Ambivalence towards England, in negatively marking out Scottish identity, has been equally evident in contemporary Scottish political culture. The heavily touted 'Doomsday Scenario' of the 1987 General Election - at which the Tory share of 72 Scottish MPs was more than halved to ten - came and went, and the Scottish Office carried on its business largely unaffected.

Inside the home ground, ASC control over space remained a good deal more prominent. Soccer was still the major centripetal site of activity for the movement, reciprocated by the latter's continuation as the most vociferous and distinctive element in the Aberdeen support. By this juncture, the South Stand had become a 'naturalised' setting for participatory support, resolving the long-standing quandary over geo-social identity for young Aberdeen fans within their own ground. Yet the declining fortunes of the footballing side were matched by the ASC's demise as trail-blazing stylists. Whilst the 'trendies' were swamping the movement within the ground, and the police and rival casuals undermining its initial status outside, Aberdeen F.C. were struggling through a barren run with only the two Scottish Cups in 1986 to parade before a revitalised Rangers and the inspired, double-winning Celtic side of 1988.

To condense developments in this period, the 'trendies' activities constituted a misappropriation of their casual forebears' legacy. The former became immersed in recapitulating stylistic content, rather than exploring the amorphous sense of enablement which had been utilised by the ASC at its inception - as the first local subculture to unify local and stylistic antagonisms, and generate challenges to some of the established symbolic hierarchies within the soccer field.

Across the broader social spectrum, as culture intermediaries, the ASC's effectiveness in grounding designer casual wear as accessible public attire, had come to some success. However, this style was strongly diluted by three-tier market segmentalisation; Aberdeen casuals themselves contributed to this process, conceding the material heights of Fila for the prosaic pragmatism of Hi-tech and Olympus. Spatially, the formation's success in establishing a new locus within the ground for younger fans, was barely offset by the forfeiture of many city central sites. Inter-subjectively, the movement was fragmenting through redifferentiation: returning to peripheral housing estates and the 'downward options' of working class culture. And the challenge which the ASC had embodied relative to long-standing Scottish soccer interests was now atrophying, nearing pruning from a scissors-effect of the old (Glaswegian soccer dominance) and the new (police measures, emerging casual gangs elsewhere).

1988-present: Chilled out by style, more or Ellesse

The major themes running through this period concern how the ASC deal with the youth cultural style currently dominant in Aberdeen and Britain generally, and the crucial correlated question of how the formation continues to conceptualise the body. Previously, the ASC had accepted practically the conventional ontology of the body, as communicative, for the two basic reasons noted earlier: the post-war youth cultural fascination with style *per se*, and the local, Scottish obsession with minimising self-disclosure. Both factors exaggerate neurotically the corporeal potential for 'communication out of character'.(34) The new style problematicising this conception is the 'techno-pop', 'Indie-dance' or 'rave' phenomenon, alluded to above in respect of the English *avant garde* (1985-88).

Empirically, 'raving' is deemed to consist of all-night dancing at clubs or 'warehouse parties' with special D.J.s/Master-mixers of the requisite sounds (extremely obscure, pure techno-pop), the full perception of which is sharpened by copious consumption of designer pharmaceutics. Inter-subjectively, 'raving' is held to favour a 'cut and paste' plagiarism musically (through such devices as sampling machines); it also promotes a pacified, distortion-free 'attitude' towards fellow ravers engaged in a wilful and collective self-hypnosis. Redhead (1990, pp.1-6) notes, for example, that in the hackneyed tabloid parlance, the 1988 'Acid House' boom became known as the 'Second Summer of Love'. Equally, the simple etiological chain of chemistry-consumption-action is reified by media-friendly for 'ravers' consuming the MDMA drug compound: taking a lead from the suppliers' argot of 'ecstacy', erstwhile rave-goers are now said to be swallowing 'the hug drug' or 'the love drug'. More relevantly, the new ontology of the body produced by the new 'rave' phenomenon defines itself against not only casual style, but concepts of 'style' and social boundaries *per se*. The communicative body - and its other-related concern with the exclusion of object from subject - is rendered redundant, replaced by the body as mirror. Through dance, the mirroring body stands as monadic and with no conception of the other, reflecting instead the predominant *zeitgeist*, to the extent of complete submergence:

> the mirroring body constitutes its objectives in its own self-reflection. Even as the body itself mirrors these objects, the objects are always already seen as mirroring the body. Other objects are all 'pre-assimilated' to the body. One size fits all, and all fits the one body.[35] (Frank, 1991, p.61).

Finally, at the emancipatory level, raving is generally viewed as possessing its greatest power at the juncture with soccer subcultural style. The post-Heysel re-evaluation of hooligan *praxis* now recovers a positive subcultural identity through the explosion of the club scene in the late 80s, and the pro-Europe fraternalism crystallised by E-consumption (Redhead, 1991, pp.105-7; Hills, 1991). Thus, raving represents a new 'episteme' with its more concerted fusion of music and soccer, and its discursive rejection of 'hooligan' behaviour through the de-differentiation of violent gang enmities.

Examining the Aberdeen casuals relationship to this phenomenon, it can be said that only technically, by accepting a vocabulary of motive favourable to embracing the style, have they retained their *avant garde* stature within post-80s Scottish youth culture. Even here it is apparent that the rest of Scotland is not being left behind: one 'rave' nightspot manager from Strathclyde declares "We've got our own crowd though - no disrespect, but they're mostly ex-soccer hooligans, that kind of background..." (*TLN*, July/August, 1991). The major 'rave' clubs in Aberdeen, as elsewhere in Scotland, testify to

179

the dominance of this narcissistic energy. In baggy tops and trousers, the majority of which are a few standardised sizes, and hair lengths ranging from skinheads to long pony-tails, patrons gyrate, swing-on-the-spot, or 'chill out', lost in the automatism of the hypnotised corporeal.

One major section of Aberdeen casuals, which had dominated one major 'rave' club until its recent closure, are unable to rationalise this subcultural reinvention fully. This grouping may possess the purchases and patois redolent of the mirroring body perspective, but structure this upon the style-centred ontology of the communicative body. Such a reading effectively confuses the requisite interpretive grids of 'casual' and 'raver' identity. The net result for those entering this hybrid grouping's spaces is a visual frisking, aimed at evaluating the newcomer's proximity to a non-existent 'Indie-dance' ideal. It would appear, however, given the above, that this compulsion to retain a stylisation of identity has at least as much to do with the North-East as subcultural biographies. The dynamics of social exclusion are such that 'door policies' are operational in some Aberdeen clubs, for style rather than security reasons. It is not unknown for these clubs to refuse admission on the grounds of the errant patron sporting unsound adornments, such as a moustache or tanned leather jacket.

Although spatially city centre clubs such as these may seem to be a compensatory recolonisation of the core, following the 1985-88 return to periphery housing estates, the problems of their 'Indie-dance' content do not terminate at the corporeal. Inter-subjectively, the ASC have significant problems in balancing the clearly defined range of 'others' of the past with their re-emergence in the anti-other present. When old casual rivals turn up in Aberdeen clubs wearing obviously 'raver' attire, there is confusion as to the required response; 'get tore in about them' as would have been recommended in the first period (1981-85), ignore them as inconsequentials (*a la* 1985-88), or be demonstrably friendly (as favoured by today's ideology), with shared biographies further amenable to this tertiary fusion of horizons. The disorientation is regularly induced by the establishment of techno clubs in each major city, which positively endorses travel from one major venue to another in Scotland (and Britain or Europe, if the finance or inclination is there). At present, this possible rapprochement of Scottish youth remains precarious, with other casual gangs experiencing this conflicting subcultural loyalty equally acutely - Hibs Casuals have recently taken to advertising this antipathy via 'Smash the Ravers' posters, or calling meetings to determine collective policy on these 'bubbles' or 'fashion victims'. The down-side of this apotheosis of mobility produces some vicarious re-enactments of soccer casual rivalry within an 'Indie-dance' context. There is the rather obvious suspicion of 'rave' hosts that old enemies are simply being 'wide' by swaggering about on their patch; for their part, the visitors' *en masse* modes of transit replicate the group dynamics and subsequent, intoxicated *mentalite* which had been a *sine qua non* for bloody battles of the past. At home, the core group of Aberdeen casuals had recently obtained a manageable fusion of 'casual' and 'raver' identities in one particular nightclub, which offered its patrons 'techno-pop' music of today and the drinking environment of clubs circa 1984. However, the aporias inherent within this dual subcultural identity have not taken long to surface; riot between casuals, bouncers and police in the 'Hoochi-Coochi' club recently occurred to match more large-scale trouble between ravers and police at raves in the south.(36) Again, Hibs casuals have been perceived by club staff as possessing a similar antipathy towards the club experience, which necessarily entails a violent result (see Giulianotti 1991c).

Obviously, the 'raver' habitus has mitigated the ASC's definition of soccer as the major centripetal concern. This is also partially a consequence of the success of the trendies, and younger groupings of participatory supporters, in displacing the Aberdeen casuals from the precise space in the South Stand that they had carved out for themselves. When fragmented casual groupings stride into the South Stand around kick-off time, they often find these seating areas annexed by an overspill of younger fans who had, ironically, heeded the casuals' raucous support, to desert the artificial home 'end' for a different soccer-watching experience. 'Casual corner' now only genuinely appears at major matches attracting large crowds, when the police are forced to accede 'no-go' areas within the ground to all types of supporters. Therefore, empirically and inter-subjectively, as illustrated by these differential experiences of access to core ground spaces, the ASC now constitute a "subculture within a subculture" (Cohen, 1956, p.12), cross-cutting youth and local soccer subcultures. This marginalisation obtains at the point where a more replete intersubjective and critical parity surfaces between the Aberdeen casuals and their cohorts in the south. Crucially, however, this equilibrium itself only pertains following the subcultural squeeze on English style hooliganism, and where the dominating body is superseded by the mirroring ones.

Beyond both soccer and macroscopic processes, the ASC's effective reproduction is challenged by the disinclination of teenagers on rival post-war housing estates to mirror the unity of a decade earlier. The intersubjective harmony of the first two periods has collapsed, with 90s teenagers from several locales involved in regular feuding on peripheries, and in the core spaces of the city centre, given the jealous guarding of the latter by a new youth subculture there which is no casual 'baby crew'. There seems to be little prospect of an 'ideal speech situation' amongst the city's youth becoming at least the majority position in the foreseeable future, even less so with soccer at its core. The fragmentation is best symbolised by the fact that the first two locales to produce subcultures that combined under the casual aegis now play host to an on-going feud between these gangs' younger siblings.

Beyond youth cultural politics, the cumulative effects of the Casuals' mediation of sports and leisurewear, and the de-differentiation of style nurtured by 'rave' culture, have ensured a visible disintegration of style boundaries in the city. Until 1991, the ubiquitous shell-suit had come to reign supreme in Aberdeen with a numeric presence unmatched elsewhere in Scotland. Casual style itself has procured further designer names, such as Duffer of St. George, Chevignon, Chipie, Champion, Boss, Katherine Hamnett and Valentino. Fila and Ellesse have enjoyed recoveries, mainly courtesy of diversification into footwear. Critically, however, this attire does not connote the violent moral imperative that its older siblings had done half a generation before. More recently, the shell-suit's status as semiotic boiler suit has become hypostatised, while ski-jackets are more regularly to be found amongst CID officers patrolling opaque-coloured football mobs. Further stylistic elitism has resurfaced simultaneously amongst the 'high' wider culture and the wealthier exponents of youth subculture. Undoubtedly the most obvious feed-through of high-priced specialist attire to the mass market in Aberdeen has been the diffusion of Berghaus jackets, whose waterproof range has a median price of approximately £250. Overall, it would appear that the casuals' predilections with designers and/or specialist labels has been a critical intermediary factor in the successful diffusion of these and other fashion signifiers to a wider social populace.

Furthermore, the cultural revivification of the Scottish central belt has drawn public attention away from the economic exigencies required for creating a positive sense of civic identity, a referent which the ASC found particularly efficacious. The embracement of Glasgow as 1990 European City of Culture, by local politicos and cultural doyens, engendered strong controversy throughout Scotland on the social justice of this award, given the appalling public housing, burgeoning drug, and embedded unemployment problems therein. An estimated 12,000 people in the Glasgow area are believed to be intravenous drug users; the city in 1991 had a 12% unemployment rate (according to government doctored statistics), the highest of Scotland's four major cities (*Economic Gazette,* December 1991). Yet, the greatest debate within the 'quality' media surrounding the formal cultural award centred upon the challenge which this represented for Scotland's erstwhile city of arts, Edinburgh. In this period, Dundee also sought to advance its public profile, christening itself 'The City of Discovery'. Aberdeen's response to these economic disclaimers has been unimaginative, and has done little but irradiate the themes of the mid-80s for civic advancement: drawing from the same stagnant well that had contained 'Glasgow's Miles Better', the North-East's image-makers brought up 'Grampian's Going Places'. Throughout Scotland, the question of constructing a new and positive sense of civic identity was further reflected in national political opinion, with a solid majority favouring constitutional change.(37) There can be little doubt that in this, as in the matter of promoting a politically flavoured cultural identity, the central belt, especially the west, has left the North-East light years behind.

Briefly, this most recent period has brought the ASC ontology a revealing examination. Having successfully carved out spaces in the city centre and the ground for greedy appropriation by both their younger and older stylistic subalterns, the advent of an incommensurable youth subcultural movement has left the formation stuck in the Scottish dubs of corporeal neurosis. The veneration of style still seeks to examine a habitus where it has no currency. Most potently of all, it appears that the next youth subcultural phenomenon which reaches Aberdeen will not be grounded in a city-wide context, intra-violence having nullified its antecedents' legacy.

Conclusion: Triumph of an instinct for comforting uniformity

I have argued that the effect which soccer casuals have had on other sections of the public - as cultural intermediaries in opening new styles, codes and spaces for their selective appropriation - has a critical cultural dimension in Aberdeen and Scotland. In the context of the debate on the nature of Scottish culture, and the catalytic role which youth culture may harbour for delivering it from subservience to English/British culture, the major Scottish youth formation of the 80s, the ASC, takes on a new analytic centrality. Its proponents are more than a heuristic for mapping out the relative merits of Nairn or Kane's respective theses, instead representing the contested issues themselves. Hailing from a city that encapsulates Nairn's sub-national *weltanschauung,* the ASC are the vanguard youth cultural formation of Scotland in the 80s, to which Kane's new identification of agency and self-empowerment in young Scots is assuredly appealing.

It will be quite apparent by this stage that I do not consider the ASC to have satisfied the full criteria of micro-political and -cultural enablement identified by Kane in the practices of the contemporary Scottish young. Even during the period of their birth, Aberdeen casuals were coming to visualise the cultural boundaries within which they would have to operate. As an Aberdonian gang, they continually experienced the paralysing unease that perhaps they were not the trendiest, not even the hardest, amongst their national contemporaries; this discomfiture was displaced by searching for the prosaic core within the plastic *avant garde,* precipitating the uniform adornment of the accessible Pringle. Even stylistically, the movement always sought a safe, single common denominator, a monocentric flavour.

Hankering for uniformity was in fact the cause of the ASC's successful mushrooming in the first period. Aberdeen remains a culturally mechanistic city, favouring a plural homogeneity: plural across time, homogeneous across space. The ASC, becoming the dominant subcultural formation, certainly were favoured by this epistemic tendency; their shelf-life would always only be measured by the length of time it took for another 'style' to be beamed up from the south, and not be the intrinsic worth of the casual project itself.

Perhaps axiomatic for a Scottish product, the ASC can even be said to have made a crucial contribution to their own demise, tightening the grip on both ends of the scissors-effect cutting into their stylistic reproduction. At the youth cultural side, the 'rave' phenomenon in Aberdeen continues to experience the same uncritical participation of the city's youth that the ASC enjoyed almost a decade earlier. But, for this style to move out of the rarefied atmosphere of these hermetic club-regulars, the new 'style' has required networking to younger minions, with 'ex-soccer hooligans' the obliging intermediaries. Similarly, for those older casuals wishing to abandon the youth subcultural scene, there is little room for manoeuvre within the 'mature' fashion segments. Having mapped out new leisure spaces of the 'smart, but casual' variety, they now find themselves lost in the multi-coloured ocean of tacky shell-suits and ski-jackets: the waterproof Berghaus may offer one last domain of continuity.

Indeed, fashion is the most obvious space which the ASC have opened up for wider appropriation, interpolating the collapse of the modernist distinction of high and low-level style, though baser shell-suits do threaten to pull this syncretism into zip-fast descent. The other visible setting to have undergone a social transformation via the casuals appropriation has been the physical space of the South Stand inside the home ground - a parochial point pitched at the first cognitive interest, but no less true for that. Again, this grouping have found themselves gradually displaced by a younger, less violently orientated grouping. Inter-subjectively, they have also been the vanguard formation in the construction of a network of Scottish casual subcultures which cock a snook at the imagery of fear and firewater previously enshrouding Old Firm supporters. Finally, in terms of their emancipatory stature, the ASC's legacy will not be longeval. Reliance upon London-centred stylistic forms was uninterrupted, their main achievement being in not falling behind the New Times as the city's built-in cultural lag would otherwise have ensured. Having been successful in amalgamating rival city gangs to procure their inception, the ASC have failed to secure their future through a 'Baby Crew', with the result that old locale-based feuds have returned with interest. Nor has there been any release from the watchful North-East practices of 'other-relatedness', the neurotics of social disclosure. With many abandoning soccer in favour of the 'rave' club scene, a misinterpretation of its constitutive 'mirroring body' according to the local and style precepts of the 'communicative body' has ensued. Comfort in knowledge of one's comparative understanding of the *avant garde* is purchased at the price of underlining the city's peripheral cultural status anew. The ASC have certainly operated as cultural intermediaries in the technical (fashion and spatial) sense; germinated the communicative nexus of both Casual formations against 70s and Old Firm fan identities, and the rival post-war estates at home. But, their lasting sub-political content was always fatally sited upon the shifting sands of North-East cultural deference, the quintessence of a disempowered Scottish cultural politics.

Notes

1. Although it may be contrary to popular belief, writers associated with post-modernist and post-structuralist social theory are homogeneous in neither history, discipline, method nor perspective (Harland, 1987, pp.184-6). Jameson (1991: xiii) argues persuasively that changing experiences of social and cultural life in late post-war capitalism initially had precipitated the meeting of 'a truly motley crew of strange bedfellows', under the clock of post-modernity.

2. At this stage, I use the term 'subculture' in an open-ended sense, as interchangeable with 'gang', in a similar manner to that used by Cloward and Ohlin (1960, pp.1-7). However, I am not persuaded by their emphases upon the subculture's 'delinquent acts' as a definitive prerequisite; or, the rather individualistic biases inherent in their application of this category (Hall et al, 1976, p.28).

3. Ian Taylor (1987, p.179), in reappraising his earlier work on football hooliganism, states:

    > ...the violence of working-class soccer supporters in the 1980s occurs within a different conjuncture in the development of class relationships in Britain to the violence of the 1960s.

    Following Cohen (1972) - which seems rather dated given his time periods - Taylor argues that the bifurcation of the British working class has produced a 'bourgeois worker' moving away from the 'older traditional worker'. Both workers, particularly the former, are viewed as oscillating towards a self-interested, racist and nationalist paranoia homologous with the cultural politics of Thatcherism. In some ways, this thesis is similar to the more jaundiced piece by Williams (1986) on the overlaps between the political xenophobia of Thatcher's first two terms, and the chauvinistic values of young, working class English fans preparing to descend on Mexico for the World Cup.

4. Certainly, this 'modernisation' of soccer subcultures may also

be seen as parallelled *mutatis mutandis* elsewhere in Europe (Horak, 1989; Moscati & Roversi, 1989). However, some restraint must be stressed in interpolating into these 'mobs', within a modernist imaginary, a differentiated element of cabalism or 'leadership' (Hobbs & Robins, 1991, p.563): hooligan subcultures are more prone to display characteristics of acephalous gang affiliation (Armstrong & Harris, 1991). Moreover, the popular accessibility of a modernist meta-narrative which requires as a categorical imperative the presence of 'leaders' within such subcultures can, of course, induce a self-fulfilling prophecy in the courts when the 'generals' are put on show (see Giulianotti, 1992).

5.   I have alluded to this relaxation of the 'casual' identity elsewhere (Giulianotti, 1991a, p.526). Yablonsky (1963, p.229) in defining the 'mob' as the least defined on his continuum of three gang structures, brings out cogently what I would suggest the transition from 'casual(s)' to 'boy'/'mob' signifies. The latter term illustrates the wider range of access-points for potential hooligans (style is hardly a barrier); the low level of leadership; and, the variable hierarchical structures internally.

6.   Aberdeen casuals originally referred to 'scarfers' as 'Christmas trees' (Allan, 1989; Giulianotti, 1989b); Hibs casuals refer to an equivalent grouping as 'sweaties' or 'cavemen' (Giulianotti, 1991c).

7.   Thrasher's (1927, p.191-2) classic study of 1,313 Chicago gangs offers a similar bifurcation of young collectives' nomenclature: "The names adopted by the gangs sometimes suggest their interests and activities, and at others reflect social patterns in their milieu." The former dimension may be seen as analogous to casual gang names' identification with the networked subculture; the latter may be interpreted as an inchoate use of locale-centred metonyms.

8.   Rangers casuals' gang name has been altered by rival casual gangs, particularly the Aberdeen casuals, to IBF (Iron Bru Firm). This renaming is premised upon the former's excessive continuity with Old Firm hooligan behaviour since the 1930s, in

using bottles as weapons (Forsyth, 1990, p.116). The choice of Iron Bru is a further calumniation of Rangers casuals maturity, and a cultural stereotypification of Glaswegians' diet.

9. Both analytically and synthetically, 'post-modernism' cannot escape the clutches of 'modernism'. The term 'post-modern' itself designates a break with, or definition against, the 'modern' (Featherstone, 1990, pp.1-11). Yet, as Jameson (1991) repeatedly maintains, the act of naming and historicising the 'post-modern' ensures that this rupture with modernity can never be complete. And then there is the modern exigency of reclaiming for cultural studies *qua* social epistemology some *raisons   d'etre* in the brunt of Baudrillard's dreaded pronouncement 'The intellectual is dead', in order to make intelligible any commentary on contemporary popular culture. The privileged vantage point of modern social theory is most effectively reclaimed through the methods of the French sociologist, Pierre Bourdieu (cf. Lash, 1990, pp.237-265).

10. For Marcuse (1964) sublimation of the Pleasure Principle is facilitated by genuinely three-dimensional culture; the 'repressive' or 'administered' society affords only two-dimensional culture, and intellectual/libidinal desublimination. The latter removes the politically critical aspect of sublimatory 'transcendence' through culture in order to secure the reproduction of the capitalist order; this is achieved by neutralising both 'artistic alienation' at the production side, and the 'estrangement effect' at the consumption side, through the mediation of cultural experiences by the 'dominant culture'. Marcuse's imaginary is formally consistent with Gramsci's (1971, p.80) notion of hegemony, which posits that the reproduction of the capitalist order is achieved through a mixture of force and, crucially, consent. The latter is obtained beyond the economic 'base' by the 'hegemonic bloc' within the superstructures of politics, culture, the bureaucracy of the Civil Society, etc. In this sense, the 'dominant culture' of the hegemonic bloc is able to control the range of political potentialities which may be produced by the intellectuals within subaltern cultural spheres.

11. I have argued elsewhere (Giulianotti, 1989a) that the main weakness in the Birmingham School's theoretical edifice is the syncretism of Althusser and Gramsci, in its conception of 'relative autonomy'. Where the Althusserian postulate of the economic structure being 'determining in the last instance' is accepted, this 'relative autonomy' is resolved most oppressively on the side of social structure and reproduction of power inequalities (see Benton, 1988). Consequently, the dubious claims of privileged epistemology aside, activity within the 'superstructures' of culture 'high' and 'popular' has all the objective import of a 3rd/4th place play-off (replay) in the Scottish Reserve League (East Section). The cultural experiences of working class youths are still regarded as 'over-determined' *a priori*. Conversely, Willis (1991, pp.156-7) argues for a less structuralist visualisation of how youth identities are put together in a microsocial sense, within Gramscian accounts of hegemony. Similarly, Fiske (1989, pp.160-2) contends that hegemony is over-stratified, whereas Foucault's conception of discourses as a 'will to knowledge' and a 'will to power' considers power as more than a top-down force, and resistance a bottom-up challenge.

12. Nairn (1981, p.158) offers this classic insight into Scottish provincialist, Presbyterian life-worlds:

> Kailyardism was the definition of Scotland as consisting wholly of small towns full of small-town 'characters' given to bucolic intrigue and wise sayings. At the first the central figures were usually Ministers of the Kirk (as were most of the authors) but later on schoolteachers and doctors got into the act. Their housekeepers always have a shrewd insight into human nature. Offspring who leave for the big city frequently come to grief, and are glad to get home again (peching and hoasting to hide their feelings). In their different ways, village cretins and ne'er-do-wells reinforce the essentially healthy *Weltanschauung* of the place.

13. McCrone (1989, 164-5) argues that although the origins of the tartan's populist success are obscure, the role of the British

aristocracy in its diffusion is undisputed. He gives as a watershed moment in the plaid's fortunes the wearing of a kilt by George IV, 'set off fetchingly by pink tights' before bemused Edinburghians in 1822.

14. William McIlvanney, Scotland's leading writer and essayist, also confesses to an intense ambivalence towards the popular cultural knowledge of Scottish fixation with football. For him, to stand out with this obsession would, presumably, undermine his claim to commentate on the political possibilities of Scottish cultural identity as this is experienced. He writes, from a formally Nairnian perspective:

> If the World Cup is the West End of football, the Scottish game is a crude and ineffectual form of group therapy in which players and fans desperately improvise towards some mutually acceptable sense of themselves. Instead of being a natural extension of our lives, an expression of ourselves, it remains the nexus of a stubborn national neurosis. (McIlvanney, 1991, p.70).

15. This is not well received by Smith (1989, p.89) in his romanticised account of *The Granite City*. Gibbon's insight into the 'bleakness, not meanness or jollity' of Aberdonian character is disingenuously countered through history, and the city's alleged reputation in the 16th century as 'blyth and blissful'. For any prosecutor of Gibbon's case, Smith's vexing defence merely begs the question about Aberdeen's later, pacified incarnation.

16. Somewhere along its historical trajectory, Aberdeen's radicalism flipped over into an orbit of the Covenant and its affinal Kailyardism (small-town gossip culture) which rendered the Scots Victorian *avant la lettre*. Harvie (1990, p.12) notes of the Scottish Covenant tradition, pluralism was never on the Scottish religious agenda throughout the 19th century and beyond:

> ...while it (Covenantism) put a strong emphasis on community involvement, it was weak on toleration...(in

Scotland) 'dissent' has generally tended to take the form...of *groupuscules* each claiming to be the legatee of the 'true Kirk', prepared to make the point by persecuting everyone else if they get the chance and meanwhile maintaining rigid discipline within their own ranks.

Covenantism itself was interpreted in the metaphorical sense, as a contract between God and the Scots as 'chosen people' (Stevenson, 1983); or, as one is prone to hear at Ibrox, 'We are the People!'

17.   A sub-narrative amongst Aberdeen's supporters has for long acknowledged their undeniable, excessive barracking of Aberdeen players born and bred in the city. One player in the mid-1950s, whose 144 goals averaged a goal every other game, virtually retired (aged 28) because of the abuse he received from home supporters (Webster, 1990, p.142-3). The local fanzine, *The Northern Light,* has devoted two lengthy pieces to mocking another local striker from the early 1960s (90 goals in 165 games). Of the three key local players in the great Aberdeen side of the early 1980s, only one left on amicable terms with the supporters, a *'bon accord'* sealed by his crippling tackle on Rangers' favourite, Ian Durrant in 1988. There is even a belief amongst older supporters that the greatest ever player to hail from Aberdeen, Denis Law, was advised by older relations in the early 1960s to avoid signing for the local club and to take this talents south to more hospitable setting - Huddersfield.

18.   Thomson (1988, pp.301-2) reports that the local moral panic about 'Teddy Boys' did not germinate until the general release of the film *Rock Around the Clock* in 1956. Conversely, both Hebdige (1988, p.70) and Davis(1990, pp.142-3) locate the emergence of the Teddy Boys subcultures in the *early* 50s, within east and south London working class youth.

19.   A trawl of texts on youth deviancy nets barely a recognition of the city's existence. Thrasher (1927, pp.50-1) notes a Chicagoan rivalry between a gang named the Aberdeens and some Polish boys known as The Murderers, though the origins

of the Scottish sobriquet is not explained. Elsewhere, there is, of course, Allan (1989), but Webster (1990, p.262) provides an interesting resumé of Allan's exceptional background within the North-East cultural aristocracy:

> ...the son of Charlie Allan, farmer and broadcaster (and ex-University lecturer and globetrotter) from Little Ardo of Methlick, and a grandson of that distinguished North-east writer, John R. Allan who ranks second only to Lewis Grassic Gibbon. His father's uncles included Sir Maitland Mackie, who became Lord Lieutenant of the county, and two of his brothers who took their seats in the House of Lords.

20. The connotations of violence between Glasgow soccer and its subcultures, as encouraged by the long history of 'bottle battles' between Old Firm fans since the 1930s (Forsyth, 1990, pp.115-122), helped to encourage prospective 'hard men' in Scottish provincial cities such as Aberdeen, to follow loyally or faithfully the respective colours of Rangers or Celtic during the post-war era (Giulianotti, 1989b). From the original Aberdeen casuals whom I have talked to as part of this research, I can only estimate that as much as 30% of the movement initially consisted of Celtic and Rangers fans whose exchange of allegiance was irreversible. A similar pursuit of a forum for violence has persuaded some Hearts fans to cross the Edinburgh divide and follow Hibernian as part of the Hibs casuals (Giulianotti, 1991c). Even in Glasgow, some original Celtic casuals have been displaced into fighting alongside Rangers casuals, following a hostile response to their activities by fellow Celtic fans (Finn, 1992).

21. In a revealingly self-indulgent piece for *Marxism Today* (August, 1991), Kane reports his hope that his daughter 'has all my intelligence"; that he himself is a 'thinker, thinker, thinker', blessed by a 'lust for knowledge'; is 'a chronic bibliophiliac' with 'exponential ambitions'; and who is appreciative of 'Jurgen Habermas: I find his notion of "communicative action" marvelously humane'.

22.   This process would appear to fit into Dunning et al's (1988, pp.199-203) conception of 'ordered segmentation', in the construction of hooligan formations. However, aside of significant criticisms of this explanation in terms of definition (Armstrong & Harris, 1992) and ubiquity of application (Giulianotti, 1991c), it should be added that this sociological description should not outlive what it seeks to explain. In Aberdeen, for example, the term 'ordered segmentation' no longer has currency, as the 'core' ASC have largely abandoned any central identification according to eco-social subculture in favour of gang association within the city centre (Giulianotti, 1989b).

23.   This process was, of course, not without its social tensions. Interaction between those from rival estates, particularly coterminous ones, could lead to established enmities resurfacing and underpinning either a reproduction of localist subcultural boundaries, or production of closer association with new, networked subcultural 'styles'. Allan (1989, p.90) recalls an ASC excursion to Glasgow, during which two erstwhile comrades, seeking casual origins in their old Sunday best:

> ...were getting into a serious argument over who started the Aberdeen Casuals, who was trendy first - Bridge of Don or Seaton, who had Pringle or Lyle and Scott jumpers back in 1980.

24.   In the first half of the 80s, Aberdeen F.C. won the Scottish League Championship three times, the Scottish Cup three times, the Scottish League Cup twice, the European Cup-Winners' Cup once, and the European Super Cup once.

25.   Again, the dichotomy of *avant garde* style and criminal activity could be intermittently difficult to synthesise. One early casual most adroit in stealing the requisite attire to order over-reached himself on one occasion, and adorned an exclusive Pringle pilfered earlier. It was quickly spotted and his business, like so many others in the early 80s, went into temporary liquidation.

26.   Lash (1990, pp.173-4) defines de-differentiation thus:

> I think that if modernism and modernity result from a process of differentiation...then postmodernism results from a much more recent process of *de*-differentiation....De-differentiation is also present in the postmodernist refusal to separate the author from his or her *oeuvre* or the audience from the performance; in the post-modernist transgression of the boundary (with no doubt greater or lesser success) between literature and theory, between high and popular culture, between what is properly cultural and what is properly social.

27.   This dependency upon the south was critical in the very genesis of the Aberdeen casuals' project, for the group of lads from one housing estate to initiate the style into the city had regularly attended matches in England, primarily those involving Tottenham. One casual who has been a major figure in the gang's development over more than a decade has stated that his main influence from England was a Spurs casual later killed in an infamous escalator incident at the Seven Sisters Tube station, which had involved Spurs and Manchester United fans (see Buford, 1991, pp.180-1).

28.   Frank (1991, p.69) states that 'dominating bodies' possess two characteristics: they are discursively considered to be exclusively male, and heavily imbued with a sense of lack, which is evinced through fear and anxiety. With the first feature, there are no problems in this context. The second is only resolved symbolically; the casual's dominating body must be considered dyadic in relation to the other on whom the body is inflicting domination, within the wider project of prosecuting the claim of 'number one'.

29.   Hibs casuals have enjoyed augmented numbers through at least two waves of 'baby crew' maturing to join the 'front-lines' ranks during the latter half of the 80s. Current Hibs casuals are somewhat uncertain about the credentials of the contemporary band of 'baby crew' now present in Edinburgh city centre, however (Giulianotti, 1991c). Celtic casuals also

have a formation distinct from the main casual grouping and which is known as the Celtic Soccer Babes.

30.   One prominent Chelsea boy who went on to contribute substantially to the dance scene of the late 80s suggested that Heysel provided both a personal and collective Rubicon for earlier casuals:

> I was sitting round at my mate's flat and at first we were laughing and shouting "get in there Liverpool." Once we realised people had died it changed. People felt they'd contributed to what happened at Heysel. (Terry Farley quoted in Redhead, 1991, p.75).

31.   The 'authoritarian populism' of the Thatcher government cranked into a higher gear with the personal intervention of the Prime Minister on football hooliganism, following her viewing on television the crowd trouble at the Luton v. Millwall match on March 13, 1985 (see Taylor, 1987). An emergency debate was held in the House of Commons the next day, at which the Environment Minister Neil Macfarlane, a former Minister for Sport, stated that the FA would be pressed for a report within one week on its plans to deal with football hooliganism. Failure by the FA to satisfy Mrs Thatcher's draconian instincts led to the germination of the ill-fated Football Spectators Bill, 1989. This legislation was passed in modified form in 1991, following the Taylor Report's criticisms of Thatcher's original plan to require all soccer fans in England and Wales to join a national membership scheme.

32.   Forsyth (1990, pp.87-8) reports the fears of the Scotland manager, Jock Stein, on this prospect. Faced with an away match against Wales that would determine whether Scotland qualified for the 1986 World Cup Finals, Stein stated on match day that his greatest concern was the possibility of Scotland fans being considered disorderly by politicians, and thereby being included in the latters' legislative remit. Combined with the tension of the match, this worry led to Stein suffering a massive heart attack and dying just after the final whistle. News of Stein's death quickly spread amongst the 20,000+

Scottish fans in Cardiff, and muted celebrations to such an extent that politically there could be no referent for bringing policy on Scottish fans in line with that for English fans.

33.   In 1981, Ted Croker, Secretary of the English FA, attempted to implement a ban on Scottish fans for the biannual match at Wembley, following an English media-led campaign against Scottish fans in the late 70s (Moorhouse, 1989). It didn't work. In 1983, he then ensured that the match was played on a Wednesday evening. It didn't work. In 1985, the government ordered that the match be switched to Glasgow, on the grounds that Scottish fans might precipitate crowd trouble. It didn't work. A year later, after the 1985 watershed, this tartan referent had been obliterated and the symbolic balance of power complete. Scottish official and popular discourses on fans used domestic and European referents to legitimate the reversal of Scottish and English fan identities. By 1989 Scotland's top-selling tabloid, the *Daily Record* (October 8), could call for the Scottish League to reconsider its invitation for the English League to send a team north, under the heading 'Return of the Thugs'.

34.   For Goffman (1959, p.168), 'communication out of character' pertains, in essence, to any verbal or non-verbal emission which might undermine or discredit a definition of the situation which one individual or team wishes to project to another individual or team.

35.   To support Frank's final point within this context, Rietveld (1991, p.21) notes the mode of ravers in favouring outsize clothing and children's dress labels. "The result was that the wearer looked like an overgrown toddler", a semiotic infantilism given referent by a reversal to pre-Oedipal sexuality and the resensualisation of the entire corporeal.

36.   At a meeting of the Aberdeen Licensing Board, the Hoochi Coochi Club was granted a two month stay of execution on its 2 a.m. licence. Particular attention was drawn to its public order problems by a senior police officer at the meeting, who stated, "The Chief Constable is so concerned that he wished to

complain because he fears for safety and public order at the Hoochi Coochi Club." The main source of this concern was a series of riots at the club, the first of which had been initiated by 'soccer casuals':

> Since then, however, there have been four other incidents, the latter involving large numbers of people using discarded or disused bottles as weapons and it took 15 police officers to quell the riot on the last occasion," said Mr Tucker. (*Aberdeen Press & Journal*, April 15, 1992).

37. A leading expert on the political sociology of Scotland reports for the period June 1990-June 1991:

> The polls carried out by MORI and ICM continue to show desire for constitutional change. The monthly MORI polls indicate that around one third of those questioned wanted some form of Independence (either inside or outside the EC) and over 40% a devolved assembly with some taxation and spending power. Support for the status quo rarely exceeded 20%. (McCrone, 1992, p.227).

Bibliography

Allan, J. (1989), *Bloody Casuals: Diary of a Football Hooligan*, Famedram: Northern.

Armstrong, G. (1992) *With the Blades: a study of Sheffield United Fans*, (forthcoming).

Armstrong, G. and Harris, R. (1991) 'Football hooligans: theory and evidence', *Sociological Review, 39, 3*.

Armstrong, G. and Hobbs, D. (1992) 'The Professional Foul: Covert Policing in Britain - the Case of Soccer', paper presented at the *International Conference: Soccer, Culture and Identity*, University of Aberdeen.

Baudrillard, J. (1983a) *In the Shadow of the Silent Majorities*, New York, Semiotext(e).

Baudrillard, J. (1983b) *Les Strategies Fatales*, Paris, Grasset.

Benton, T. (1988) *The Rise and Fall of Structural Marxism*, London, Macmillan.

Bernstein, R. J. (1976) *The Restructuring of Social and Political Theory*, London, Methuen.

Bourdieu, P. (1984) *Distinction: a Social Critique of the Judgment of Taste*, translated by R. Nice, London, Routledge & Kegan Paul.

Buford, B. (1991), *Among the Thugs*, London, Secker & Warburg.

Chapman, W. D. and Riley, C. F. (1949) *Granite City: a Plan for Aberdeen*, Report to Aberdeen City Council.

Clarke, J. (1978) 'Football and working class fans: tradition and change', in R. Ingham (ed), *Football Hooliganism: the wider context*, London, Inter-Action.

Cloward, R. A. and Ohlin, L. E. (1960) *Delinquency and Opportunity: a theory of delinquent gangs*, New York, The Free Press.

Cohen, A. K. (1956) *Delinquent Boys*, Glencoe, The Free Press.

Cohen, P. (1972) 'Subcultural conflict and working class community', *Working Papers in Cultural Studies 2*, Birmingham, CCCS.

Cosgrove, S. (1991) *Hampden Babylon*, Edinburgh, Canongate.

Davis, J. (1990) *Youth and the Condition of Britain: images of adolescent conflict*, London, Athlone.

Dunning, E. et al (1988) *The Roots of Football Hooliganism*, London, Routledge.

Featherstone, M. (ed.), (1990) *Global Culture*, London, Routledge.

Featherstone, M. (1991) *Consumer Culture & Postmodernism*, London, Sage.

Feldman, A. (1991) *Formations of Violence: the narrative of the body and political terror in Northern Ireland*, Chicago, University of Chicago Press.

Finn, G. (1992) 'Sectarianism and soccer: adolescent social identities and traditions of change and continuity', paper presented at the *International Conference: Soccer, Culture and Identity*, University of Aberdeen.

Fiske, J. (1989a) *Understanding Popular Culture*, London, Unwin Hyman.

Fiske, J. (1989b) *Reading the Popular*, London, Unwin Hyman.

Forsyth, R.(1990) *The Only Game*, Edinburgh, Mainstream /McEwan's Lager.

Frank, A. W. (1991) 'For a Sociology of the Body: an Analytical Review' in M. Featherstone et al (eds.), *The Body: Social Process and Cultural Theory,* London, Sage.

Frith, S. (1988) 'Art Ideology and Pop Practice', in C. Nelson and L. Grossberg (eds.), *Marxism and the Interpretation of Culture,* London, Macmillan.

Giulianotti, R. (1989a) 'A Critical Overview of British Sociological Investigations into Soccer Hooliganism in Scotland and Britain', *Working Papers on Football Violence No. 1,* University of Aberdeen.

Giulianotti, R. (1989b) 'A Participant Observation Study of Aberdeen Football Fans at Home and Away', *Working Papers on Football Violence No. 2,* University of Aberdeen.

Giulianotti, R. (1991a) 'The Tartan Army in Italy: the case for the carnivalesque', *Sociological Review,* 39, 3.

Giulianotti, R. (1991b) 'Scotland, Drink and Drugs: another generation of casualties?' *E.U.I Colloquium Papers,* (forthcoming publication).

Giulianotti, R. (1991c) 'Keep it in the Family: an outline of Hibs Casuals' Social Ontology', (forthcoming publication).

Giulianotti, R. (1992) 'Taking Liberties: Hibs Casuals and Scottish Law', (forthcoming publication).

Goffman, E. (1959) *The Presentation of Self in Everyday Life,* Harmondsworth, Penguin.

Gramsci, A. (1973) *Selections from the Prison Notebooks,* London, Lawrence & Wishart.

Grossberg, L. (1988) *It's a Sin,* Sydney, Power.

Habermas, J. (1978) *Knowledge and Human Interests,* Second Edition, translated by J. Shapiro, London, Heinemann.

Hall, S. et al, (1976) *Resistance through Rituals,* London, Hutchinson.

Harland, R. (1987) *Superstructuralism,* London, Methuen.

Harvie, C. (1990) 'The Covenanting Tradition', in G. Walker and T. Gallagher (eds.) *Sermons and Battle Hymns: Protestant Popular Culture in Modern Scotland,* Edinburgh, Edinburgh University Press.

Hebdige, D. (1979) *Subculture: The Meaning of Style,* London, Methuen.

Hebdige, D. (1988) *Hiding in the Light,* London, Routledge.

Hills, G. (1991) 'Whatever happened to the likely lads?', *The Face,* 2, 39.

Hobbs, D. and Robins, D. (1990) 'The Boy Done Good: Football Violence, Changes and Continuities', *Sociological Review, 39, 3.*

Horak, R. (1989) ' A Brief History of Juvenile Soccer Fan Subcultures in Austria', *Sociological Review, 39, 3.*

Jameson, F. (1991) *Postmodernism or, the Cultural Logic of Late Capitalism,* London, Verso.

Lash, S. (1990) *Sociology of Postmodernism,* London, Routledge.

Leatherdale, C. (1986) *The Aberdeen Football Champion,* Edinburgh, John Donald.

Marcuse, H. (1964) *One Dimensional Man,* London, Routledge & Kegan Paul.

Marsh, P. (1978) *Aggro: the illusion of violence,* London, Dent.

Marxism Today, various dates.

McCrone, D. (1989) 'Representing Scotland: Culture and Nationalism', in D. McCrone et al (eds), *The Making of Scotland,* Edinburgh, Edinburgh University Press.

McCrone, D. (1992) 'Opinion Polls in Scotland, June 1990-June 1991', in L. Paterson and D. McCrone (1992) *The Scottish Government Yearbook 1992*, Edinburgh, Edinburgh University Press.

McIlvanney, W. (1991) *Surviving the Shipwreck*, Edinburgh, Mainstream.

Moorhouse, H. F. (1984) 'Professional Football and Working Class Culture: English theories and Scottish evidence', *Sociological Review*, 32.

Moorhouse, H. F. (1989) 'We're Off to Wembley: the history of a Scottish event and the sociology of football hooliganism' in D. McCrone et al (eds.) op cit.

Moscati, R. and Roversi, A. (1989) 'Football Hooliganism in Italy', *E.U.I. Colloquium Papers*, 227/89 (col. 31).

Murray, W. (1984) *The Old Firm*, Edinburgh, John Donald.

Nairn, T. (1981) *The Break-Up of Britain*, 2nd. edition, London, NLB.

Payne, J. (1975) 'Housing Deprivation in Aberdeen', *Focus*, September edition.

Redhead, S. and McLaughlin, E. (1985) 'Soccer Style Wars', *New Society*, August 16, 1985.

Redhead, S. (1986) *Sing When You're Winning*, London, Pluto.

Redhead, S. (1990) *The End-of-the-Century, youth and pop towards 2000*, Manchester, Manchester University Press.

Redhead, S. (1991) *Football with Attitude*, Manchester, Wordsmith.

Rietveld, H. C. (1991) 'Living the Dream: analysis of the rave phenomenon in terms of ideology, consumerism and subculture', *Unit for Law and Popular Culture Working Papers*, Manchester Polytechnic. A revised version of this paper is now in Steve Redhead (ed.), (1993) *Rave Off*, Aldershot, Ashgate.

Robins, D. (1984) *We Hate Humans*, Harmandsworth, Penguin.

Smith, R. (1984) *The Granite City*, Edinburgh, John Donald.

Stevenson, D. (1983) *The Covenantors*, Edinburgh, Saltire Society.

Taylor, I. (1971) 'Soccer Consciousness and Soccer Hooliganism' in S. Cohen (ed.), *Images of Deviance*, Harmondsworth, Penguin.

Taylor, I. (1987) 'Putting the boot into a working class sport: British soccer after Bradford and Brussels', *Sociology of Sport Journal*, 4.

Taylor, I. (1989) 'Hillsborough: 15 April 1989. Some personal contemplations', *New Left Review*, 177.

Thomson, M. (1988) *Silver Screen in the Silver City: a history of cinemas in Aberdeen 1896-1987*, Aberdeen, Aberdeen University Press.

Thrasher, F. M. (1927) *The Gang*, Chicago, University of Chicago Press.

Walker, G. (1990) '"There's not a team like the Glasgow Rangers": Football and religious identity in Scotland', in G. Walker and T. Gallagher (eds.), op cit.

Webster, J. (1990) *The Dons: The History of Aberdeen Football Club*, Revised edition, London, Stanley Paul.

Williams, J. (1986) 'White Riots: the English football fan abroad' in A. Tomlinson and G. Whannel (eds.) *Off the Ball: The football World Cup*, London, Pluto.

Williams, J. (1991) 'Having an away day: English football spectators and the hooligan debate', in J. Williams and S. Wagg (1991), *British Football and Social Change: Getting into Europe*, Leicester, Leicester University Press.

Willis, P. (1990) *Common Culture*, Milton Keynes, Open University Press.

Yablonsky, L. (1962) *The Violent Gang*, New York, Macmillan.